REWRITING THE SELF

The fundamental issue of identity has been endlessly explored by philosophers, poets, priests, psychologists, and men and women generally. Whilst the question has stayed the same, the answers offered have changed over time. This book examines changing notions of selfhood from a historical perspective.

The overarching perception of *Rewriting the Self* is that the received version of the 'ascent of Western man' needs to be rethought in the light of the critical cultural analyses of today. Rereadings are offered of classic texts like those of Descartes, but wider perspectives are also presented. These assess the discursive construction of the self in the light of political, technological and social changes.

The range of the book is large, both in the number of models of personal identity discussed and the differing viewpoints from which they are examined: the eye/I is perpetually contested. Chronologically the book spans from Petrarch to the present, taking in the Renaissance, Enlightenment, Romanticism, Modernism and Postmodernism.

Rewriting the Self arises from a seminar series held at the Institute of Contemporary Arts in London. The accessibility and freshness of these presentations has been preserved in the contributions to this book. *Rewriting the Self* represents a rare coming together of leading academics from different fields, and offers a stimulating and controversial account of the meanings and histories of identity and the self.

REWRITING THE SELF

Histories from the Renaissance to the Present

Edited by Roy Porter

London and New York

First published 1997
by Routledge
11 New Fetter Lane, London EC4P 4EE

Simultaneously published in the USA and Canada
by Routledge
29 West 35th Street, New York, NY 10001

Typeset in Baskerville by Keystroke, Jacaranda Lodge,
Wolverhampton
Printed and bound in Great Britain by
Biddles Ltd, Guildford and King's Lynn

British Library Cataloguing in Publication Data
A catalogue record for this book is available from the British Library

Library of Congress Cataloguing in Publication Data
Rewriting the self : histories from the Middle ages to the present /
edited by Roy Porter
Based on a seminar series held at the Institute of
Contemporary Arts, London, Eng., spring 1995.
Contents: Representations of the self from Petrarch to Descartes /
Peter Burke — Self and selfhood in the seventeenth century /
Jonathan Sawday — Self-reflection and the self / Roger Smith —
Religious experience and the formation of the early Enlightenment
self / Jane Shaw — The European Enlightenment and the history of
the self / E. J. Hundert — The death and rebirth of character
in the eighteenth century / Sylvana Tomaselli — "Another self in
case" : gender, marriage, and the individual in Augustan literature /
Carolyn D. Williams — Feelings and novels / John Mullan
— Romantic travel / Roger Cardinal — " —As a rule, I does not
mean I" : personal identity and the Victorian woman poet / Kate
Flint — Mapping the self : gender, space, and modernity in
mid-Victorian London / Lynda Nead — Stories of the eye / Daniel
Pick — The modern auditory I / Steve Connor — Assembling the
modern self / Nikolas Rose — Death and the self / Jonathan
Dollimore — Self-undoing subjects / Terry
Eagleton.
1. Self (Philosophy)—History. 2. Self (Philosophy) in
literature—History. 3. Identity (Psychology)—History.
I. Porter, Roy, 1946–
BD450.R4448 1997
126′.09—dc20   96–15698
ISBN 0–415–14279–2
0–415–14280–6 (pbk)

CONTENTS

v

CONTENTS

PLATES

CONTRIBUTORS

Peter Burke is Professor of Cultural History, University of Cambridge, and Fellow of Emmanuel College. His books include *The Italian Renaissance* (3rd edn., 1987); *Popular Culture in Early Modern Europe* (2nd edn., 1994); *The Fabrication of Louis XIV* (1992), and *History and Social Theory* (1992).

Roger Cardinal is Professor of Literary and Visual Studies at the University of Kent at Canterbury, where he is currently Head of the School of Arts and Image Studies. He has published widely on literature and painting in nineteenth- and twentieth-century Europe (*German Romantics*, 1975; *Figures of Reality*, 1981; *Expressionism*, 1984; *The Landscape Vision of Paul Nash*, 1989), and he co-edited *The Cultures of Collecting*, 1994 with John Elsner. Author of *Outsider Art* (1972), he is an international authority on self-taught art.

Steven Connor is Professor of Modern Literature and Theory and Director of the Centre for Interdisciplinary Research in Culture and the Humanities at Birkbeck College, London. He is the author of books on Dickens, Beckett and Joyce, as well as of *Postmodernist Culture: An Introduction to Theories of the Contemporary* (Oxford: Blackwell, 1989, 2nd edn., 1996), *Theory and Cultural Value* (Oxford: Blackwell, 1992) and *The English Novel in History, 1950–1995* (London: Routledge, 1995).

Jonathan Dollimore is Professor of English in the Humanities Graduate Research Centre at the University of Sussex. His books include *Radical Tragedy: Religion, Ideology and Power in the Drama of Shakespeare and his Contemporaries* (1984, 2nd edn., 1989); (with Alan Sinfield), *Political Shakespeare: Essays in Cultural Materialism* (1985, 2nd edn., 1994), and *Sexual Dissidence: Augustine to Wilde, Freud to Foucault* (Oxford: Clarendon Press, 1991). He is currently engaged in a project on *Death. Desire and Mutability*.

Terry Eagleton is Thomas Warton Professor of English Literature at St Catherine's College, Oxford. He has written four plays, produced in Ireland and London and to be published in 1997, and is author of *The Illusions of Postmodernism* (Blackwell, 1996). He also writes on literary theory.

Kate Flint is Reader in Victorian and Modern English Literature and Fellow of Linacre College, Oxford. She is author of *The Woman Reader 1837–1914* (1993) and of numerous other works and articles on Victorian and early twentieth-century literature and art history. She is currently completing a book entitled *Victorian Visuality*, and her next major research project is on the place of America in the Victorian cultural imagination.

E. J. Hundert is Professor of History at the University of British Columbia and is currently working on a book on theatricality and Enlightenment social thought. His *The Enlightenment's 'Fable': Bernard Mandeville and the Discovery of Society* was published by Cambridge University Press in 1994.

John Mullan is Lecturer in English at University College, London. He is author or *Sentiment and Sociability* (Oxford University Press), and has edited Daniel Defoe's *Memoirs of a Cavalier* (1991) and *Roxana* (1996). He has recently completed an anthology of memoirs of Shelley and edited a CD-ROM database of eighteenth-century fiction.

Lynda Nead is a Senior Lecturer in the Department of History of Art, Birkbeck College. She is author of *Myths of Sexuality: Representations of Women in Victorian Britain* (Blackwell, 1988); *The Female Nude: Art, Obscenity and Sexuality* (Routledge, 1992), and *Chila Kumari Burman: Beyond Two Cultures* (Kala Press/Arts Council, 1995). She is currently working on a book on modernity and visual culture in mid-Victorian London.

Daniel Pick is Reader in History at Queen Mary and Westfield College, London. Author of *Faces of Degeneration: A European Disorder, c. 1848–1918* (Cambridge: Cambridge University Press, 1989) and *War Machine: The Rationalisation of Slaughter in the Modern Age* (New Haven, Conn: Yale University Press, 1993), his research concentrates upon the cultural history of nineteenth- and twentieth-century Europe.

Nikolas Rose is Professor of Sociology at Goldsmiths College, University of London. His most recent books are *Inventing Our Selves: Psychology, Power and Personhood* (New York: Cambridge University Press, 1996) and *Foucault and Political Reason: Liberalism, Neo-Liberalism and the Rationalities of Government* (London: UCL Press, 1996) co-edited with Andrew Barry and Thomas Osborne. He is currently working on a study of twentieth-century psychiatry entitled *In the Name of Mental Health.*

Jonathan Sawday is a Senior Lecturer in the Department of English at the University of Southampton, where he teaches Renaissance literature and culture. He is co-editor of *Literature and the English Civil War* (Cambridge University Press, 1990), and author of *The Body Emblazoned: Dissection and the Human Body in Renaissance Culture* (Routledge, 1995).

Jane Shaw is Fellow and Tutor in Ecclesiastical History at Regent's Park College, Oxford University. She completed her Ph.D. at the University of California at Berkeley in 1994, and is currently writing a book on religious experience in Enlightenment England.

Roger Smith is Reader in the History of Science at Lancaster University. He is author of *Trial by Medicine: Insanity and Responsibility in Victorian Trials* (1981); *Inhibition: History and Meaning in the Sciences of Mind and Brain* (1992), and of the forthcoming *Fontana History of the Human Sciences* (1997).

Sylvana Tomaselli is a former Research Fellow of Newnham College, Cambridge. An intellectual historian working predominantly, but not exclusively, on the seventeenth and eighteenth centuries, she has written on such topics as mind–body dualism, the history of women, and population theories. Her publications also include a translation of Jacques Lacan's *Seminar II: The Ego in Freud's Theory and in Psychoanalytic Technique*, edited by Jacques-Alain Miller, prepared and annotated by John Forrester (Cambridge University Press and Norton, 1988). With Roy Porter she edited *Rape: An Historical and Social Enquiry* (Blackwell, 1986; pb 1989; Portuguese translation, Rio Fundo Editora, 1992), and *The Dialectics of Friendship* (Routledge, 1989).

Carolyn D. Williams, MA B.Litt. (Oxon) is a Lecturer in the Department of English at the University of Reading. She has written *Pope, Homer, and Manliness* (1993) and a large number of articles on life and literature in the early modern period.

PREFACE

In addition to the acknowledgements from Roy Porter, and in danger of over-doing things, I would like to add some thanks and appreciations: to Roy Porter himself, for his seemingly effortless fluency and erudition; to Sonu Shamdasani, whose work for the ICA in psychoanalysis and philosophy is always bold and original; to Alan Read at the ICA, with whom I share the pleasure of business; to Jessica Pearce, our fabulous intern, who helped pull things together; and to the contributors to *The Making of the Modern Psyche* series of talks which stimulated this volume, including those who were too busy to write for the book but still gave us their time and words: Jeremy Adler, Natalie Eastman Davies, and Lisa Jardine. We are privileged at the ICA in having an audience whose intelligence and feistiness impresses all speakers. I thank them for their commitment, engagement, and outspokenness, for keeping things alive.

We invited our speakers to recreate a sense of what it was to be alive in the period under examination (over four nights, we galloped through as many centuries) and to speculate on the history of the twentieth century. Our aim was not to read earlier times in relation to current concerns, but to get under the skin of epochs – to read them from inside out. The diverse perspectives of the speakers reminded us that notions of selfhood have been constantly made, unmade, and remade over the centuries. With the help of a few anachronistic anchors, the essays here offer a complex set of histories to issues which we, in the solipsistic twentieth century, may consider to be uniquely contemporary – the notion of identity as a masquerade or performance, the problematics of vision and visibility, encounters with paranormal phenomena, and the aesthetics of technology.

ICA talks offer an independent forum outside academic or professional institutions, open to all. The essays here, learned but not laboured, capture this spirit.

Helena Reckitt
Deputy Director of ICA Talks

ACKNOWLEDGEMENTS

This book arises out of a seminar series held at the Institute of Contemporary Arts in London in the Spring of 1995. I am very grateful to all those connected with the ICA who had the idea, who then helped in many ways to turn idea into reality, and who subsequently encouraged the idea of a book. My thanks in particular to Sonu Shamdasani, who first approached me with the possibility, to Alan Read, the director of talks at the ICA, and to Helena Reckitt, without whose drive, energy and enthusiasm everything would have been much less fun.

As editor, I would like to pay tribute to all those who contributed to the series and who have then, with such good humour, put up with my bullying so as to knock this book into shape. I would like especially to thank Ed Hundert and Peter Burke, who, being on another continent, were unable to give talks at the ICA but who have nevertheless been willing to produce essays for this book. Thanks to you all! And also to Heather McCallum of Routledge, for seeing the germ of a book in an oddity of a proposal, and then keeping faith with things.

And, finally, my thanks, as always, to Frieda Houser at the Wellcome Institute, who has coordinated the compilation of this book with her habitual unflappable efficiency, and to Jean Runciman, as ever, for her superb index.

Roy Porter
March 1996

INTRODUCTION

Roy Porter

> And who are you, said he?
> Don't puzzle me, said I
> (Laurence Sterne, *Tristram Shandy*)

WHO AM I ?

The Greeks believed they were the playthings of fate, Christians saw themselves as miserable sinners, Descartes thought that man was a thinker, liberals stressed self-determination, Romantics self-expression, while Freud invited you to go and lie upon the couch. The fundamental issue of identity has been endlessly posed by philosophers, poets, psychiatrists, and people at large. But if the question has stayed the same, the answers have changed over time. And so this book explores changing notions of selfhood from a historical perspective.

THE AUTHORIZED VERSION

There's a standard way of telling the story of the self, one that embodies and bolsters core Western values. Its climax is in the fulfilment of the cherished ideal of 'being yourself' (or as Polonius put it in *Hamlet*, wearying his son Laertes with unwanted advice, 'above all things, to thine own self, be true'). In other words, the secret of selfhood is commonly seen to lie in authenticity and individuality, and its history is presented as a biography of progress towards that goal, overcoming great obstacles in the process. Achieving autonomy implies inner character-building, typically through emancipation from external constraints like religious and political persecution, or the fetters of hidebound convention. That ideal of self-realization, gloriously expressed over a century ago in John Stuart Mill's *On Liberty*, still carries a powerful appeal, and it squares with other values – democracy, freedom of speech, equal opportunities – which we all hold dear and to which all Western regimes at least pay lip-service.

Popular ideas of identity thus presuppose some real 'inner self', and one that is 'whole' – a 'divided self' is seen as sick. Favourite ways of

1

imagining its biography include the blossoming of a seedling into a flower or the development from baby to adult or dependency to self-sufficiency. These organic metaphors are reflected in a popular historical narrative purporting to trace the rise over time of true individuality.

It's a tale that begins with the fabled dawn of consciousness. 'Primitive societies' are assumed to have operated through a sort of 'tribal' mentality, when all thought-processes were collective and all activities communal. In other words, the 'savage mind' was so completely in the grip of super-natural and magical outlooks, ritual and custom as to preclude any genuine individuality. It was the golden age of Greece, the story continues, that brought the first stirrings of real individual consciousness, asserted in defiance of tribal taboos and the inexorable decrees of the gods; philoso-phers like Socrates began to give expression to ideals of inner goodness and conscience. Such new convictions proved so threatening to traditional values that even the sophisticated Athenians made Socrates drink the hemlock; while the plays of Aeschylus, Sophocles and Euripides show how the struggle between the individual and fate could only end in tragedy. Under the iron rule of Roman emperors, stoic philosophers like Seneca were to find the ultimate expression of self-determination in suicide.

The age of faith likewise took certain steps towards asserting the sovereignty of the inner self. Christianity's core doctrine of a unique, eternal soul inspired those brave acts of personal integrity, modelled on Christ's crucifixion, which were the stuff of martyrs; and St Augustine's *Confessions* (397–401) gives a remarkable self-portrait of the soul as guilty sinner. But the Catholic Church was less interested in self-exploration than in teaching how mankind's first parents, Adam and Eve, had been punished for disobedience – had not the early theologian Tertullian insisted that 'we have no need for curiosity, after Jesus Christ, nor for investigation, after the Gospel'? The lesson of Original Sin at the Fall was that devout Christians must obey the Commandments; selfishness was the archetype of all sin and Lucifer's fate showed how rebellion (*non serviam*) would be crushed. Self-denial was the supreme good, as expressed in monastic rule; saints and mystics transcended their selfishness in divine love, John of the Cross seeking the 'annihilation of the self' (Charles Wesley too would later aspire to being 'lost in Thine immensity'). All such Christian ideals of stamping down pride and vanity through submission, and selflessly serving in the *Corpus Christi*, the community of the faithful, harmonized with the feudal doctrine that everyone had his or her pre-ordained place in a hierarchical order of lords and serfs, masters and men; the whole was greater than the part.

In standard accounts of what, with obvious Darwinian echoes, has been called 'the ascent of man', it is the Renaissance that signals the truly decisive breakthrough for individualism. As Peter Burke points out in his essay below, leading historians and art critics since Darwin's contemporary, Jacob Burckhardt, have acclaimed Renaissance Italy as the time and place when mankind – by which was implicitly meant literate, gifted, elite males – began to liberate itself from the chains of custom, conformity and the Church, taking a fearless leap forward into self-discovery and self-fulfilment. The literary and scholarly movement called humanism rejected the theological dogma of man as a loathsome sinner required to abase himself before God, and began to take delight in man himself, the apex of creation, the master of nature, the wonder of the world. New cultural genres – the portrait (above all the *self*-portrait), the diary and the biography (especially the *auto*-biography) – reveal heightened perceptions of individuality, the ego glorying in its own being.

A new sense of personal singularity, a fearless impulse to explore that distinctiveness, radiates from the sixteenth-century French essayist, Michel de Montaigne, who posed the elemental question: *Que sçais-je?* (what do I know?), and then tried to answer it through honest introspection. Infinitely curious, that great sceptic suggested that man possessed an *arrière boutique toute nostre* – a room behind the shop all our own: in other words, every individual's mind was a distinctive store-room of consciousness, a personal new world, awaiting exploration. Montaigne retired early from public life to examine his own psyche. He might have rubbed along well with Hamlet, for such questions of identity are what Shakespeare has his moody, brooding, introspective hero soliloquize upon: who precisely is this paragon of animals yet quintessence of dust? The soliloquy's key role in Renaissance drama itself marks a new limelighting of the individual.

Yet, like Socrates and the Christian martyrs, Hamlet too has to die, as also do all the other great overreachers portrayed by Renaissance playwrights – think of Marlowe's Faust and Tamburlaine. Evidently the coming of the individual still had a long way to go. Of great significance in this respect is the ambivalence of Protestantism, as Jane Shaw investigates (see Chapter 4, this volume). Along with other pioneering sociologists of modernization, Max Weber argued in his celebrated *The Protestant Ethic and the Spirit of Capitalism* (1904–5) that the Reformation spurred a new individuality, thanks to the Reformers' doctrine of the priesthood of all believers: individual salvation must be a personal thing, a matter of faith; it could not be dispensed by priests or bought with bribes. Hence Protestantism forced believers to go in for soul-searching – Puritans were noted for their spiritual diaries. Yet the themes of guilt, sin and submission remained central; Calvin himself stressed predestination and had heretics burned; and arguably it was not till Nietzsche proclaimed 'God is dead' that man could fully come into his own as a truly liberated autonomous being.

Historians of Western philosophy have often identified the seventeenth century as the great divide, the point from which rationality could serve as the foundation-stone of the self-determining individual. According to that reading of the psyche's progress, it was René Descartes (1594–1650), born in France but living in the Netherlands, who staked out a new role for the individual by making the basis of his *Discourse on Method* (1637) the proposition: *cogito ergo sum* (I am thinking, therefore I am): my own consciousness is the one thing of which I can be sure, and hence the one fixed Archimedean point in the universe. Not God or nature, but the ego, the conscious self, thereby becomes the source of understanding, and so of everything else (as Roger Smith shows in Chapter 3, this volume).

In medieval thought, as may be seen from Dante's *Divine Comedy*, dating from the early fourteenth century, the human condition had been understood through a panorama of the whole sphere of creation and its macrocosm/microcosm correspondences. That cosmology was now reversed by an act of self-reflective thought – literally, in Descartes' case, while meditating alone in a small room with a stove – man was rethinking the universe around him. Indeed, in an astonishingly daring stroke, Cartesian dualism claimed that man was perfectly unique in creation: everything else, the entire animal kingdom included, was mere 'extension'; that is, matter blindly governed by the laws of mechanics and mathematics; man alone, under God, had a conscious mind, could *know himself* and so understand the meaning of things.

Descartes' dream of the uniqueness of human interiority (self-aware thinking) invited later introspective philosophers further to probe the mechanisms of the mind. The question of who we were now hinged upon how our thinking processes worked: identity became a matter of intellect. The highly influential philosopher, John Locke, argued in his *Essay Concerning Humane Understanding* (1690) that the mind is not like a furnished flat, prestocked with innate ideas, but like a home gradually put together from scratch out of ceaseless mental acquisitions. The self is thus the product of experience and education: 'of all the men we meet with', the English empiricist insisted, 'nine parts of ten are what they are, good or evil, useful or not, by their education.' We are what we become – or, in Wordsworth's later *aperçu*, the child is father to the man. Different parents, different surroundings, different stimuli will produce different selves. Identity is thus unique but contingent, the product of perpetual accidents. By implication Locke thus gave his philosophical blessing to human diversity, change and progress, and it is no accident that he became the philosophical mascot to that archetypal eighteenth-century fictional auto-biographer of indirection, the eponymous hero of Laurence Sterne's novel, *Tristram Shandy* (1759–1767).

The new Lockian psychology awakened a bold vision of man making himself – viewed both as the *producer* but also as the *product* of social development and the civilizing process. Man was no longer to be pictured as an Adam, created by God with all his faculties fully implanted; rather the new Enlightenment myths favoured the model of the self-made man; they made their mark on Marx. Drawing on Francis Bacon's championing of science as the key to human progress, many *philosophes* spoke of man as *faber suae fortunae*, the author of his own destiny. New prominence was given to dynamic and evolving notions of consciousness, built upon Locke's suggestion that the mind began as 'white paper, or wax, to be moulded and fashioned as one pleases'; interaction with nature and the restless dialogue of needs and wants gave man the capacity to progress towards perfectibility, according to the optimistic new social theories proposed by thinkers like Condillac, Turgot and Condorcet in France, Priestley, Erasmus Darwin and Godwin in England, and Fichte, Herder and Hegel in Germany.

This standard story of the self is not without its sub-plots and complications. One centres on that great enigma, Jean-Jacques Rousseau, a provoking solitary who took his stand on painful honesty in his auto-biographical *Confessions* and in many other soul-searching works: 'I know my own heart' he proclaimed, and, knowing it, felt obliged to bare it, good and bad, to all the world, in a compulsion for self-exposure that released a ceaseless confessional stream from poets, artists, geniuses, drunks, drug-addicts and drop-outs – witness works like Thomas De Quincey's *Confessions of an English Opium Eater* (1822).

He was quite unlike any other person, Rousseau insisted: he had masochistic leanings, he was addicted to vices like masturbation, and had abandoned all his infants to an orphanage. In Rousseau, and all the more so with the Marquis de Sade, the anatomy of the psyche discovered psychopathology – a heart of darkness – and spurred the urge to reveal, in the name of truth, what formerly had been judged better left unknown or at least unsaid. Formerly a sin, self-centredness was being transformed into the *raison d'être*, the pride and glory of the modern psyche.

This new and seemingly inexhaustible fascination with baring the soul reminds us that, as discussed by John Mullan and Carolyn D. Williams (Chapters 7 and 8, this volume), it was during the eighteenth century that the novel established itself as the literary vehicle for the minute exploration of intense inner consciousness, particularly when cast in the form of a first-person narrative. Classics like Goethe's *Wilhelm Meister* (1796) took as their very subject the tortured development (*Bildung*) of the hero's character. The odyssey of self-discovery became, as Roger Cardinal shows (Chapter 9, this volume), the key Romantic metaphor, with its wanderer protagonist finding a spiritual epiphany through arduous effort. Romantic love privileged the heart; 'sensibility' became essential to good-ness and beauty; and in the cult of the man and lady of feeling, every sigh, blush and teardrop proved the exquisite tuning of the superior soul.

The individual also moved centre-stage in many other domains of eighteenth-century thinking. Cast as the autonomous bearer of rights he became the basic building block in a political liberalism that rebutted old Divine Right and absolutist theories with the declaration that the individual was prior to the state. Society was the product of free men (as ever, the male gender was taken for granted) contracting together in the state of nature to set up a political society to protect fundamental rights to life, liberty and property.

In a parallel move, Enlightenment economic theories also took as base-point the private property-holder – the possessive individualist or Robinson Crusoe figure. Finding classic expression in Adam Smith's *Wealth of Nations* (1776), political economy envisaged the market-place as an arena of sovereign operators, each pursuing personal profit through cut-throat competition. Thanks to what Smith called the 'hidden hand', enlightened self-interest, pursued without hindrance, would providentially advantage all; the result would be, in Jeremy Bentham's utilitarian formulation, the greatest happiness of the greatest number. What a spectacular reversal of the old theology! The Church had rejected selfishness as sin. But Enlightenment propagandists and philosophers like Bernard Mandeville and David Hume were now contending that the rational hedonism of *homo economicus* was good both for the individual and for society at large. Self-love and social were the same, sang the poet Alexander Pope, while (as explored by E.J. Hundert in Chapter 5, this volume) Mandeville revelled in the paradox that private vices were public benefits. With her faith in market forces and conviction that there was 'no such thing as society, only individuals and families', Mrs Thatcher was somewhat echoing these eighteenth-century thinkers – though, by praising 'Victorian values', she got the century wrong.

New Enlightenment individuality climaxed in the American Constitution and in the 'Liberty, Equality and Fraternity' of the French Revolution itself (its outcomes, the Terror and the Napoleonic Empire, betrayed the aspirations). The revolutionary era moreover inspired *Sturm und Drang* and Romanticism in literature and the arts, pitching individualism on to even higher planes. Rejecting the cash nexus and the despotism of polite conventional taste Romanticism idealized the outsider, the Bohemian artist, the Byronic rebel, bardic visionaries – and even victims like Dr Frankenstein's monster. Romantic social critics loathed bourgeois respectability; the world was too much with us, Wordsworth complained; urban man was alienated; and communing with nature was the way to get back in touch with one's self. Life must be a journey of self-discovery. That could be bitter – a *Winterreise*; but the road was not to be refused. In their comparable ways, Schiller and Shelley, Coleridge and Chateaubriand, Hölderlin and Hazlitt each espoused a creed of the sacredness of individual development, in pursuit of what Keats called the holiness of the heart's intentions. Self-development was thus assuming a religious ethos, while in the philosophy of Hegel, the dialectical strivings of mind or spirit (*Geist*) towards autonomy or full self-awareness fused personal development with spiritual destiny: Goethe's *Faust* (1808) offers a dramatic parallel.

Through the nineteenth century, Romantic drives to self-understanding and realization found further expression. Bleak philosophers like Schopenhauer and Nietzsche centred their tragic visions on the lone individual, solipsistically enduring or enjoying utter isolation from the universe and society. Decadent *fin de siècle* poets dwelt upon their inner consciousness, often stimulated by dreams, drugs or drink. Academic psychology meanwhile turned the subject into an object for scientific investigation and, through the invention of systematic testing, focused attention upon the meaning of individual differences.

Above all, the quest for the ultimate self seemed to make a crucial breakthrough with the 'discovery of the unconscious'. The upstaging of the Cartesian *cogito* was not a new thing with Sigmund Freud, but it was he who actually theorized the unconscious. Psychoanalysis argued that the rational understanding proudly cultivated by the Renaissance humanists, Descartes' prized *ego cogitans*, was not after all master in its own house, not the real thing. What truly counted was what had hitherto lain concealed, an unconscious profoundly repressed and hence expressed only in foreign tongues or obliquely and painfully by means of illness, hysteria and nightmare. Neurotics especially needed to be put in touch with this repressed self, re-integrating it within a healthy whole.

Freud thereby opened up new horizons of selfhood, or rather delved into the psyche's ocean depths, uncovering a submarine population of dark desires and dangerous drives. Self-discovery had become a journey into inner space. Exploration of this seemingly alien realm was to have the profoundest implications for modern psychiatry, art and literature – think of surrealism or the stream-of-consciousness novel. And, crucially important, Freud claimed he had hit upon a crucial new truth (or one long silenced): the self's ultimate secret was sexuality.

Depth psychology thus gave new edge to Polonius' advice. Because the Freudian psyche might not be very pleasant to behold, ruthless honesty became more essential than ever, nothing should be concealed or rationalized away. This imperative of truth was no less fundamental to one of the key philosophical movements of the twentieth century, existentialism, whose oracle, Jean-Paul Sartre, stressed the paramount need to combat the 'bad faith' of the unexamined life, and all its duplicitous deceptions. The movement beginning with Renaissance autobiography culminated, it thus appears, in existential angst, the finest hour of subjective individualism. Meanwhile, on a less exalted plane, the present century was spawning scores of creeds and cults, building on Freud and similar experts, and claiming to help people to understand themselves, maximize their potential, like themselves, express themselves and, of course, *be* themselves. Ours is the age of the 'me generation', doing your own thing.

THE SELF THROUGH FRESH EYES?

Narratives of this kind – of how the West discovered a unique self unknown to former times, an inner psyche unfamiliar in other cultures – carry a huge appeal and underpin familiar thinking. They shape our image of the medieval peasant, of the Romantic poet – and of ourselves. And who can deny they contain a measure of truth? After all, much of our artistic and intellectual heritage – Petrarch and Rilke, Milton and Mill, love poetry and liberalism – amounts to defences and celebrations of the uniqueness of the outpourings of the individual imagination and heart. Yet the tale also has the ring of myth, even an air of soap-box rhetoric, especially when recounted as an epic in which the heroic self is portrayed as surmounting ridge after ridge until it reaches its peak of perfection in our own times. That's a story flattering to ourselves, and perhaps all the more so when, as Jonathan Dollimore argues (see Chapter 15, this volume), an additional twist in the tale hints that ours is also an age of special psychic crisis. Looked at closely, however, it also proves a story full of loose ends and begged questions. And so it's time to rethink our received grand saga of the self, and that is what this book begins.

Key aspects of the odyssey of identity just sketched are addressed by various of the contributors. The chapters in this book cover the Renaissance and Protestantism, Descartes and Rousseau, the Enlightenment and Romanticism, Freud and Thomas Mann, Marx and Weber, psychology and psychotherapy. And in so doing they challenge old assumptions and suggest new possibilities. Here a couple of examples will suffice: addressing the new Renaissance formulations of self, Peter Burke reveals how the medieval mind was more individualistic than Burckhardt believed, and Humanist outlooks more conventional. The standing of Descartes as the founder of a new philosophy is central to the pair of essays by Jonathan Sawday and Roger Smith; but while reaffirming the importance of the Cartesian *cogito*, both suggest his radical philosophy will only be fully understood if it is set in its wider cultural contexts – for instance, contemporary artistic commitment to the business of anatomizing ('autopsy' literally means looking into one-self), or the striking preference for privacy in the bourgeois Netherlands where he lived. The profound writings of Norbert Elias on 'the civilizing process' have likewise pointed to the ties between psychological change and new opportunities for solitude and interiority provided by trends in material culture – books, mirrors, individual bedrooms and so on.

Here and elsewhere the contributors get away from the heroic struggles of the old escapologist self, and seek to put developments in their historical and cultural contexts. Thus John Mullan and Kate Flint both consider the new 'I' or voice created and presupposed by literary genres (the novel and dramatic verse), while Daniel Pick and Steve Connor explore the crucial role played by new technologies (respectively those concerning the eye and the ear) in furthering new concepts of the 'I': without the camera or the gramophone, the twentieth-century *ego* would have had very different sensory and conceptual parameters.

In particular, conventional assumptions about linear and inevitable progress are disputed in this book. The notion of an ascent from some primordial collective psychological soup to a sharply defined individual identity now seems a question-begging and self-serving leftover of Victorian fanfares of progress. The horrors of the twentieth century have demolished the assurance of earlier individualists like Herbert Spencer that individuality automatically spelled moral improvement. We can now clearly see that modern individualist cults in the West, especially the USA, were in large measure reactions first to Fascism and then to Soviet propaganda in the Cold War era. With Communism collapsed and Western democracies unsure about future paths (do we want to be coldly competitive, or caring?) it is a good time to reflect upon our myths of the self.

This shaking of confidence in progress frames some of the revisionist accounts below, which accentuate the darker side and ambivalences of former philosophies of the self. E.J. Hundert analyses the ambiguities of the fashionable Enlightenment image of the self performing its part in the drama of the *theatrum mundi.* Each individual got his role, true; but the theatrical image implied that all was artifice, an 'act': tear away the mask and what was there? – another mask, or nothing at all? Certain Enlightenment figures like Diderot loved toying with the idea that reality was in truth but illusion, while Rousseau regarded it as the ultimate reproof of modern *mores.* Other eighteenth-century figures like Mary Wollstonecraft, as Sylvana Tomaselli shows, were as uneasy as Rousseau that the new individualism was but the disguised self-indulgence of a frivolous and morally bankrupt society, devoted to rapacity among men and a glamorized narcissism among women.

Again: working within the Lockean tradition, Augustan satirists and philosophers like David Hume were (as Carolyn D. Williams explores) deeply troubled by the possibility that the individual was nothing more than an unstable heap of impressions. Under such circumstances, what guarantee was there that the same person would wake up as the one who went to sleep the night before? (Perhaps only that false friend, memory.) It is surely no accident that the sceptical philosopher David Hume himself suffered what we would today call a nervous breakdown, as did his successor, John Stuart Mill.

The problematic nature of psychological individualism has had lasting repercussions. In the eighteenth century, Locke's idea that man is made not given (nurture not nature) served a progressive role – it was a promise of liberation; in the Victorian era it focused attention on the importance of childhood in individual development; but in modern times this doctrine of the malleability of man played into the hands of Skinnerian

9

stimulus–response behaviourism, totalitarian brainwashing and other advocates of social science conditioning.

Freud was fully aware of the ambiguous implications of science for the psyche, of the tension between self-knowledge and self-possession. He was wholly committed to pursuing to the limit the anatomy of the self, while having to disabuse himself and others of the Victorian optimism that such new knowledge would automatically make us freer and happier. The science of the self would rather shatter man's self-esteem:

> Humanity has in the course of time had to endure from the hands of science two great outrages upon the naive self-love. The first was when it realized that our earth was not the centre of the universe, but only a tiny speck in a world-system of a magnitude hardly conceivable; this is associated in our minds with the name of Copernicus, although Alexandrian doctrines taught something very similar. The second was when biological research robbed man of his peculiar privilege of having been specially created, and relegated him to a descent from the animal world, implying an ineradicable animal nature in him: this transvaluation has been accomplished in our own time upon the instigation of Charles Darwin, Wallace and their predecessors, and not without the most violent opposition from their contemporaries. But man's craving for grandiosity is now suffering the third and most bitter blow from present-day psychological research which is endeavouring to prove to the 'ego' of each one of us that he is not even master in his own house, but that he must remain content with the veriest scraps of information about what is going on unconsciously in his own mind. We psycho-analysts were neither the first nor the only ones to propose to mankind that they should look inward; but it appears to be our lot to advocate it most insistently and to support it by empirical evidence which touches every man closely.
>
> (Sigmund Freud, *Introductory Lectures on Psycho-analysis* (1916–17), in *The Standard Edition of the Complete Psychological Works of Sigmund Freud*, Vol. xvi, trans. and ed. J. Strachey *et al.*, London: The Hogarth Press and Institute of Psycho-Analysis, 1953–74, p. 285).

Yet, for all his anxieties, Freud was in one fundamental respect a traditionalist: he believed there was indeed an inner truth – albeit a terrifying subterranean battleground of the id, ego and super-ego – waiting to be discovered, interpreted, and even healed. Or, to put this another way, the reason why Shakespeare and others could write romances and comedies of 'mistaken identity' was precisely because they believed that such mistakes could actually be undone and true identity would eventually be revealed: deceptions would end, the masks would come off.

What has been especially striking in recent times, however, is the rise of new philosophies challenging the very idea, ensconced since the Renaissance, of a core (if elusive) inner personal identity. Crucial here have been the speculations of deconstructionists, Derrideans and post-modernists, and, most influentially of all, the work of Michel Foucault. In a series of books published over the course of twenty-five years, Foucault challenged liberal belief in human agency, championing and popularizing the notion of the 'death of the author'. Conventional understandings of subjectivity – individual writers and readers, having minds of their own and exercising free will through thought and action – all were deluded. Rather Foucault argued for the primacy of semantic sign systems, cognitive structures and texts. We don't think our thoughts, they think us; we are but the bearers of discourses, our selves are discursively constructed. Within this frame of analysis, any notion of the ascent of selfhood is but idle teleological myth, a hagiography of humanism. Such was for Foucault essentially the Romantic fallacy, blossoming in the nineteenth century before collapsing in our own era, partly thanks to the devastating Nietzschian critique – the death of 'God', Foucault suggested, reversing standard interpretations, entailed the death of 'man' as well. The validity and implications of this Foucauldian analysis of the decentring or dissolution of man are assessed in several chapters in this book, in particular those by Steve Connor, Nikolas Rose, Jonathan Dollimore and Terry Eagleton, who also evaluates Wittgenstein's somewhat analogous demolition of the inner and private subject (the notorious 'ghost in the machine' fallacy).

The anti-humanist Foucault maintained that the conventional story of the self was but anthropocentric piety. Even more scandalously, he and his followers were to argue that the new individualism gaining ground during the Enlightenment was in truth – contrary to the claims of its champions and to customary understanding – not an emancipation from social fetters but the very means by which the state locked subjects into bureaucratic and administrative systems, by stamping them with a clear and distinct identity (subjectivity). Civil registration required the documenting of names, births and deaths; police mug-shots and fingerprinting were introduced – unique to the individual and useful mainly as means of social identification: they'd got your name and number. Continuing controversy in Britain over the proposed introduction of compulsory identity cards illustrates the point: what has been truly difficult to achieve in modern times is not identity but anonymity. The implication is that our prized individuality is truly a tool of social control, being, argues Nikolas Rose, subject to manipulation through those 'psy sciences' which have been so spectacular a feature of the modern scene, prescribing for personalities. These questions of the discursive construction of the self are also examined from a technological point of view by Daniel Pick and Steve Connor.

WHERE THE SELF STANDS

Traditional liberal–progressive tellings of the ascent of man have thus been critiqued by those who suggest that the esteemed liberal self is just a construct, a trick of language, a rhetorical ruse. The literary historian Stephen Greenblatt has portrayed Renaissance man as 'self-fashioning', as if the self were essentially a suit of clothes; by extension, the much trumpeted 'discovery of the self' – supposedly the divesting of artifice, confronting the naked truth about ourselves – is similarly reduced to yet another stratagem, or at least to a mode of 'social construction'.

Liberal orthodoxy has been further assailed of late by a battery of feminist critiques. Lumped together, their thrust is that the telling of the 'discovery of the self' has been mystificatory, because it has always covertly taken males as its subject. The 'true self' has been imagined in terms of the masculine self, utterly ignoring the fact that humans have, linguistically and culturally, always in reality been gendered, with quite different attributes ascribed to the 'opposite sexes'. Not least, the normative image of the emergent thrusting and self-sufficient ego has served to legitimate crudely macho stereotypes. In response feminist critiques have emerged, calling the traditional saga of the self into question on the grounds that it has essentially mirrored and reinforced myths of masculinity. Several chapters in this volume – notably those by Carolyn Williams, Sylvana Tomaselli, Lynda Nead and Kate Flint – dissect the role played by gender in shaping paradigms of identity, showing how influential expectations, like the Victorian 'separate spheres' notion of 'public man, private woman', have dictated what selves are permissible.

The twilight of the twentieth century is a good moment to be rethinking the sense of self. The Old Testament God told Moses: 'I AM THAT I AM' but few of us mortals can feel so confident about ourselves these days. In the US and UK, right-wing governments have been stridently proclaiming the merits of socio-economic individualism, with the backing of sociobiologists who insist that the selfish gene is nature's way. And there is no shortage of propaganda for a galaxy of styles of self-fulfilment, self-expression and psychotherapy. But these ideological campaigns are being advanced against a backdrop of the erosion of established identities, associated with the disintegration of traditional patterns of family life, employment, gender roles, education and other social institutions. The introduction of new drugs – Ecstasy, Prozac, etc. – may herald a new age in which the chemical modification of the brain calls into question old assumptions about defined individual character. The controversy in the US about repressed and recovered memory syndrome – the multiple personality alleged to follow from childhood sexual abuse – hints that we may be facing a future in which traditional models of a stable and permanent personality may lose their applicability. And, as Jonathan Dollimore argues, death has once more become a key player in the game, partly as a result of AIDS.

Not least, we live in the age of the computer, the Walkman, of artificial intelligence, virtual reality and the threatened or promised cyberspace revolution. If machines will think like us (and feel?); if cyberspace supplants the inner space of personal consciousness, what will happen to the privileged realm of our psyche? Will there follow a dissolution of the traditional ego-boundary consciousness, with perhaps a 'reversion' to a 'tribal' – but now electronic – consciousness? We may be glimpsing the end of the tradition which the following chapters explore.

FURTHER READING

Philippe Ariès and Georges Duby (general eds), *A History of Private Life*, vol. i, *From Pagan Rome to Byzantium*, ed. P. Veyne, trans. Arthur Goldhammer (Cambridge, MA: The Belknap Press, 1987); vol. ii *Revelations of the Medieval World*, ed. George Duby, trans. Arthur Goldhammer (Cambridge, MA: The Belknap Press, 1988); vol. iii, *Passions of the Renaissance*, ed. Roger Chartier, trans. Arthur Goldhammer (Cambridge, MA: The Belknap Press, 1989); vol. iv, *From the Fires of Revolution to the Great War*, ed. Michelle Perrot, trans. Arthur Goldhammer (Cambridge, MA: The Belknap Press, 1990); vol. v, *Riddles of Identity in Modern Times*, eds Antoine Prost and Gerard Vincent, trans. Arthur Goldhammer (Cambridge, MA: The Belknap Press, 1991).

William Barrett, *Death of the Soul. Philosophical Thought from Descartes to the Computer* (Oxford: Oxford University Press, 1987).

Jacob Burckhardt, *The Civilization of the Renaissance in Italy* (Oxford: Phaidon, 1981; 1st edn, 1859).

Ian Burkitt, 'The Shifting Concept of the Self', *History of the Human Sciences*, vii (1994), 7–28.

Michael Carrithers, Steven Collins and Steven Lukes (eds), *The Category of the Person* (Cambridge: Cambridge University Press, 1985).

S.D. Cox, *'The Stranger Within Thee': The Concept of the Self in Late Eighteenth Century Literature* (Pittsburgh: Pittsburgh University Press, 1980).

Norbert Elias, *The Civilizing Process*, vol. 1, *The History of Manners* (New York: Pantheon, 1978); vol. 2, *Power and Civility* (New York: Pantheon, 1982); vol. 3, *The Court Society* (New York: Pantheon, 1983).

Henri F. Ellenberger, *The Discovery of the Unconscious: The History and Evolution of Dynamic Psychiatry* (New York: Basic Books, 1970).

Michel Foucault, *La Folie et la Déraison: Histoire de la Folie à l'Age Classique* (Paris: Librairie Plon, 1961); trans. and abridged as *Madness and Civilization: A History of Insanity in the Age of Reason*, trans. Richard Howard (New York: Random House, 1965; London: Tavistock, 1967).

Michel Foucault, *The Order of Things: An Archaeology of the Human Sciences* (London: Tavistock, 1970).

Michel Foucault, *The Archaeology of Knowledge*, trans. A.M. Sheridan Smith (London: Tavistock, 1972).

Michel Foucault, *Discipline and Punish: The Birth of the Prison*, trans. A. Sheridan (London: Allen Lane, 1977).

Michel Foucault, *Histoire de la sexualité:* vol. 1, *La volonté de savoir* (Paris: Gallimard,

1976); trans. Robert Hurley, *The History of Sexuality: Introduction* (London: Allen Lane, 1978; New York: Vintage Books, 1985).

Stephen Greenblatt, *Renaissance Self-Fashioning: From More to Shakespeare* (Chicago: University of Chicago Press, 1980).

Ian Hacking, 'Multiple Personality Disorder and its Hosts', *History of the Human Sciences*, v (1992), 3–32.

Elie Halévy, *The Growth of Philosophic Radicalism*, trans. Mary Morris, 2 vols (London: Faber and Gwyer Ltd, 1928; 2nd edn, 1934).

T.C. Heller *et al.* (eds), *Reconstructing Individualism: Autonomy, Individuality and the Self in Western Thought* (Stanford, CA: Stanford University Press, 1986).

Christopher Lasch, *The Culture of Narcissism: American Life in an Age of Diminishing Expectations* (New York: Norton, 1979).

Stephen Lukes, *Individualism* (Oxford: Basil Blackwell, 1973).

J.O. Lyons, *The Invention of the Self: The Hinge of Consciousness in the Eighteenth Century* (Carbondale, ILL.: Southern Illinois University Press, 1978).

C.B. MacPherson, *The Political Theory of Possessive Individualism: Hobbes to Locke* (Oxford: Oxford University Press, 1964).

Lois McNay, *Foucault and Feminism: Power, Gender and the Self* (Cambridge: Polity, 1992).

John N. Morris, *Versions of the Self: Studies in English Autobiography from John Bunyan to Stuart Mill* (New York: Basic Books, 1966),

Camille Paglia, *Sexual Personae* (London and New Haven: Yale University Press, 1990).

John Passmore, *The Perfectibility of Man* (London: Duckworth, 1968).

Anthony Smith, *Software for the Self: Culture and Technology* (London: Faber, 1996).

Patricia Meyer Spacks, *Imagining a Self: Autobiography and Novel in Eighteenth Century England* (Cambridge, MA: Harvard University Press, 1976).

C. Taylor, *Sources of the Self. The Making of Modern Identity* (Cambridge: Cambridge University Press, 1989).

Part I

RENAISSANCE AND EARLY MODERN

1

REPRESENTATIONS OF THE SELF FROM PETRARCH TO DESCARTES

Peter Burke

Cogito ergo sum: I think, therefore I am. Philosophers have often pointed out that this argument of Descartes, in his *Discourse on Method* (1637), is a circular one, since the 'I' of 'I think' assumes exactly what the writer is trying to prove. From the point of view of a cultural historian, however, this passage remains important as a celebrated affirmation of the importance and the unity of the self.

It is often claimed that this modern idea of the self goes back to the Renaissance, in the sense of the period of European cultural history which stretches from Petrarch to Descartes, from the early fourteenth century (at least in the case of Italy) to the early seventeenth. If this chapter were being written in the age of Jacob Burckhardt, its main thesis would be simple and clear. When he published his essay on *The Civilization of the Renaissance in Italy* in 1860, the great Swiss cultural historian was confident that a central development in Italian culture in that period was what he called 'individualism' or 'the discovery of man'.

Burckhardt's contrast between the Middle Ages and the Renaissance was a dramatic one. In the Middle Ages, according to him, people were aware of themselves only as members of a group; in the Renaissance, on the other hand, 'man became a spiritual individual and recognized himself as such'. The rise of self-awareness or subjectivity was reflected by the rise of autobiographies and portraits. In its concern with the individual self, according to Burckhardt, Italy was the first modern culture. Italy was a model for the rest of Europe as Europe would later be for the rest of the world.

However, all these statements are problematic, as historians have become aware in the last thirty years or so. Problematic from at least three points of view: geographical, sociological and chronological. In the first place, we cannot assume the uniqueness of the Western self without examining Japanese autobiographies, Chinese portraits and so on. I shall return to this problem at the end of this chapter. In the second place, there is the sociological problem: whose self? Burckhardt's examples came from a tiny minority of Italians, generally upper-class males.

In the third place, Burckhardt's contrast between the Renaissance and the Middle Ages was too sharp. On one side, he underestimated the importance of the preoccupation with the individual self in the Middle Ages, especially from the twelfth century onwards. On the other side, he exaggerated this preoccupation during the fifteenth and sixteenth centuries. In the Italy of this time there is no lack of evidence of identification with family, guild, faction or city. In different contexts, people saw themselves or presented themselves as Florentines (say), as Italians, as Christians, as males, as soldiers and so on. Identities were not single but multiple.

It is also necessary to raise the question whether changes in the sense of individual identity were connected with the cultural movement we call the Renaissance, or whether they simply happened at the same time. In certain cases, as we shall see, classical examples were taken as models, but some writers of personal documents were probably unaware that the Renaissance was taking place.

CONCEPTS OF THE SELF

In any case, the very concept of 'the self' is not as simple as it looks. Burckhardt was particularly concerned with self-consciousness and its expression in literature (biographies and autobiographies) and art (portraits and self-portraits). He assumed, as many people have done before and since, that these expressions of the self were transparent. However, this assumption has been undermined by many twentieth-century literary, historical and sociological studies. Their authors view the outward expressions of the self as so many facades and stress the strategies and conventions of 'self-presentation', 'self-stylization' and 'impression management'. They are interested not only in the person but also in the 'persona', the mask which the individual wears in public, the role which he or she is playing.

More recently, these studies, of which Erving Goffman's *The Presentation of Self in Everyday Life* is the most famous, have been undermined in their turn. The idea of self-presentation implies a fixed self operating behind the facade. By contrast, a cluster of recent books emphasize 'self-fashioning' (as Stephen Greenblatt puts it in a study of Renaissance England), or the 'reconstruction' or even the 'invention' of the self, which is now assumed, in the wake of the French psychoanalyst Jacques Lacan, to be a linguistic, cultural or social construct.

The ideas of self-consciousness, self-expression, self-presentation and self-fashioning do not exhaust the conceptual problems awaiting a historian of the Renaissance self, or better, of the variety of 'Renaissance selves'. Self-knowledge, self-confidence, self-cultivation, self-examination and self-reliance also deserve to be considered. So does self-respect, an idea which was usually formulated in this period in terms of 'honour'.

So too does self-control. According to the Dutch historian Johan Huizinga, emotional instability was characteristic of Europeans in the late Middle Ages, a 'perpetual oscillation between despair and distracted joy, between cruelty and pious tenderness'. Building on Huizinga's foundation, the German sociologist Norbert Elias argued that the consolidation of the centralized state in the early modern period led to a consolidation of the self. Political stability led to psychological stability. Elias illustrated the trend to self-control in an unforgettable way with examples of increasingly strict table manners taken from 'conduct books', a popular literary genre in the fifteenth and sixteenth centuries and one to which Erasmus and other Renaissance humanists contributed.

If we are not to lose ourselves in this forest of concepts, we need to turn for orientation to the language used during the period itself. Renaissance humanists were much concerned with self-knowledge. 'Know thyself', they reiterated in different languages, *gnothi seauton, nosce teipsum, erkenne Dich selbst* and so on. As Sir John Davies put it in his poem *Nosce teipsum* (1599), 'My self am centre of my circling thought / Only myself I study, learn and know.'

Equally important was the presentation of self to others. 'Giving a good impression of oneself' (*dar buona impression di sé*) was a central theme of one of the most famous books in Renaissance Italy, Baldassare Castiglione's *Book of the Courtier* (1528). Around the year 1600, a number of European writers, including Francis Bacon, discussed the twin arts of simulation and dissimulation. There was also considerable interest in what was occasionally called 'psychology', especially in character-types and psychological disorders, notably melancholy (regularly discussed from Marsilio Ficino in the later fifteenth century to Robert Burton in the early seventeenth).

The uniqueness of the individual was also a concern at this time. According to Castiglione, 'Master Unique' (*Messer Unico*) was the nickname of a poet at the court of Urbino. John Donne claimed that in his day 'every man' 'thinks he has got to be a Phoenix', in the sense that there 'can be / None of that kind of which he is, but he', while social roles such as 'Prince, subject, father, son' had been forgotten. The claim is remarkably similar to Burckhardt's later remark that in the Middle Ages 'man' was only conscious of himself as a member of some general category, while in the Renaissance a sense of the individual developed.

'Sincerity' was another Renaissance concept, a word which came into regular use in English in the late sixteenth century, as the American critic Lionel Trilling pointed out. Shakespeare used the terms 'sincerity', 'sincere' and 'sincerely' thirteen times in his printed works (Sidney and Jonson used the terms twice each, while Milton, by contrast, used them forty-eight times in his prose works alone). The advice Polonius gives Laertes in *Hamlet* 'to thine own self be true' may have been a common-place but it was a relatively new commonplace. What is more, the term 'sincere' was becoming a fashionable one in other languages during this period, notably Italian and French (Montaigne was one of the first recorded users). Like the literature on simulation and dissimulation, the rise of the new term suggests that people were becoming more aware of the difference between an inner and an outer self, a difference which was given its classic formulation by Descartes at the end of the period in his famous contrast between mind and body, unkindly described in our own day as the doctrine of 'the ghost in the machine'.

As the examples cited above suggest, the sources for the study of Renaissance selves are manifold. Besides essays such as Montaigne's, plays like Shakespeare's, and dialogues such as Castiglione's, there are biog-raphies, autobiographies, diaries, travel journals, letters. This literary evidence may be supplemented by painted and sculpted portraits and self-portraits. In this chapter I shall examine a few of these sources of information about self-consciousness, looking especially at changes over the long term. The reader should try to bear in mind the fact that the same texts and artefacts have been viewed by different scholars as examples of self-expression, self-presentation or self-invention.

BIOGRAPHY AND AUTOBIOGRAPHY

Biographies were not unknown in the Middle Ages. Lives of the saints were common, and lives of laymen were written from time to time. In the ninth century, a biography of the emperor Charlemagne was written by his chaplain Einhard. In the thirteenth century, the French nobleman Joinville wrote a biography of Louis IX of France. In the fifteenth century an anonymous follower of Bayard wrote the biography of his master, the knight 'without fear and without reproach'.

However, the interest in biography had been much stronger in ancient Greece and Rome, especially in late antiquity. Plutarch wrote his parallel lives of famous Greeks and Romans at the beginning of the second century. Suetonius wrote his biographies of Roman emperors at about the same time, while Diogenes Laertius wrote his lives of philosophers in the third century.

These lives attracted much interest during the Renaissance and they inspired modern imitations, first in Italy and later elsewhere. Petrarch wrote the lives of a number of illustrious men on the model of Jerome's *De viris illustribus*. His friend Boccaccio wrote lives of Dante and Petrarch on the model of the life of Virgil by the Roman critic Donatus. In the fifteenth century a Florentine bookseller, Vespasiano da Bisticci, wrote the lives of the famous men of his day (many of them his clients). In the sixteenth century, two famous collections of biographies were published: Paolo Giovio's lives of princes and generals and Giorgio Vasari's lives of Italian artists. It became increasingly common to provide famous books with an introductory biography of the author, as if his life was the key to the work.

Women too were the subjects of biographies. Boccaccio wrote the lives of more than a hundred illustrious women, from Eve to Queen Joanna of Naples, via Semiramis, Juno, Venus, Helen, Artemisia, Portia and Lucretia. Jacopo Filippo Foresti, an Augustinian hermit from Bergamo, published a collection of lives, *On Certain Famous Women* (1497), including the Renaissance scholars Isotta Nogarola and Cassandra Fedele. Vespasiano included the life of Alessandra de' Bardi in his collection, comparing her to the ancient Roman matron Portia for her piety and courage.

Outside Italy, few biographies were written before the sixteenth century, but then the trickle turned into a flood. For example, a biography of Dürer was published in 1532, the first Northern European biography of an artist. A biography of Erasmus was published in 1540, only four years after his death. The French humanist Theodore Beza published a biography of his master Jean Calvin in 1564. In England, one thinks of William Roper and Nicholas Harpsfield on Thomas More, of George Cavendish on Cardinal Wolsey (all written in the 1550s), and of Fulke Greville on his friend Philip Sidney. The popularity of the French and English translations of Plutarch's *Lives* is another sign of the interest in intimate biographical details. Plutarch was one of Montaigne's favourite authors precisely because his biographies dealt with private as well as public affairs, with the inner as well as the outer life of his subjects.

The autobiography or what some historians call the 'ego-document' (a broader category including diaries, journals, memoirs and letters) is potentially at least even more revealing of the self. Before 1500, auto-biographies and memoirs were relatively rare, despite a few famous examples such as Petrarch, the humanist pope Pius II, the pious Englishwoman Margery Kempe, and the French diplomat Philippe de Commynes.

It is obviously dangerous to argue from the rarity of ego-documents before 1500 that self-consciousness was undeveloped, since modern Western links between writing and self-examination are not universal. The kinds of text produced in a given culture are related not only to its central values but also to local assumptions about the uses of literacy (and we must not forget that only a minority of the population of Renaissance Europe was able to write).

When ego-documents exist, on the other hand, they are valuable testimonies to the kind of self-image current in a particular milieu, as two examples may suggest. Petrarch's autobiography, the *Secretum*, takes the form of a dialogue between 'Franciscus' and 'Augustinus' and so bears

21

witness to its author's sense of a divided or fragmented self. Again, in Florence the tradition of memoranda (*ricordanze*) went back to the fourteenth and fifteenth centuries. These texts were not quite account-books, not quite diaries, not quite local chronicles, not quite family histories, but something of each of these. They illustrate a form of self-consciousness in which the boundaries between the individual, the family and the city were less sharp than they became centuries later.

After 1500, ego-documents became more common and more personal. In Italy one finds not only such famous examples as the autobiographies of the Florentine sculptor Benvenuto Cellini and the Milanese physician Girolamo Cardano, but also a host of minor figures including the apothecary Luca Landucci, the tailor Sebastiano Arditi and the carpenter Giambattista Casale.

Outside Italy, sixteenth-century examples of autobiography include the emperor Maximilian (who employed ghost-writers), St Teresa, St Ignatius, the French soldier Blaise de Monluc, the Swiss family Platter (which produced three texts in three successive generations), the German burgomaster Bartholomew Sastrow, and the English musician Thomas Whitehorne.

Why should the autobiographical habit have developed at this time? It might be argued that the city, which offers alternative ways of life, encourages a sense of individual choice. The sixteenth century was an age of urbanization. It was also an age of travel, and travel encourages self-consciousness by cutting off the individual from his or her community. A famous account of a visit to Brazil begins as follows: 'I Hans Staden of Homberg in Hesse proposed, if God willed, to see the Indies, and with this intention I travelled from Bremen to Holland.'

The sixteenth century was also the first century in which print became part of everyday life. It was the age not only of the rise of the autobiography or journal but also of fictional narratives in the first-person story, such as the picaresque novel in Spain or the sonnet-sequences of Sidney, Shakespeare and others. These examples suggest the importance of the diffusion of printed models for the creation of a new or sharper sense of self, as well as for the breakdown of inhibitions about writing down the story of one's life.

Why were specific texts produced? In the case of autobiography, the explanation is usually given in the first paragraph or so of the text (it is one of the conventions of the genre). They offer an interesting body of answers, which are worth taking seriously even if we do not take them literally. They range from the 'modesty formula', claiming that the text was produced at the request of someone else (often a son, as in the case of Thomas Platter and Sir James Melville, sometimes disciples, as in the case of Ignatius Loyola), to Cellini's immodest assertion that 'Every man who has done something worthwhile' – such as himself – 'should write an account of his life with his own hand'. In the case of biography, fame was again the spur or one of the spurs. Another purpose was to offer exemplars to the reader, or in the language of modern psychologists, 'role models' or 'ego ideals'. The lives of the saints, for instance. Again, Antonio de Guevara's *Dial of Princes* (*Reloj de Principes*) was a biography of Marcus Aurelius written in order for princes such as Charles V to regulate their conduct as if by a clock.

A variety of models and styles was available. There was the impersonal style, for instance, exemplified by the 'commentaries' of Pius II or Monluc or the English soldier Francis Vere (in the manner of Julius Caesar). A different form of impersonality can be found in the majority of *ricordanze*, listing births, marriages and deaths, noting prices, the weather, news which arrived in the city and so on. There was also a more personal, confessional style in the manner of St Augustine, whose example was followed by Petrarch, among others, and also by St Teresa, who began by remarking that 'If I had not been so wicked, the possession of devout, god-fearing parents together with the favour of God's grace, would have been enough to make me good.' A secular form of the confessional model can be found in the diary of a young Florentine patrician Girolamo da Sommaia, narrating his sexual exploits to himself, recording them for safety's sake in the Greek alphabet, and describing his 'sweetness with Francisca' (*dolcetudine con Francisca*), 'sweetness of Isabella without paying' (*Dolcetudine di Isabella senza soldo*) and so forth.

Today it may seem odd or even contradictory that the biography or autobiography of the unique individual should follow a pattern, but for readers and writers of the Renaissance, who were taught to model themselves on the exemplary figures of antiquity, there was no paradox. Following a model had the advantage of imposing order on apparent chaos, turning random events into a story with a plot, with a beginning, middle and end. All the same, something which we would regard as valuable – how much, we shall never know – must have been sacrificed in the process of fitting new lives into old categories.

A similar tension between stereotype and spontaneity or authenticity can be found in another form of self-presentation, the letter. The private letter is perhaps the personal document *par excellence*, expressing the thoughts and emotions of the moment at the moment, rather than recollecting them in tranquillity in autobiographies and journals. Leading figures of the Renaissance such as Petrarch and Erasmus put a good deal of themselves into their letters; indeed, both men used letters as a tool of self-presentation or self-fashioning. All the same, letters followed literary conventions. Indeed, Cicero's letters were studied in some Renaissance schools as a good example of the way to write prose. A number of treatises on letter-writing were printed in the sixteenth and seventeenth centuries. In Italy there was a fashion for printing the letters of famous people such as the writer Pietro Aretino, the critic Pietro Bembo, the actress Isabella Andreini. There were also anthologies of letters (including one of letters by women).

The Italian treatises and anthologies were one channel by which the style and values of the Italian Renaissance reached other parts of Europe. Montaigne claimed to own a hundred books of letters, and it is likely that these collections helped him and other readers to express, present and fashion their selves. Montaigne remains one of the most memorable examples of Renaissance self-awareness. For his time, he placed unusual stress on the need for privacy, for what he called 'a room behind the shop which is completely our own', *une arrière boutique toute nostre*. He was sceptical of the claims of other people to know an individual, pure guesswork according to him, but he was not sceptical about self-knowledge. His *Essays* offer a more vivid portrait of an individual than most autobiographies of his time – or indeed since. Defending his enterprise – and it is revealing of the values of his day that he felt the need to defend his enterprise – Montaigne made a comparison between autobiography and self-portraiture, taking the example of René of Anjou. 'Why is it not legitimate for every man to portray himself with his pen, as it was for him to do it with a crayon?'

PORTRAIT AND SELF-PORTRAIT

Material culture was, and is, an important vehicle for expressing views of the self. Palaces and country houses expressed the self-images of their owners, all the more effectively when they were decorated with the owner's coat of arms, badge, device, name or initials, as in the case of the famous 'EH' (Elizabeth of Hardwick), on the parapet of Hardwick House in Derbyshire. Painted and sculpted portraits, which became increasingly numerous in the course of the Renaissance, can also be read as expressions of the sitter's self-image (or at least of the artist's image of the sitter's self-image). The multiplication of portraits and self-portraits after 1500, in parallel with biographies and autobiographies, seems to support Burckhardt's suggestion that there was an increase in self-awareness in the course of the Renaissance. Like texts, images sometimes followed exemplary models with which later artists identified themselves. One Italian artist, Bandinelli, portrayed himself with features resembling those of Michelangelo. Another, Jacopo Bassano, represented himself as Titian.

As in the case of texts, recently recovered ancient artefacts such as the busts and coins of Roman emperors encouraged the growth of interest in physical appearance as an expression of the inner self. The concern with fame was reflected in portraits and biographies alike. In the fourteenth century, Petrarch was consulted about the decoration of a room in Padua with portraits of 'illustrious men', presumably because of his book on the subject. In the sixteenth century, the biographer Paolo Giovio collected four hundred-odd historical portraits of 'famous men' (including at least seventeen women) for the museum in his villa near Como. Collections of biographies were sometimes illustrated with portraits. It was also at this time that the works of famous writers came to be furnished not only with biographies of the author but also with engraved portraits, usually as frontispieces.

It should be added that the cult of the outstanding individual did not appeal to everyone. Some upper-class Venetians, for instance, were suspicious of this form of individualism and cultivated an alternative, communal tradition. In 1421, the patrician Francesco Barbaro complained to the humanist Guarino of Verona that it was impossible to erect a monument in Venice to a naval hero. The mercenary leader Bartolommeo Colleoni paid for his own equestrian monument, which survives to this day, but the Venetian government found an excuse not to erect it on Piazza San Marco, where he wanted it, and had it placed in a less conspicuous square.

It is time to turn to the self-portrait. Although earlier examples can be found (like that of René of Anjou, quoted by Montaigne), the rise of the self-portrait was a sixteenth-century trend, related not only to self-awareness but also to the rise in the status of the artist. In Italy, one thinks of the old Titian, for instance, or of the young Parmigianino regarding himself in a convex mirror. In Germany, the early sixteenth century has been described by Joseph Koerner as 'the moment of self-portraiture', the examples including Hans Holbein, Lukas Cranach and Albrecht Dürer, who also kept a journal. The habit of signing paintings also became more common at this time.

The growing concern with the uniqueness of the individual, already mentioned, is revealed by increasing demands for verisimilitude, for a 'likeness', to be found in commissions for funeral effigies. There was a shift from contracts which stipulated only 'a man armed' or 'a fair gentle-woman' to demands for a likeness. In the case of printed series of portraits, a genre which became popular around the middle of the sixteenth century, a claim to realism or historical accuracy was sometimes explicit in the title, as in the case of Pantaleon's *Wahrhaffte Bildnisse* (1562) or Pacheco's *Verdaderos retratos* (1599). Paradoxically enough, the most reliable evidence for this concern with veracity consists of absences. In a collection of images of scholars edited by Theodore Beza in 1580 the compilers left a blank for the German humanist Reuchlin, for instance, because they were unable to discover a likeness.

Portraits became increasingly individualized, and displayed more and more of the sitter, literally and metaphorically, as the fifteenth and sixteenth centuries progressed. It is likely that the rise of portraits of famous people both reflected and encouraged the rise of an interest in their personalities. A sixteenth-century satire on the cult of Petrarch describes one of his admirers not only as visiting the places where Petrarch and Laura had lived, but also as trying to obtain portraits of them both.

However, if we examine the uses of the portrait in the Renaissance, or at any rate their location (which is easier to document), it is to discover that most of these objects were originally hung in groups, including members of a particular family or holders of particular offices (bishops, doges and so on). Sitters were surrounded if not weighed down by such accessories as robes, crowns, sceptres, swords, columns, curtains and so on, accessories which represented particular social roles. These practices suggest that the identities supported by the paintings were collective or institutional rather than individual. In short. there is an apparent contradiction between two types of explanation of the significance of the portrait, two perspectives. If we take a broad, comparative view, a view from a distance, we can hardly fail to notice the parallel rise in the numbers of portraits in biographies in Italy and certain other European countries after 1500. On the other hand, in 'close-up' the picture looks rather different, since the uses of the portrait were more often institutional than individualistic.

There is a similar contradiction between the care taken by some artists and scholars to record or discover the features of certain individuals, and the lack of interest shown by others. A late fifteenth-century chronicle published in Nuremberg used the same woodcut to portray Homer, the prophet Isaiah, Hippocrates, Terence, the medieval lawyer Accursius and the Renaissance philosopher Filelfo. Again, more than fifty years later, the anonymous illustrations to a collection of biographies produced by the Swiss humanist Heinrich Pantaleon several times reproduced the same image to serve as the portrait of different individuals. It may not be too much of a surprise to find the rulers 'Tuisco' and 'Eric' given the same features, since they came from remote periods. However, Einhard, the biographer of Charlemagne, was conflated with the sixteenth-century humanist Johann Reuchlin. Still more of a scandal, in the sense of a stumbling-block to our understanding of the Renaissance, is the use of the same woodcut to represent two sixteenth-century figures, the humanist Gemma Frisius and the painter Albrecht Dürer – Dürer of all people, a man whose many self-portraits suggest his obsessive concern with his appearance, not to mention a relatively widespread knowledge of his face.

CONCLUSION

Three general points may be worth emphasizing at the end of this brief survey.

The first concerns the variety of Renaissance selves or conceptions of the self. A remarkably wide range of people portrayed themselves in autobiographies, journals and diaries (to say nothing of letters): northerners and southerners, men and women, nobles and commoners. In Spain, the autobiographies of soldiers were almost common enough to form a sub-genre of their own, the most famous example being Alonso de Contreras. The majority of the surviving texts come from members of social elites, but apothecaries, tailors, carpenters and even peasants are also represented. Most documents are the work of males – but exceptions include Margery Kempe, St Teresa, Charlotte Arbaleste (wife of the Calvinist noble Philippe de Mornay), and Marie de Gournay (a disciple of Montaigne), while the Flemish painter Catherine van Hemessen portrayed herself in 1548. A possible task for future research in comparative history and literature would be to determine whether men and women, Catholics and Protestants, soldiers and civilians, patricians and plebeians developed their own styles of self-representation.

The second point concerns the possible explanation for the rise of concern with the self between Petrarch and Descartes, or at least its expression in texts and other artefacts. Reference has already been made to the rise of travel and of towns, but something must also be said about religion. Students of British autobiography, which took off at the end of the sixteenth century, have sometimes evoked the spirits of Protestantism and Puritanism, linking the texts to everyday habits of examination of conscience. The example of Elizabethan Puritan diaries such as those of Richard Rogers and Samuel Ward, written 'to know my own heart better', as Rogers put it, and to record examples of pride, cowardice and other sins and weaknesses, would seem to support this conclusion. However, it is weakened if not completely undermined by the many Catholic examples of the genre, far more than could be cited in this chapter. Introspection and self-examination were not Protestant monopolies at this period, as the examples of Saints Teresa and Ignatius (among others) show. These practices were part of the preparation for confession.

In accounting for change in this period, my own emphasis would fall on the increasing availability of ancient models, including Christian antiquity (above all, the *Confessions* of St Augustine) as well as pagan (the *Commentaries* of Caesar and so on). The rise of the autobiographical habit was not an inexplicable change in 'spirit' but a chain reaction, in which certain texts awoke or restructured perceptions of the self, while these perceptions in turn created a demand for texts of this kind. More elusive is the explanation for what appears to be a changing sense of self between Petrarch and Descartes, both more unified than before and more sharply distinguished from the outside world of family and community. The parallel between these developments and the rise of the centralized nation-state is an intriguing one.

The third point concerns the relation between the new sense of the self and what is often described as Western individualism. It is often assumed, at least in the West, that autobiographies and diaries are a uniquely occidental genre, or were until their imitation by Indians, Japanese and others in recent centuries. This assumption is false. In Japan, for example, a number of personal diaries were produced by noble ladies from the eleventh century onwards, the most famous examples being Murasaki and Shonagon. In India, the Mughal emperor Babur wrote his memoirs early in the sixteenth century. In China, a cluster of autobiographical texts, as well as a few portraits, was produced by scholar-officials and by monks at the time of the fall of the Ming dynasty in the middle of the seventeenth century. As in the case of Christianity, certain forms of Buddhism appear to have been conducive to self-examination.

In short, we need to free ourselves from the Western, Burckhardtian assumption that self-consciousness arose in a particular place, such as Italy, at a particular time, perhaps the fourteenth century. It is better to think in terms of a variety of categories of the person or conceptions of the self (more or less unified, bounded and so on) in different cultures, categories and conceptions which underlie a variety of styles of self-presentation or self-fashioning.

2

SELF AND SELFHOOD IN THE SEVENTEENTH CENTURY

Jonathan Sawday

> I'll never
> Be such a gosling as to obey instinct, but stand
> As if a man were author of himself,
> And knew no other kin.
>
> Shakespeare, *Coriolanus* (c. 1609)

The World (I mean not the earth onely . . . but all the *Universe*, that is, the whole masse of all things that are) is Corporcall, that is to say, Body; and hath the dimensions of Magnitude, namely, Length, Bredth, and Depth; also every part of Body, is likewise Body, and hath the like dimensions; and consequently every part of the Universe, is Body; and that which is not Body is no part of the Universe; and because the Universe is All, that which is no part of it is *Nothing*; and consequently no where.

> Thomas Hobbes, *Leviathan* (1651)

AUTONOMY

'Reconstructing individualism is not an easy task' begins the sociological theoretician, Niklas Luhmann, in a recent (1986) assault on just this problem. 'It is not easy because it has been tried before', he warns. Not the least amongst the immense difficulties involved in charting the historical dimension of such abstract terms as 'individuality', 'autonomy', 'subjectivity', 'selfhood', and (even) 'personality' is the problem posed by language itself. The rich, post-Freudian vocabulary of self-reflection upon which we now draw is, by definition, of relatively recent origin.

How, then, can we construct a 'History of the Self'? Of course, we cannot trust dictionaries, not even the *Oxford English Dictionary*, to establish the currency of an idea; they merely record the isolated observation of a certain word, used at a certain moment, in a certain literary (that is, written rather than spoken) context. Nevertheless, the *OED* does afford one tantalizing glimpse of a possible history of selfhood. Of the prefix formation 'self-', the dictionary observes:

Self- first appears as a living formative element about the middle of the sixteenth century. . . . The number of *self-* compounds was greatly augmented towards the middle of the seventeenth century, when many new words appeared in theological and philosophical writing, some of which had a restricted currency of about fifty years (e.g. 1645–1690).

This Burckhardtian narrative, where the concept of 'self' is held to be virtually invented in the Renaissance, might prompt the question of whether or not it was coincidence that, during a period of intense political and social unrest, a new vocabulary of 'ipseity' appeared to emerge in England. Certainly, in English usage, the term 'selfhood' is first recorded in the climactic year 1649, as a rough translation of Jacob Boehme's 'icheit' or 'meinheit'. But the word is anchored, in a theological sense, to an entirely negative set of ideas. 'Selfhood' in the mid-seventeenth century did not, in fact, suggest the modern idea of ipseity – the quality of having or possessing a 'self'. Rather it expressed the inability to govern the self. 'Selfhood' was the mark of Satan; it was a token of the spiritually un-regenerate individual, in thrall to the flesh rather than the spirit. 'When self or particular love rules,' wrote the leveller leader, Gerard Winstanley in 1650, 'then this earth is brought into bondage, and sorrow fills all places.'

Later in the century, John Milton was to explore the language of negative selfhood in *Paradise Lost* (1667). The rebel angels, in Book V of the poem, claim to be 'self-begot, self-raised', an echo of their ambition, at the outset of the poem, 'to reascend / Self-raised, and repossess their native seat'. What will exclude the rebellious angels from divine grace, as God explains in Book III of the poem, is the fact that they fell 'Self-tempted, self-depraved'. Selfhood, we might conclude from this kind of reading of *Paradise Lost*, indicates an absence of God, a state of spiritual isolation, rather than the presence of reflective enquiry.

Milton's vocabulary of self-reflexivity also hints at the troublesome link between self-reflection, or self-scrutiny, and what Luhmann describes as 'the devotional movement of the seventeenth century, which privatized the attempt to achieve salvation'. 'Autonomy' from God, from the divine plan itself, is what the rebel angels seek in Milton's poem. 'Autonomy' is what God insists his angelic and human creatures already possess, since he has created them 'free to chose'. 'Autonomy' appears to be both the consolation prize and the punishment for Eve's and Adam's transgression at the end of *Paradise Lost*. The penultimate word of the poem, in the course of perhaps the most famous exit in English literature, is 'solitary'. Providence, it is true, is still to be their 'guide', but as 'autonomous subjects', Eve and Adam choose a 'solitary way' through the world; the immediacy of the divine nexus between the human creatures and God has been shattered.

We might contrast this poetic evocation of a lonely entrance into a psychologically (as yet) undiscovered country, with the socio-historical response to the problem of 'selfhood'. Adam is told, at the close of *Paradise Lost*, that he will possess a 'paradise within' which will far surpass the external paradise of Eden. The passage, then, towards the autonomy promised at the end of the poem is also a voyage into the interior. Outward observance will be abandoned in favour of an ever-more intense 'inward' scrutiny of the human psyche. As Luhmann writes, in his description of the 'devotional movement' (of which *Paradise Lost* is a late but crucial manifestation):

> religious care was no longer care for others. It did not require praying for others, monastic conditions, or supererogatory works. Instead it was care for one's own sole salvation.

Etre devôt, c'est vouloir se sauver et ne rien negliger pour cela ('to be devoted means to want one's own salvation, and to neglect nothing in pursuit of that end'). Although Luhmann's authority for this evidence of the jealous policing of the boundaries of the individual's 'soul' proves to be a late seventeenth-century Jesuit writer (Pierre de Villiers), such fierce pursuit of the individual psyche has long been associated with a predominantly Protestant mode of thought. Moreover, Luhmann's account of the 'privatized' attempt to achieve salvation echoes by far the most influential account of the historical formation of individuality written in recent years: Stephen Greenblatt's *Renaissance Self-Fashioning* (1980). When Greenblatt writes of the 'essential relationship between private property and private selves', then the private 'self' indeed appears to be a place of domestic retreat, an *inner-sanctum*, whose doors are closely bolted against the public, urban world. 'Withdraw your selfe into your selfe,' Montaigne was to advise in his *Essays* of 1580, 'but first prepare your selfe to receive your selfe.' The Protestant emphasis on 'inward' experience, the 'inner anxiety' associated with Calvinism, the perpetual distrust of 'interior' motivation, accompanied by an equal fascination with the 'inner' voice of conscience, all of these elements in the so-called psychology of Protestantism, are mirrored in Montaigne's sceptical, Catholic investigation of his own 'personality'.

No matter how difficult the task of 'reconstructing individualism' might be, the starting point suggested by Montaigne is the very idea of 'interiority'. But what did 'interiority' amount to in the period? If it was a concealed place of refuge for Montaigne writing in the 1570s, then it was also a dangerously troubling landscape for a radical such as Winstanley in the mid-seventeenth century, or even for a more orthodox Puritan divine such as Richard Sibbes, who wrote, in 1635: 'We carry that within ourselves that, if it be let loose will trouble us more than all the world besides.' 'Interiority' and 'selfhood' in the seventeenth century may be linked, somehow; but what was the nature of that link?

AUTOPSIA

'Protestant emphasis on inward grace,' writes Greenblatt, 'tends to obscure the implication of the body.' The image of the suffering Christ, Greenblatt continues, may manifest itself in 'somatic imitation', where the believer's own body and the physical body of the incarnate Christ seem to shade into one another. The believer may even find himself or herself seeking to re-enact the passion, the gestures of suffering, the physical pain of the crucifixion to a point where the identification with Christ 'lies deeper than literary artifice, pastoral consolation, or religious doctrine'. 'Spit in *my* face you Jewes, and pierce *my* side / Buffet, and scoffe, scourge, and crucifye *mee*' (my emphasis), thus John Donne begins his 'Holy Sonnet' XI, written c. 1609–1610. What one critic (John Carey) has termed Donne's 'need for suffering' may also be the mark of a well-rehearsed pattern of replication: an emotional and cathartic identification of one's physical existence with the identity of the 'man of sorrows'.

But this 'somatic imitation' could manifest itself in an altogether more dispassionate sphere, and one which takes us close to the core of the relationship between 'selfhood' and the sense of embodiment. At the beginning of the seventeenth century, in the same year (1603) in which Montaigne's *Essays* and Shakespeare's *Hamlet* were first published in England, a remarkable enquiry into the nature of interiority was conducted in one of the most striking devotional paintings of the age. In some sense, however, to call Caravaggio's *Incredulity of St Thomas* (Plate 2.1) a 'devotional' painting is impossible, such is the profound scepticism which informs the work. Furthermore, there may be a hint of autobiography in Caravaggio's image, though not of the kind associated with Donne's attempt to slide his own personality into the drama of the crucifixion. The painting's subject – a sceptical enquiry into the 'truth' of the resurrection – in many respects echoes events in Caravaggio's own life at the time of the composition. For Caravaggio, too, had been the subject of an enquiry, though of a rather different kind to that depicted in *The Incredulity of St Thomas*. In September 1603 Caravaggio had been arrested on a charge of libel, imprisoned in the Tor di Nona at Rome, tried, and then released, after just a fortnight in gaol, following the intervention of the French ambassador. Condemned, Caravaggio nevertheless found himself restored to freedom at the hands of a higher, arbitrary authority. The libel charge had been occasioned by the publication of scurrilous verses directed towards a rival and inferior artist: Giovanni Baglione. In 1602 Baglione had been preferred to Caravaggio for the commission to paint a *Resurrection* for the Jesuit church, Il Gesù, in Rome. It is clear, then, that the 'truth' to be established in the painting was the veracity of the very subject which Caravaggio's rival – Baglione – had unveiled in the Jesuits' church on Easter Sunday 1603. It was as if Caravaggio, sceptically, was revisiting the

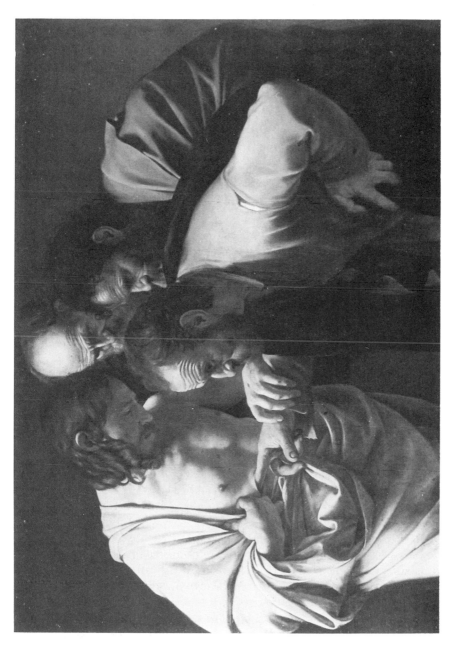

Plate 2.1 Michelangelo Caravaggio, *Incredulity of St Thomas*. Reprinted by permission of the Preussische Schlösser und Gärten, Berlin-Brandenburg, Potsdam

subject matter *he* had wished to paint for the Jesuits: the corporeal fact of the resurrection and, by extension, the reality of the doctrine of the incarnation.

Studying the *Incredulity of St Thomas*, it may come as no surprise to learn that Caravaggio failed to win the commission to paint a resurrection for the Jesuits. By the time he had completed this painting, Caravaggio's notion of a 'religious' image had already worried Counter-Reformation churchmen. His reputation for painting in a style which was neither sacred, nor profane, but a hybrid of the two (*trà il devoto, et profano*), had attracted uneasy commentary among potential ecclesiastical patrons. In this respect, the *Incredulity of St Thomas* might almost be read as a gauntlet thrown in the face of counter-reformation orthodoxy. For Caravaggio had chosen to explore the central mystery of the Christian faith – the incarnation and the resurrection – with what might, tendentiously, be termed an almost Protestant literal-mindedness.

The art historian Howard Hibbard has described the painting as expressing a 'surgical detail' which is almost 'unbearable'. That surgical detail is compounded out of a series of striking effects associated with the human body: the probing, sceptical finger, which stretches the unhealed wound cavity; the attentive yet abstracted attitude of St Thomas (as though he were a physician, concentrating on some pulsating inner organ whose presence can be detected only by touch); the hand of Christ which, ambiguously, both guides and restrains his inquisitor's hand; the furrowed concentration of the witnesses to the operation who seem entirely oblivious to any hint of religiosity or faith at this moment; even the suggestion (from St Thomas' awkward pose) that the chief investigator of the incarnation suffers from an arthritic hip. These effects, or mannerisms, conspire to produce that realism for which Caravaggio was celebrated by his contemporaries.

Admired and copied, the *Incredulity of St Thomas* was one of the most widely known of Caravaggio's private pictures, though the identity of the patron who commissioned it is still uncertain. What astonished Caravaggio's contemporaries, as they surveyed this and other works, was the artist's attention to the details of nature, to the possibility of re-creating lifelike forms and expression which *appeared* to be unmediated by the devices of art, to an extent (in the case of his religious subjects) which constantly hovered on the edge of blasphemy. 'Naturalism', 'imitation of nature', 'true to life' – these were the terms with which Caravaggio's art was described in the seventeenth century. It was as if a new genre of painting had been uncovered which was later to be exploited, most famously, by Rembrandt in his 'anatomical' paintings of 1632 and 1656. That genre was the memorialization of the investigation of corporeality itself.

The comment on Caravaggio's tendency to mix the 'sacred' and the 'profane' in a manner which many of his contemporaries found profoundly unsettling adds a further twist to the painting's genesis. Caravaggio's image glances over its shoulder to the long tradition, in Christian iconography, of Christ in 'self-demonstration', palpating his wound, or displaying the scars of the crucifixion to his onlookers. Later, this 'demonstrative' form of image would result in that baroque fascination with the exposure of the 'sacred heart'. But in this image of 1603, Caravaggio also seemed to be responding to a new emphasis, in the realm of science or natural philosophy, on the vital importance of personal experience of the phenomena which were under investigation. In the field of medicine and anatomy, such a stress on direct, visual, sensory experience at the expense of the textual study of Galen and classical and Arabic medical commentary, involved the cultivation of 'autopsia' – literally, seeing for oneself.

The extent to which, in the early modern period, a scientific culture of 'personal experience', and the pieties of 'self-identification' with the pain of Christ's passion, support, or even merge into, one another is still little understood by cultural historians. The popular idea of a fundamental dichotomy between a fideistic pattern of thought as opposed to a 'scientific' world view still dominates our thinking. Yet, in Italy, as much as in Holland or England, Caravaggio and his contemporaries inhabited that 'culture of dissection' which was celebrated in the ornate theatres of anatomy that were springing up all over Europe. Later, in Holland, which became a leading centre of anatomical discovery, Rembrandt, in common with his contemporaries, was to explore the 'culture of dissection' in his own accounts of 'autopsia', of which the 1632 *Anatomy of Dr Tulp* is the most important manifestation. In the new theatres of anatomy, what may be defined as an aesthetic *and* scientific commitment to the study of corporeality flourished, whose effects were far-reaching. A single illustration may suffice. Vasari, in his best-selling *Lives of the Artists* (1550) recounts the story told of Bartolommeo Torri, a minor painter from Arezzo, who is said to have sequestered limbs and other human members under his bed. Living in squalor amidst the detritus of his anatomical studies, Vasari wrote that Torri thus lived 'like a philosopher'. The simile is revealing. Rather than surround himself with the works and commentaries of Plato, Aristotle and their humanist heirs, the 'new philosopher' who is also the 'new artist' surrounds himself with the vestiges of physicality. Corpses rather than a *corpus* of texts have become the object of his attention.

Torri's devotion to the study of the human body, though carried to an almost perverse extreme, was not an isolated instance. Like the great anatomists of the period, who complemented their spectacular, public demonstrations with more illicit forays into the countryside in search of bodies, the artists of the previous generation – Leonardo, Parmigianino, Piero di Cosimo, Rosso – flayed and eviscerated human corpses, scavenged for remains in cemeteries or from the gibbet, and conducted secretive, nocturnal dissections. There is a suggestion, even, that the work of a particularly famous anatomist was treasured in a way that saints' relics might be preserved. At the time of his death, in 1669, Rembrandt, for example, possessed 'four flayed arms and legs anatomized by Vesalius'. The limbs must have been over one hundred years old by the time Rembrandt's possession of them is recorded, since Vesalius had died in 1554.

This devotion to the minute observation of the natural world was to become part of the folklore surrounding Caravaggio's life. In the eighteenth century, for example, a sensational story was told of Caravaggio by the painter-priest Francesco Susinno. In the composition of Caravaggio's *Resurrection of Lazarus* (1609), Susinno records:

> in order to give the central figure of Lazarus a naturalistic flavour [Caravaggio] asked to have a corpse dug up that was already in a state of decomposition, and had it placed in the arms of the workmen who, however, were unable to stand the foul odour and wanted to give up their work . . . those unlucky men were forced to continue their job and nearly die.

Whether or not Susinno's account is to be trusted (and a degree of doubt is warranted: a few lines later Susinno recounts how Michelangelo 'nailed a poor man to a wooden board and then pierced his heart with a lance, in order to paint a crucifixion') the story is illustrative of the extraordinary commitment to corporeality which was now expected of the artist, as much as it was to be encouraged among the scientists.

'Embodiment', then, is the object of enquiry in Caravaggio's depiction of St Thomas searching the wounds of his saviour. In this respect, Caravaggio's St Thomas is, in essence, replicating the task of the artist. The goal of the artists' studies was mastery of the difficult process by which they would be able to offer a convincing rendition of 'embodiment' in their works. But 'embodiment' now meant far more than the representation of the surface appearance of the body. It involved the artist in suggesting the complex, dynamic quality of the body's internal organization. To this end, the artists had to master the art of 'autopsia' – or seeing for oneself. Susinno's story of Caravaggio forcing his workmen to arrange themselves around a decomposing corpse is a perfect illustration of 'autopsia'. 'Autopsia', of course, was the guiding principle of the post-Vesalian anatomists whose fame was spreading all over Europe, a mirror of the fame enjoyed by the successful artists of the period, who might even find themselves sharing (as did Vesalius and Rosso) the same patrons.

The most sustained, certainly the most influential, example of the application of 'autopsia' in the earlier seventeenth century was to be found in the work of the Englishman, William Harvey. In 1602, having gained his MD at Padua after two years' residence in Italy, Harvey returned to England to begin the anatomical work which would eventually result (in

1628) in the publication of *Exercitatio Anatomica De Motu Cordis et Sanguinis in Animalibus* at Frankfurt. *De Motu Cordis* ('Of the Motion of the Heart and Blood in Animals') is, in essence, a sequence of experimental 'proofs', via 'autopsia', of the hypothesis that the body contains a dynamic circulatory system. Harvey and Caravaggio's St Thomas thus share a similar dedication to proof. In the Gospel account, the sceptical, enquiring St Thomas demanded much more than rumour, hearsay and recorded authority before believing in the truth of Christ's corporeal presence. In similar fashion, Harvey, in the opening chapter of *De Motu Cordis*, stressed the primacy of his own experience in the analysis of phenomena. It was 'the use of my own eyes instead of through books and the writings of others' which led him, he writes, to abandon his pessimistic meditation 'that the heart's movement had been understood by God alone'. St Thomas's words as recorded in St John's Gospel (the basis for Caravaggio's painting) – 'Except I shall see in his hands the print of the nails and put my finger into the place of the nails and put my hand into his side, I will not believe' (John 20: 25, Douai version) – might also stand as the credo of Harvey himself, or of any post-Baconian philosopher, as he set about the laborious business of demonstrating the 'truth' of the dynamic systems within the newly fashioned human interior.

Indeed, in Chapter 4 of *De Motu Cordis* we read of an experiment which, almost uncannily, may appear to be the direct scientific counterpart of the scene which Caravaggio has shown St Thomas performing. 'In an experiment carried out on a dove' Harvey writes:

> after the heart had completely stopped moving . . . I spent some time with my finger, moistened with saliva and warm, applied over the heart. When it had, by means of this formentation recovered – so to speak – its power to live, I saw the heart . . . move, and contract and relax, and – so to speak – be recalled from death to life.
>
> (Trans. Kenneth Franklin.)

Perhaps it was the presence of a dove, whose symbolic association with the Holy Spirit, and hence with the divine *pneuma* itself, would not have escaped an orthodox Anglican such as Harvey, which caused the anatomist to hesitate in this description. The hesitation in Harvey's formulation ('so to speak . . . so to speak'), as though he were grasping for the precise term with which to describe this extraordinary moment, is not only a function of his notoriously cumbersome Latin, but suggests a kind of inner struggle to escape out of the dominant religious metaphors which encode this passage from death to life. But for a man such as Harvey – pious, devout, politically and religiously conservative – the language of resurrection was impossible to evade. The heart of the dove twitches, momentarily, into life once more. The movement recalls Caravaggio's St Thomas, sceptically probing, with his finger, into the thoracic cavity of the risen Christ, and it looks forward to Rembrandt, delicately flexing the lifeless hand of an executed criminal. In the seventeenth century, a new, and astonishing, vision of the human body had been uncovered. 'In the human interior', St Augustine had written, 'truth resides'. But what kind of 'truth' of human interiority were the sceptical scientists of the age of Caravaggio and Harvey now uncovering, and how did their sceptical interrogation of 'nature' mesh with that religious experience of 'inwardness' which, later in the seventeenth century, Milton was to explore poetically in the fabrication of his human creatures?

SELF-REFLECTION

'Interiority', whether considered as a psychological or a somatic phenomenon, is based on a distinction between 'inside' and 'outside'. Such a distinction is crucial to modern, Western accounts of individuality. At the beginning of this century, a Melanesian, asked what his culture had received in its encounter with Europeans, is said to have replied: 'What you have brought us is the body.' Is the body, in some obscure fashion, a cultural product? Surely not. 'Most people,' R. D. Laing claimed in his study of 'dis-ordered' personalities which was *The Divided Self* (1959), 'feel they began when their bodies began and that they will end when their bodies die.' The 'embodied' person, Laing continues:

> has a sense of being flesh and blood and bones, of being biologically alive and real: he knows himself to be substantial. To the extent that he is thoroughly 'in' his body, he is likely to have a sense of personal continuity in time. . . . The individual thus has as his starting-point an experience of his body as a base from which he can be a person with other human beings.

The sense of being 'embodied', one might assume, is surely trans-cultural, even trans-historical. Yet, unlikely as it may at first appear, this account of embodiment is strikingly similar to modern accounts of a purely cultural phenomenon: the development of the portrait in the Renaissance. The development of portraiture has often been associated, by cultural historians, with the emergence of 'individuality' in the period; and sometimes more than 'individuality'. Commenting, in 1934, on one of Dürer's many self-portraits, the German art historian Hugho Kehrer wrote that what was represented was:

> more than an individual likeness. This representation of the I is at once a spiritual self-analysis and self-dissection. One could say, that in that hour of Dürerian self-observation the German Renaissance awoke.

Dürer's 'autopsia' here is taken as a founding moment not only in psychological or even cultural terms, but in terms of an awakening *national* history. 'Self-observation', however, is more usually held to be the preserve of the speculative 'I', rather than the collective 'we'. Nevertheless, Kehrer's sense of a 'self-dissection' encapsulates the idea of 'autopsia' we have been tracing. At the beginning of the sixteenth century, Dürer gazes into a convex mirror, and he sees . . . 'himself'.

Or does he? Was such an unmediated access to the 'self' actually possible in the period? In his self-images of 1503 (Plate 2.2) and 1512 (Plate 2.3), Dürer was to survey his own body, in its totality, under the special conditions of sickness. The 1503 self-portrait, produced, it is generally agreed, with the help of a large flat mirror (itself an expensive rarity in the early sixteenth century) appears to show the artist as fully 'embodied'. Dürer's body is now subjected to a ruthless, almost scientific examination. It is as if, having risen exhausted from his sick-bed, he is now surveying the distorting effects of illness on his own body. To use the word 'scientific' of this portrait, however anachronistic, seems appropriate. What cannot be seen cannot be represented. What can be represented is *only* what can be seen.

Recalling R. D. Laing's comments on 'embodiment' as a key element in the constitution of selfhood, it is difficult to resist the conclusion, then, that Dürer's self-image is indeed a moment of 'awakening' for the self. Here is 'autopsia' at its most extreme and self-reflective. But the portrait may also be part of a more complex, fideistic process of the reaffirmation of identity as a fully 'embodied' individual within a larger community. Recalling that the 1503 drawing was made either during, or soon after, a period of illness, we should note how illness, in the early modern period, was not merely a somatic state, but a crucial period during which the faith of the believer was put to the test. The sick person was not advised to expect recovery, as we, in the late twentieth century, might reasonably anticipate recovery. Where, today, illness is an aberration, and death a failure of technology as much as it is a fact of life, in the early modern period sickness was part of the constitution of one's existence. Thus the sick person was advised to prepare both for their imminent extinction as an individual and the urgent possibility of their joining a new community: the community of the dead. In such moments, we can only speculate on the enormous psychological importance of the remembrance, even the re-enactment, of the gestures of proof by which Christ affirms the 'truth' of his own resurrection and incarnation – his full embodiment. And this gesture of 'proof' appears in shadowy form in Dürer's self-images. Joseph Leo Koerner, in his recent and masterful study of Dürer's self-portraits, has argued that, in his 1503 'mirror' image, the artist has reinscribed the wound of the spear in Christ's side at the crucifixion on to his own body. Above Dürer's right hip, an area of skin has been drawn so as to suggest the trauma of a wound.

Peter Burke has commented on the psychological penchant for artists of

Plate 2.2 Albrecht Dürer, *Self-portrait* of 1503. Reproduced by permission of the Kunstsammlungen zu Weimar, Graphische Sammlung, Schlossmuseum

the Renaissance to exhibit symptoms of what he terms 'social deviancy'. But Dürer, as far as we know, was no Benvenuto Cellini – he did not engage in sensational street brawls in which he might have been wounded. But his scrupulous 'scientific' pictorialism had taught him to draw *only* what he could see, and therefore he had 'seen' a wound on his body. At this point we might reflect on Dürer's peculiar sense of 'embodiment' in this image. For all that the drawing seems to concentrate on the details of 'embodiment', the truncated body is oddly disturbing, as though it is not (yet) fully corporeal. It seems to emerge from, and yet also merge into, the rough area of unprepared background. Is Dürer dead or alive in this image? Is he stumbling back into full 'embodiment', or is he anticipating his own bodily resurrection? The drawing may well appear to be a confirmation of Dürer's 'identity', but what, then, is the nature of such an identity?

Over a hundred years later, in the course of his fatal illness of 1631, John Donne was to anticipate the experience of death by having himself drawn as though dead, but waiting for his resurrection. After his last, sensational sermon, Donne retired to his chamber to await his death. But this was no passive rite of solitary endurance. Rather the sick-room was a hive of activity. Having ordered charcoal fires to be bought to his sick-room, and a large wooden urn to be constructed, Donne wrapped himself in his winding sheet and balanced on this precarious perch while his image was drawn on to a piece of board. The image was then set before him for him to feast his eyes upon while he waited for his own death. The image (which later was transformed into the stone sculpture in St Pauls Cathedral) showed Donne's 'lean, pale and death-like face', Izaak Walton records. His face 'was purposely turned towards the East from when he expected the coming of his and our saviour Jesus.' Donne's auto-icon of mortality, though it is not, technically, a self-portrait, nevertheless fulfils the function of helping the individual to pass the crucial psychological moment for which the *ars moriendi* – the art of dying – was a rehearsal. In a similar fashion, Dürer's self-image, with its oblique memorialization of the resurrection, is part of the process by which illness, sickness and eventual extinction were re-enacted. Hence the question: Is Dürer celebrating his recovery from illness, or memorializing his passage away from embodiment?

We can see this ambiguity more explicitly in the later image, drawn during a further bout of illness in 1512 (Plate 2.3). Now, Dürer maps the sacred imagery which Caravaggio was later to exploit in his painting of St Thomas directly on to his own body. The finger points – as Christ makes Thomas point – to the place where his body endures pain, as the inscription at the top of the drawing indicates: 'There where the yellow spot is and the finger points, there it hurts me' (*Do der gelb fleck ist vnd mit dem finger drawff dewt, do ist mir we*). But the image is much more than a clinical self-diagnosis. For the combination of the traditional posture, and Dürer's

41

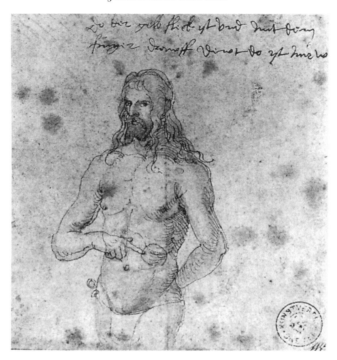

Plate 2.3 Albrecht Dürer, *Self-portrait* of 1512.
Reproduced by permission of the Kunsthalle, Bremen

affirmation that 'where . . . the finger points, there it hurts me' may be understood as a generalized meditation on Christ's passion, interiorized to the point where it has become part of the subjective experience of the individual believer. Where Christ is wounded, all humanity is wounded. Much later, in the seventeenth century, the English Catholic devotional poet, Richard Crashaw, would seize on this image in his meditation on Christ's words in John 10:9 – *Ego sum ostium* ('I am the door'). The wound in Christ's side is the 'door' through which all believers must pass to enter the kingdom of heaven. Dürer, however, is more self-reflective than Crashaw was to be. Pointing to his own wound, Dürer has re-enacted Christ's passion; he has discovered the Christ within.

But from a purely physiological standpoint, as commentators on the drawing have long recognized, Dürer appears to be pointing to his spleen, the seat of melancholy in Renaissance psychological theory. That the self-image may also function as an 'accurate' (in twentieth-century terms) record of illness is not precluded by its participation in a network of sacred imagery. So, this representation of an artist's individual pain *and* the pain of Fallen humanity may still, in Joseph Leo Koerner's words, 'articulate . . . a subjective state and the constitution of his character'; and perhaps we might add to Koerner's analysis the observation that the drawing also represents the condition of being an artist, since melancholy was held to be the dominant humour in the 'personality' of those given to such rapt self-reflection. 'Where it hurts me' may also be the location of artistic prowess. Self-reflection, then, even the self-reflection of the self-portrait, could be a complex exercise in identification of oneself within a larger, fideistic framework of belief. The moment of Dürer's 'self-analysis, self-dissection . . . self-observation', we might conclude, does not suddenly reveal a vista of autonomous selfhood. What it does reveal, however, is the complex nature of the engagement with 'embodiment' in the period – an engagement which the 'new science' of the seventeenth century was supposedly to force into redundancy.

THE THINKING THING

The body, art historians agree, still lies at the core of the development of Renaissance portraiture. By now, however, it may also be appreciated what complex layers of cultural forces came to shape the way people 'saw' their bodies. John Pope-Hennessy remarks that the Renaissance portrait is:

> the story of how eyes cease to be linear symbols and become instead the light-reflecting, light-perceiving organs we ourselves possess; how lips cease to be a segment in the undifferentiated texture of the face, and become instead a sensitized area through whose relaxation or contraction a whole range of responses is expressed; how the nose ceases to be a fence between the two sides of the face, and becomes instead the delicate instrument through which we breath and smell.

In this account, the portrait reflects not so much a history of representation as it traces a history of the body – the history of how 'they' (the subjects of Renaissance portraits) appear to end up with the same organs that 'we ourselves possess'. Thus the portrait appears to 'evolve' in an almost Darwinian fashion; from crude, two-dimensional studies in profile, the portrait evolves into complex, 'higher' forms of three-dimensional, volumetric individuality. This progressive narrative of 'ascent' is also often (sometimes unconsciously) utilized in the field of literary history. For example, in England, the Elizabethan and Jacobean soliloquy, it has been argued, offers a convincing illusion (in the theatrical sense) of a 'free-standing individual'. No longer anchored to alliterative verse, as Catherine Belsey remarks, the 'flexible and fluent iambic pentameter' promises psychological 'fullness' – an evocation of 'interiority' not to be discovered in earlier literatures. Macbeth, Hamlet or Othello do not, of course, 'think' in any meaningful sense. Rather, Shakespeare (together with his con-temporaries) appears to have grasped the possibility of dramatizing the thinking process: we witness a psychologically convincing representation of the unfolding of thought.

In psychological terms, as R. D. Laing's account suggests, a fully realized sense of 'selfhood' or 'ipseity' depends on a grasp of a sense of one's own 'embodiment'. In aesthetic terms, a convincing register of individuality can only be displayed through an understanding of the techniques of trans-cribing three-dimensional 'corporeality' on to the two dimensions of painted canvas, wood, copperplate or fresco. Embodiment and selfhood thus appear to represent two sides of the same coin, and both are said to have their origin in the period of the European Renaissance.

But what of the new science of 'autopsia'? How was corporeality to be shaped when the scientists, artists and writers, well-versed in identifying themselves within the larger framework of Christian symbolism, began to see the body as, in some fashion, cut loose from the scaffolding of devotion and piety? One response was struggle, and then flight back to older certainties, as Donne's 'Anniversary' poems of 1611–12 demonstrate. Or one could simply throw up one's hands in confusion, and thus imitate Robert Burton in his 'Digression of the Air' to be found in that otherwise most densely corporeal of texts *The Anatomy of Melancholy* (1621). Sir Thomas Browne's response was to mount an aggressive attack on his own sense of embodiment, via a neoplatonic exultation, in an effort to reassert his own sense of selfhood. 'The world that I regard is my selfe', Browne wrote in 1643, 'it is the microcosme of mine owne frame'. But this somatic definition of the self soon collapses: 'that masse of flesh that circumscribes me, limits not my mind: that surface that tells the heavens it hath an end, cannot persuade me I have any.

Browne was no Cartesian. Yet his distinction between a circumscribed body and a boundless mind might be thought of as a clear expression of the dualism associated with Descartes. And Descartes' philosophy of 'self-hood' (and, as we shall see, Milton's struggle with that philosophy) begins and ends with corporeality. Descartes' work of the 1630s and 1640s, particularly while he was resident in Holland, can be thought of as a prolonged sequence of meditations on both the origin and location of human identity, pursued through the devices of 'autopsia'. It may seem perverse at this point to claim that, in England, the equivalent of Cartesian 'autopsia' can be discovered in Milton's poetry, since Milton, notoriously, was no friend to the new philosophy of the seventeenth century. Technology, invention, discovery, in Milton's political poetics, are ideas associated with the absolutist, monarchical world of Hell.

But Milton *was* possessed with the problem of 'ipseity', or selfhood, and the relationship of those vexing concepts to the idea of 'embodiment'. Nor would we expect anything less from a poet who undertakes to demonstrate the entire scope of God's providential plan for humankind. At some stage, then, in *Paradise Lost*, Milton had to confront the very questions which were now being probed in the anatomy theatres and the artists' studios. What did 'embodiment' amount to? What was the relationship between the sense of being 'embodied' and the nature of 'selfhood'? The answer (even for Milton) was obscure, if not impossible to fathom. In Book VIII of *Paradise Lost*, Adam opens his account of emergence into a positive sense of 'selfhood' with an acknowledgment both of the philosophical scope of the enquiry and the impossibility of arriving at any satisfactory conclusion:

> For man to tell how human life began
> Is hard; for who himself beginning knew?

Adam's hesitation, as he embarks on his somewhat foreshortened auto-biography, contrasts with the autopsic certainty of Satan earlier in the poem, when, like a sceptical Cartesian philosopher, the fallen angel seems to pose exactly the same question that Adam is now pondering: 'Who saw when this creation was?' asks Satan; 'Remember'st thou / Thy making, while the maker gave thee being?' In the absence of 'autopsia' – seeing for oneself – Satan can only conclude, irrationally, that since 'we know no time when we were not as now' the answer to the riddle of origin is (as we have seen) negative 'selfhood' or spiritual isolation: God's creatures are 'self-begot, self-raised'.

Satan's query, however, is not quite the same as Adam's, and nor (speaking philosophically) is it quite as subtle. For Satan the 'proof' of being is located either in visual experience ('Who saw . . . ?') or memory ('Remember'st thou . . . ?'). For Adam, however, the problem is one of knowledge ('who . . . knew?'). To which the answer, of course, is that God knows. But the question may also be thought of as a reversion to the familiar classical motto of the philosophers and anatomists of the sixteenth and seventeenth centuries: *Nosce Teipsum* (Know Yourself), the motto of the science of 'autopsia'.

Adam's question, then, initiates an 'autopsia' in its fullest sense. What he pursues is what Descartes, in his *Rules for the Direction of Mind* (begun in the 1620s but not published until after his death), would term '*scientia*': 'certain and evident cognition'. A sceptical 'autopsia' is the starting point for such an enquiry, and this is precisely what Adam proceeds to conduct on himself. However we translate the 'seipsum' of Adam's question, then, what Milton actually describes is little less than a Cartesian enquiry into the relationship between mind and body. Adam awakes from sleep, in a warming and liquid 'balmy sweat', and looks towards the sky. But then he is 'raised' (with the suggestion not only of religious justification, but also Cartesian, not to say Harveian, mechanics) by a 'quick instinctive motion' to his feet. Like the heart of the dove which, in 1628, Harvey had warmed and moistened and thus called into life, so Adam springs into motion. Around him, too, is a world of motion – of bodies endowed with life. But it is towards himself that he must now turn:

> Myself I then perused, and limb by limb
> Surveyed, and sometimes went, and sometimes ran
> With supple joints, and lively vigour led.

Adam's 'self', at this moment of conscious awakening, or of the awakening of consciousness, appears to be fully embodied. To peruse the 'self' is to 'survey', limb by limb, the corporeality of his own individuality. And yet he is not a complete 'person'. For once this vigorous self-demonstration of the 'machinery' is over, Adam turns to the more pressing problem of the relationship between the body and the self. And in the moment of reflection on his own autonomy, the unified sense of selfhood – the conviction of autonomy – is abandoned, never to be regained: 'But who I was, or where, or from what cause, / knew not'. 'How came I thus, how here?' he asks of the inanimate nature which surrounds him. Milton's compressed syntax manages to convey two distinct questions: 'How did "I" come to exist. . . . How did I come to exist here?' Adam supplies his own answer 'Not of my self'. The 'self', then, cannot be the source of the cogitating, enquiring, reasoning power which Adam now knows himself to possess. And later in the narrative even the term 'my self' will become problematic when Adam greets the suddenly corporeal Eve as 'my self / Before me'.

'Personal continuity in time', Laing writes, is a function of feeling oneself to be 'in' a body. But a sense of personal continuity in time is precisely what Adam lacks. He has no history at this point, and he appears to have no future. For no sooner are his philosophical enquiries completed with the conviction that, since the 'self' cannot be the source of his being, then his being must be attributed to 'some great maker', than he feels himself to be dissolving 'untroubled' and 'insensible' into his 'former state' of non-being. In the subsequent dream (and Descartes' rhetorical deployment of the dream experience may come to mind at this point), Adam will meet his maker, and the philosophical scepticism he has hitherto displayed will be quietened with the words 'Whom thou sought'st I am'. God's words in *Paradise Lost* are, of course, a reinscription of the reply to Moses in Exodus 3:14 – 'I am that I am.' But it is also difficult to resist the sense that Milton is also trying to quieten Descartes, whose Adamic enquiry into the constitution of his sense of selfhood had resulted in the formulation of the *cogito* of 1637: *je pense, donc je suis* ('I am thinking, therefore I am').

Descartes' self-reflective conviction of existence lasts only as long as the subject continues to reflect on the problem of existence. The *cogito*, as is clear from its context, should not be translated as 'I think' (i.e. I am a thinking person) 'therefore I am'. Rather, Descartes' sense is better conveyed in the somewhat clumsy formulation: 'while I am conscious of being involved in thought, I am conscious of existence.' Consciousness of existence, and hence the proof of existence, is momentary. Like Adam in

Paradise Lost, the 'autopsia' which Descartes performed in his meditations showed him that he has no stable knowledge, but merely a sequence (in John Cottingham's words) of unrelated 'flashes of cognition'. He must move, then (and again the parallel with Milton's enquiry is striking) from the sensory experience of the world available through *cognitio* (mere cognition, such as Satan possesses) to *scientia* – a stable body of knowledge. Inner conviction of his own existence, Descartes argued, is merely the prelude to a conviction of the existence of God.

There is no evidence that Milton had ever read a word of Descartes' philosophy. Neither is it likely that Harvey and Milton would have had much contact with one another, particularly in the light of their respective political allegiances during the last years of Harvey's life. And yet, in their different spheres, the anatomist, the philosopher and the poet proclaim themselves to be devotees of 'autopsia' – of seeing for oneself. Adam's enquiry into his own sense of 'selfhood' faithfully reflects the Cartesian process of philosophical self-interrogation summarized in the second of Descartes' meditations 'On the Nature of the Mind' (published in 1641) in the following phrase: 'I, who am certain that I am, do not yet know clearly enough what I am.' Milton, of course, went no further in his enquiry before introducing the creature to its maker, and then to its reflection in the 'other self' which is Eve. But Descartes, in contrast, continues: 'What, then, did I formerly think I was? I thought I was a man. But what is a man? Shall I say a rational animal? No . . . what then am I? A thing that thinks.'

The results of Descartes' 'reduction' of the human being to little more than a self-reflective machine lead us to the conclusion of this chapter about 'self' and 'selfhood' in the seventeenth century. But even Descartes himself drew back from the monstrous conclusion towards which Cartesian philosophy tended: the creation of 'l'homme machine'. 'Everyone feels that he is a single person', Descartes wrote, in 1643, in a letter to the Princess Elizabeth of Bohemia, as he tried to reassure the Princess that the 'notion of a union which everyone has in himself without philosophizing' is genuine. But of course, such unreflective unity was no longer enough once the body – that core of individuality – had been so ruthlessly probed. The dictionary tells us that, in England, the 'self' emerges, grammatically, as a 'living formative element' at some point around the middle of the sixteenth century, and reaches its apogee in the mid-seventeenth century. Is this, then, the period when the modern idea of 'selfhood', or at least an 'integrated rhetoric of the self', emerges? Cultural evidence, beginning with Dürer's earlier images of himself as Christ in sickness, but then moving though Caravaggio's cool enquiry into the core of Christian faith, Donne's imaginative participation in the key moment of the trial of belief, and (later) his rehearsal of his own extinction, Harvey's secular resurrectionist experiments, Milton's enquiry into the knowledge of being, and even the emergence of Descartes' mechanistic philosophy, suggest a more complex picture. What was 'born' in the period was not 'selfhood' but the modern idea of 'corporeality'. 'Autopsia' – the science of seeing 'for oneself' – was also the science of seeing 'teipsum', of seeing yourself. But no one, in the seventeenth century any more than today, saw themselves as abstract 'subjects' or 'personalities'. Rather, they saw themselves, as we now see ourselves, 'embodied'. The point, however, was that 'embodiment' was no more 'natural' than the idea of 'selfhood'. 'Embodiment' was a culturally fashioned object, a product of a Europe-wide artistic, philosophical and scientific programme which spanned nearly 150 years. Laing's assertion that 'the individual . . . has as his starting-point an experience of his body' may well be true. We cannot conclude, however, that the 'experience of the body' is simply all there is in the process by which we find ourselves to 'be a person with other human beings'. For 'embodiment' as much as 'selfhood' may itself be subject to a shifting history, which is as much a product of culture as it might be of nature.

3

SELF-REFLECTION AND THE SELF

Roger Smith

René Descartes (1596–1650) is the pivotal figure in many histories of psychology. He appears as the man who established mechanist ways of thought about nature, the explanation of nature by matter and motion, and then began to apply such thought to what we hold to be human. Modern natural scientists often look back to Descartes and see the beginning of a true appreciation of human nature at one with the material universe. They accept that Descartes himself remained sincerely committed to the existence of the soul, a rational and immortal principle, but – from the perspective of the modern materialist – judge his position to involve an inconsistency which modern science is busy removing. Whether such discussions are true to Descartes, to history and to nature is another matter, and the modern materialist's story has elements of myth-making. Nevertheless, there were new mechanist natural philosophies of nature in the seventeenth century, Descartes was their most influential philosophical spokesman and there are good reasons to look here for major elements of modern views of what we are.

Not the least of the questions thrown up by Cartesian philosophy concerns the reality of the individual 'self' or person. This language of the self has a historical character and is not fixed. A new sense of self in the seventeenth century is a crucial part of what is distinctive, modern and Western. Modern people are preoccupied by personal feelings, personal wealth, personal fulfilment, personal health, personal privacy and much else 'personal' besides. This gives much of the twentieth century human sciences, like psychology and sociology, their subject matter. There is much less agreement about how, why and when these preoccupations arose. It was a long-term historical process. But the seventeenth century was a time when there was a considerably increased sense of self connected to developments in natural and moral philosophy as well as society and culture more generally.

In the late twentieth-century literature on the self, some of which is historical and some of which is stimulated by experience of a fragmentation of self-identity, there is no simple conclusion about whether or not a distinctive Western sense of self developed in the early modern period. The question needs to be clarified. If we step back, we can ask what notion of the individual and of the self there was in this age, as we can ask this question of every age, rather than seek the origins or the invention of individuality or the self, as if reference to 'the individual' or 'the self' denotes only one kind of thing. This does not imply acceptance of a trans-historical self. It merely suggests there are different notions of the individual and the self, with the implication that there can be no one origin, development or invention. It therefore does not make sense to refer, without qualification, to 'the discovery of the self' in the seventeenth century. It is obvious that Christian belief presumed the category of the person, which denoted someone who possesses an immortal soul, while Roman law presumed that civil society consists of individuals endowed with agency and hence responsibility. Since medieval society rationalized the maintenance of order in terms of Christianity and jurisprudence, this society, in some sense, acknowledged the reality of individuals. Yet this does not tell us how far this reality was internalized as a conscious subjective sense of self-identity and how far different types of people used a language that represented experience of an inner self. To what extent, for example, did a person react to social events in terms of individualized subjective feelings?

Most modern people, when they use the category of the 'person', especially in the context of the human sciences, ignore the theological dimension. This is badly ahistorical when projected back on to the seventeenth century. There was an extensive medieval and early modern literature that discussed the nature of the person in terms of the individual rational and immortal substance or soul. This related what it is to be an embodied person to questions of Christ's body, a passionately significant topic relevant to the dogmas of the Trinity and of transubstantiation. When philosophers like Descartes and, later, John Locke (1632–1704), who sometimes look modern to us, discussed what they meant by a person or self, their views were understood at the time in theological terms. Much of the controversial character of the new natural philosophy stemmed from this. Locke was notably innovative, and he was much criticized, when he detached the question of personal identity from the theology of the Trinity and associated it with consciousness. When the term 'personality' became current in psychology in the late nineteenth century, the word was already in use in Christology, the theology that concerned the personhood of Christ.

For whatever reasons and to whatever degree, there was a heightened sense of self in the seventeenth century. Whatever the subsequent modifications and intensifications of the sense of self by Romantic writers, by urban society or by modernist art or philosophy, it is possible in the late twentieth century to grasp and identify with the individualizing content of seventeenth century expression. This is not so easy to do for the medieval period. This construction of an expressive language of self, which took place in the domains of theology and jurisprudence but also went beyond these domains, created possibilities for psychological experiences, along with psychological terms and concepts, and hence helped make possible the modern human sciences. There could, after all, be no psychology unless there is a psychological subject.

Descartes' vivid use of 'I' when he wrote philosophy establishes a point of departure from which to explore the early modern self. His *Discourse on the Method of Rightly Conducting One's Reason*, first published in 1637, is remarkable not least for the directness and persistence with which sentences begin with 'I'. Descartes' method to arrive at knowledge was a form of biography: he stressed what 'I' have experienced in 'my' education and what 'I' have concluded as a new foundation for truth. The point is not that Descartes was egotistic. The point is that he chose the 'I' as the hero of the story. He invited readers to reflect as he had done, to find in their own 'I' the grounds for truth

> For my part, I have never presumed my mind to be in any way more perfect than that of the ordinary man . . . I shall be glad nevertheless, to reveal in this discourse what paths I have followed, and to represent my life in it as if in a picture, so that everyone may judge it for himself.

This differed from the language of earlier scholastic philosophy, in which the personal 'I' was used in disputation but only to serve deductive argument or textual exegesis, that is, to serve an impersonal subject. Medieval and Renaissance Aristotelian philosophers considered reason and morality as general conditions of being not as personal acts. Descartes' 'I am, therefore I exist' rings down the centuries as an individual assertion.

It is significant that, when Descartes turned inwards to examine his individual mind as a source of knowledge, he represented this as an individual act, not an act characteristic of life in a certain community of people. He stressed self-examination as an individual as opposed to a social performance. This was a taste of what was to come when introspection and the examination of mental content provided a new psychology in the late nineteenth century with subject matter: the representation of mind in terms that ignored the social constitution of what is represented.

Yet it must be questioned whether Descartes really did have a modern sense of the individual 'I'. The style in which he presented himself was heavily rhetorical. Further, when he wrote about his 'I', he referred to the soul as thinking substance; he denoted something universal and characterized by a reasoning nature, and he did not necessarily refer to an individual consciousness. Descartes claimed, for example, that the soul necessarily always thinks but he did not claim that an individual soul is always conscious. Descartes used the Latin word *cogitare* or the French word *penser* when he discussed the soul's qualities, rather than words equivalent to the modern English word 'consciousness'. All the same, even if rhetorically, he portrayed himself as the hero of his philosophical story. Further, he discussed self-control of the passions as the means necessary for the individual to reason rightly, and we should perhaps look for the roots of the modern 'I' in the discourse on the passions rather than the discourse on reason. Yet again, however, the discourse on the 'self'-control of the passions was embedded in Classical and Christian moral philosophy. To picture and train the passions was an ancient art, for which Latin authors like Cicero or Seneca, as well as Christ, provided a language. To moderate the passions requires a reflective stance, and perhaps much of the modern 'I' grew in this discipline. The reference to 'consciousness' as definitional of the self came later; in the English-speaking world, this was after the work of Locke.

Other writers – the best known is Montaigne – turned, like Descartes, to the world of reflection as a world in which at least something could be certain to be true. Half a century before Descartes, the *seigneur* Michel de Montaigne (1533–1592), surrounded by violent political and religious conflict, wrote the *Essais* which continue to be admired for their detached, amusing, reflective view of customs and events as elements in the constitution of his own self. In his much quoted Preface 'to the reader', he claimed that 'I want to appear in my simple, natural and everyday dress, without strain or artifice', and he concluded that 'I am myself the substance of my book'. We do not have to believe this rhetoric about the exposure of his 'nakedness' to see that he still made his subjective self the source of knowledge about the human subject. If the object of knowledge is himself, as he said, 'no man ever came to a project with better knowledge and understanding than I have of this matter, in regard to which I am the most learned man alive'. This is the definitive pre-Freudian conviction. He set up the self as the basis for a wider learning: 'Every man carries in himself the complete pattern of human nature.'

Montaigne did not expect women or the ordinary people to possess the same reflective means to knowledge. Rather, he observed, 'the true advantage of the ladies lies in their beauty; and beauty is . . . peculiarly their property.' Thus, when he claimed the self as his own starting point, he denied the same quality of self to others. When he defined beauty he did so as beauty appears outwardly to men and not as it is subjectively experienced by women. Whenever the self is discussed, we find a principle of differentiation, a way to draw distinctions as well as to describe something that is supposedly foundational to the human world.

Montaigne chose to express himself in 'essays', a medium which he developed and popularized as a way to fit words to experience. Since he rejected the possibility of a unified world-view and scorned the religious fanatics who slaughtered to establish such unity, he exploited a medium appropriate for the diverse bits of *his* experience that could, he felt, constitute knowledge. A treatise may claim to be universal, but an essay must claim to be particular. The form of the essay mirrored the disjointed nature of the author's experience. Later, empirically minded natural philosophers like Francis Bacon (1561–1626) and Robert Boyle (1627–1691) adopted the essay as an appropriate form to use in order to describe the plain particulars of nature, to escape the artifice of language and to avoid the grandiosity that went with the formulation of world-views.

Montaigne and Descartes were independent scholars whose livelihoods depended on private wealth or patronage. This points to another dimension of the heightened sense of self. Though 'the rise of capitalism' is a phrase no longer in vogue since that 'rise' appears in different places in Europe anywhere from the thirteenth to the twentieth century, the use of capital in the seventeenth century did generate wealth, and this wealth did support art, scholarship and moral philosophy. These cultural productions stressed individual attributes and qualities. Wealth, of course, mainly or exclusively benefited elites – 'polite society' – though these were as diverse as the courtiers at Louis XIV's Versailles and the members of the Watch in Amsterdam. Economic and political power promoted individual display – of learning as well as of dress – in the courts, country houses and merchant homes of the age.

One sign of the growth of reference to individual status was that the portrait came into its own as a genre of European painting, exemplified by the work of Hans Holbein at the court of Henry VIII of England and of Diego de Silva y Velazquez, at the court of Philip IV of Spain. The portrait, with its roots in the Renaissance, certainly represented its subject as king, pope, infanta or merchant prince, but it also created an individual presence, a self. The desire for glory and fame led rulers and would-be rulers to grandiose displays of individuality. The Italian Renaissance master Benvenuto Cellini created evidence of his skill and then wrote down what he had done, for all to read as well as see, in an autobiography. This was an example of what the nineteenth-century historian Jacob Burckhardt called 'the most zealous and thorough study of [a man] himself in all forms and under all conditions'. The French historian of ideas Georges Gusdorf suggested that the technology of the mirror, perfected and marketed by Venice in the early sixteenth century, first enabled people literally to reflect on a whole picture of themselves. By contrast, before the sixteenth century, blown glass mirrors magnified what was near their surface and this made it difficult for people to see their whole appearance. In all of this, there was an enrichment of the sense of self.

Quiet reflection on the 'I' as a subject achieved unparalleled beauty in the Low Countries in the seventeenth century. Jan Vermeer's painting of a young woman reading a letter enables us to see a person who is actively self-absorbed. One self has spoken to another in the letter; and the viewer 'sees' intimacy, just as, with the written letter, intimacy became a refined reflection and the letter a route to self-discovery. The painter has taken the eye around a curtain to look at the woman's private world, and he has illuminated her by light from an open window, the leaded panes of which reflect the woman's self-absorbed face. The painting's subject is the subjective self; we cannot know what is in the letter but we do know the woman's quiet sensibility. In Rembrandt's self-portraits, created at about the same time, the painter boldly presented a challenge to the viewer about what it is to be Rembrandt as well as a picture of what the artist thought he looked like. These powerful pictures remain a profound emblem of the self. Much earlier, Montaigne put the writer's case for the self-portrait: 'Authors communicate with the world in some special and peculiar capacity; I am the first to do so with my whole being, as Michel de Montaigne, not as a grammarian, a poet, or a lawyer.'

Though portraiture heightened the dignity and value of a person as an individual, it did not cease to represent its subject as a person in a social position, as a person who stands for a type of man or woman or even for humanity as a whole. There were portraits of Indians, slaves, servant girls, peasants, madmen and animals, as well as kings and bankers. When art cultivated and enriched the language of individuality it also cultivated the language of social differentiation. The 'I' recognized beneath the clothes and skin was also a social entity.

Except in rare instances, such as Rembrandt's self-portraits, the new language of the self was weighted with reference to a person's social position and responsibilities. The language of Catholic states tended to re-express belief that a person's identity is subordinate to collective political entities of church and state. In contrast, the language of some Protestant communities placed a heavy and even oppressive emphasis on the self as a moral agent; this is the stock image of the Puritan. Protestant values heightened awareness of a direct relationship between each individual fallen soul and God's omnipotent will. This related to and was sometimes in conflict with a political and social stress on the web of individual rights and obligations under natural law, the law given by God to the world as its nature. There was much anxious attention to everyday conduct, to business and domestic matters and to ordinary things, to the particulars of the individual life. As God's will created the world, it appeared to be an act of worship as well as an instantiation of God's law for the creation to be morally serious in the daily round. The Protestant sensibility, notably evident in New England, encouraged belief in the inward self as a responsible agent, and it understood this responsibility to lie equally in relation to the God-given soul and to the God-given material world. The Protestant work ethic united inward and outward responsibilities and enhanced the growth of the individual, self-conscious self. In economic terms, Protestants extolled the individual's prudent management of capital, labour, property and time. These expectations about individuality were very unevenly distributed. Power in much of Europe continued to rest with the Catholic Church and Catholic monarchs, with a feudal aristocracy and with new states and their autocratic rulers, rather than with individuals. The 'I' flourished in spaces between institutions, as in Descartes' meditations or in the domestic order of Dutch merchants.

Responsibility to God's creation, work, economic activity, new technology and new science fostered an instrumental view of the self. There was a conception of a person as a practical agent, an individual whose identity and worth, subjectively and socially, resides in being able to do things, to act on nature, self or society to achieve practical ends. The archetypical instrumental relationship involves an individual in actions whose form responds to the requirements of technology. From this perspective, the new philosophies of nature – most obviously, Cartesian mechanical philosophy – are not just theories about nature but attitudes towards nature. Critics argue that these attitudes made for a distanced, objective and sometimes mechanistic relationship towards nature and, as hopes spread for a science of man, towards women and men as well. Thus, the individuality achieved in the seventeenth century was an individuality that often oriented the person in an instrumental way in her or his relationships. Knowledge, it seemed, was knowledge when nature and human nature were subject to prediction and control.

Printed works, common since the early sixteenth century, included many 'conduct books' directed at self-control. The book itself, like the letter, significantly enhanced a person's capacity to become self-absorbed and self-aware, that is, to become individual. The book and the letter were the material medium of private thought, sensibility and improvement. Descartes wrote about human life and published his thoughts as 'these things are worth noting in order to encourage each of us to make a point of controlling our passions' so that 'even those who have the weakest souls could acquire absolute mastery over all their passions if we employed sufficient ingenuity in training and guiding them'. Conduct books, especially in Puritan culture, sharpened self-reflection, sometimes to a painful degree. Boyle, who played a pivotal role in the legitimation of the new natural philosophy in England, referred to three 'books' which carry authority – nature, scripture and the conscience. The conscience, he believed, lies in each person and can be known by the use of right reasoning about moral things. From this perspective, the self is a book of truth comparable to the books of nature and of God's word.

A sense of self reached its height in the diary, the book written by oneself for oneself as a means of self-reflection and self-control. Serious Puritans recommended the diary as a discipline for the soul's steady contemplation of its proper ends. The parish minister at Coggeshall in Essex, Ralph Josselin, kept a diary through the difficult years of the reign of Charles I. There, amidst the seemingly endless round of his wife's confinements and in the confusion of his family's and his own ailments, he worried about the meaning of daily events for the salvation of his soul. The diary recorded external events and, more significantly, struggled to make a pattern out of events by their assimilation into a moral and spiritual narrative of the diarist's self. In the more libertarian atmosphere of 1660s Restoration London, Samuel Pepys, a civil servant at His Majesty's Admiralty, recorded in volume after volume all the vicissitudes and delights of daily life. The grand and the banal lay side by side, each in its own way worthy of record since each experience was uniquely and irreducibly Pepys' own.

Pepys was perhaps more troubled by his bladder stones than by his soul, but whether diarists recorded bodily or spiritual grief and joy they enriched the scope of subjectivity. Some historians suggest that the subjective sphere so marked out and valued for its distinctive and immediate truth characterizes modernity. If so, then it is surely not coincidental that modern science and modern consciousness developed side by side. The shift towards the understanding of what is outward in mathematical and mechanical terms, the shift for which Descartes is emblematic, seems also to have involved a shift towards understanding what is inward in terms of a private world of qualitative truth and feeling. This language that divides outward and inward is itself metaphorical and part of how the modern self is imagined.

However subjective a diarist's record, it was also a social record; the language, even the choice of the diary as a medium, derived from and shared in the wider culture. An individual who explored her or his own subjectivity did so in a society that valued such sensibility and self-responsibility. An outward sign of this was a refinement of manners and greater delicacy in public with regard to eating, excreting, cleanliness and the body generally. Society as a whole, bodily expression and subjective sensibility all slowly changed in conjunction with each other, with major differences between women and men, between social groups, between town and country, and between court and plebeian culture. The literature on conduct and manners sought to create Christian gentlewomen and gentlemen, to individualize control, to make social control self-control and to cultivate refined subjectivity. The English Puritans, like those who travelled to establish New England, and the later German Pietists, who pressed readers or listeners to consider the state of their souls, made the connections between social order and subjective order most clearly. But the theatre of Molière or of Restoration England also made much of the same play between social custom and individual character, and comedy and plot relied frequently on the disruptive individual body.

All this, it appears in the twentieth century, differentiated and dignified the psychological dimension in human life. Nobody expressed it in such terms in the seventeenth century. Words like 'consciousness' and 'self-consciousness' were unusual in English until late in the century. Nevertheless, the expression 'human nature' came into common English usage, and this language took for granted that there is a relationship between an individualized subjectivity and a shared or common nature. This was a different language for reflection on what it is to be human than the scholastic language of intellective and sensitive souls. Modern thought adapted the ancient language of the soul, humours, temperaments and spirits, but it also added a new discourse about human nature, mind and subjectivity. This new discourse stressed self-reflection and self-control, it individualized refined social values and it lay the basis for modern subjective sensibility.

ACKNOWLEDGEMENT

This chapter is adapted from a section of my forthcoming book, *The Fontana History of the Human Sciences* (London: Fontana, 1997), with the permission of HarperCollins Publishers Ltd.

Part II

ENLIGHTENMENT

4

RELIGIOUS EXPERIENCE AND THE FORMATION OF THE EARLY ENLIGHTENMENT SELF

Jane Shaw

One of the great stories – perhaps *the* great story – of the modern West is that of the rise of the rational self and a corresponding decline in religious belief. Some three hundred years ago, in that period from approximately the late seventeenth century to the mid-eighteenth century, it is said that reason came to triumph. As the new philosophy and developing scientific methods began to take hold, an understanding of man as rational, autonomous and in control of the universe emerged In this world-view, revelation, the mystical, belief in miracles and the supernatural all came to be rejected in favour of an understanding of the world as operating by observable laws of nature. It is the story of the rise of rational man. Intellectual historians of the mid-twentieth century, such as Paul Hazard, wrote of this time that:

> The most widely accepted notions, such as deriving proofs of God's existence from universal consent, the historical basis of miracles, were openly called in question. The Divine was relegated to a vague and impenetrable heaven somewhere up in the skies. Man and man alone was the standard by which all things were measured. He was his own *raison d'être*. His interests were paramount.

The intellectual history of the rise of the rational self, as represented by Hazard, is essentially and necessarily built on a study of the philosophical and theological texts of a small, educated elite. More recently, social historians have turned their attention to 'popular' religious culture which they have presumed to be different and separate from the intellectual culture of the elite. They have, for the most part, retained the notion that such an Enlightenment self came to predominate, and that it came to predominate initially among the elite. They have therefore generally suggested that the ideas of the elite won out, a sharp division between elite and popular occurred and such elite ideas eventually trickled down to the masses, who either accepted them unquestioningly or ignored them and

61

went about their 'superstitious' religious practices regardless. We receive a picture of events whereby such an elite Enlightenment self was formed in splendid intellectual isolation, and yet nevertheless came to predominate. Thus in social histories of religious and popular culture at this time, the notion of an enlightened, rational self is kept intact, while religious belief and practice are relegated to the world of the masses – the lower orders, women and all 'irrational' others. In short, neither intellectual nor social historians have given any place to religious experience or practice in the *formation* of such an Enlightenment self. This is a rather crude telling of the story, but nevertheless, some version of this story has proved remarkably persistent both in general and more learned conceptions of 'our' history of the last three hundred years.

In the past few decades, this great story of modernity, of the rise of the rational self, has been attacked by the French poststructuralists and their Anglo-American followers. They have, for example, attempted to show that such a rational man is not the autonomous self he claims to be, but that he is, rather, a *subject*, subjected to social, cultural, psychic and political forces which construct not only his sense of him-self, but the very language in which he expresses that sense of self. These insights have opened up the possibility of exploring how such a 'rational self', far from being free or autonomous, was circumscribed and defined by factors such as gender, education, social status and ethnicity. Nevertheless, while performing *this* act of deconstruction, the majority of these poststructuralist thinkers have kept intact the claim that religion declined in this period generally known as the Enlightenment. In short, they have been willing to undo one side of the equation – the notion of the rational self – but not the other: that both the impetus for and the evidence of that rational self's emergence was the rejection of religious beliefs which relied on the supernatural, revelationary and miraculous.

If we are to deconstruct *that* notion then we need to consider the possibility that religious practice and religious experience played a part in the formation of the rational 'self' which has traditionally been seen as setting itself apart from any real religious considerations. This chapter suggests – through the telling of a miracle story from the late seventeenth century – that religious experience and religious practice were central to the *formation* of such a rational, Enlightenment self, in the early Enlightenment period in England. It does *not* suggest that all Enlightenment philosophers had religious experiences which affected their work (though it would be possible to argue that some did); rather, it suggests that such events as miracles (or claims of miracles) formed the body of evidence upon and through which men who were engaged with the new philosophy tested its possibilities and, in the very practice of the new scientific and philosophical methods, emerged as 'rational selves'. In turn it also suggests, albeit more briefly, that in their testing and categorization of such stories, the modern notion of 'religious experience' also began to emerge, some two hundred years or so before William James' famous formulations about, and categorizations of, religious experience in *Varieties of Religious Experience* (1902). In short, this early Enlightenment period saw the creation of the mutually dependent categories of both 'rational self' and 'religious experience'.

A theoretical entry into this historical venture is the work of Michel de Certeau, a Jesuit historian who was much influenced by French post-structuralism. His work stands out as different from that of many of the poststructuralists because of his willingness to address our modern and postmodern preconceptions about religion and in his reading of both the theological canon and archival materials on everyday religious practice.

In his challenge to this picture of the rise of rationality and the resulting secularization, de Certeau seeks not only to undo such a history but also to ask *why* such a history has been written. He seeks to lay bare its ideological frame in terms of historical method and asks how we might (re)write such a history in the future. He sees the way forward primarily, in this context, in linking thought to practice. Noting the split which historians have maintained, for this period, between theology and religious practice in his *The Writing of History* he asks: 'how can a sociology of behavior and a history of doctrines be articulated?' He claims that this 'relation has yet to be clearly specified'. He continues: 'The analysis of documents concerning religious practices in the seventeenth centuries and eighteenth centuries must have some relation with the analysis of ideological and symbolic discourses.'

De Certeau's analysis suggests that we need to relate the intellectual developments which led to the formation of the rational self to the religious practices from which that 'self' has been distanced, simultaneously questioning the division between elite and popular. De Certeau seeks to do this for France in this period by examining religious practice, especially cases of possession and mysticism, and yet he retains the division between the elite and the 'masses' as that division has been traditionally conceptualized. He does not question that there was a

> growing divergence in the seventeenth century and even more in the eighteenth between, on the one hand, the rapid autonomy of the 'philosophes' in respect to religious criteria, and, on the other, the calm persistence, indeed the objective extension, of religious practices in the mass of the nation during the same period.

There may, indeed, be certain factors in the case of France which make this division between elite and popular likely: specifically, the role of the Roman Catholic Church and its heavy influence on – even control over – rural and popular religion, and the antagonistic relationship between the Church and the philosophes. Nevertheless, we must note – hazards of translation aside – that de Certeau (perhaps unwittingly) keeps intact the language of the literary and sociological methods in his very critique of it. He speaks of the philosophes having 'rapid autonomy' (which we might interpret as change, as progress above and beyond the super-stitious beliefs of the church) and of the religious *practices* of the masses 'calmly persist[ing]' (i.e. they persist despite the intellectual changes going on above them). That is, the masses *practise* religion – indeed their practices do not change – while the elite *thinks* about religion and experi-ences Enlightenment. De Certeau therefore replicates this story of the rise of rationality, the rise of rational man, at the same time that he seeks to undo it. As I have said, this may be the only possibility in the case of France.

I want now to turn to late seventeenth-century England and ask of religious culture there de Certeau's question: 'how can a sociology of behavior and a history of doctrines be articulated?' For I want to make the claim that his questions and method can, perhaps, more successfully be applied to the case of early Enlightenment England. Why? Let us turn briefly to the different cultural circumstances of England and France. First, while the established church of France – the Roman Catholic Church – would not be formally dismantled until the French Revolution at the end of the eighteenth century, the Church of England had already been overthrown for a while, during the Civil War of the mid-seventeenth century. Thus competing churches and religious groups gained attention and power, and after the restoration of both the monarch and the Church of England in 1660, England quite quickly had to develop a policy of religious toleration. Second, the Church of England was, in the 1660s, still rather weak and did not have the influence or inclination to enforce a kind of conformity of religious practices. Third, the Church of England did not have the kind of antagonism towards the development of science that the Roman Catholic Church had had. It was with memories of what happened to Galileo, and of the Roman Catholic Church's resistance to science in general, that philosophers and theologians developed their scientific interests in the more tolerant Protestant Low Countries and England. In England, the 'scientific revolution' was developed, at least in part, by clerics. There was no particular antagonism – at this time – between religion and science. Indeed, many historians have argued that the Protestant emphasis on an individual's authority in observing and inter-preting knowledge for him- or herself was crucial for the development of the modern scientific method. This may suggest a rapid popularization of the scientific method, a point I shall be pursuing in this chapter. It has been suggested that just as this sense of individual authority spread among Protestants in the previous century, so it spread quickly with regard to observing the world along scientific lines. As J. Paul Hunter puts it: 'although the doctrine that everyone could be his or her own priest originated as a credo about received texts, it was quickly applied to the Book of Creation as well.'

Fourth, there existed, also, a political toleration – arising out of the mixed government of monarch and parliament – which allowed the free circulation of ideas in print, in coffee houses and public houses, in philosophical and reading societies. This is the reason that Habermas' first 'ideal type' of public sphere is late seventeenth-century and early eighteenth-century England, not France. In England (unlike France) printing flourished, so that periodicals, newspapers and pamphlets were produced quickly and in great numbers. Thus, Habermas claims, this kind of public sphere did not begin to develop in France until the middle of the eighteenth century. Furthermore, the Enlightenment really got going in *England*. While the Enlightenment and its origins are often primarily traced to the French philosophes, in fact those philosophes pointed to England as the source of their ideas. Historians of this period – especially historians of religion – are increasingly making this point, and are indicating that later developments in France have rather overshadowed our perception of where that intellectual movement which we call the Enlightenment took place. With all this in mind then, let me turn to a particular case of a religious event, and public responses to that event, in early Enlightenment England.

Late seventeenth-century England was full of wondrous and unnatural events: miracles and ghosts, prophecies and providences. In 1668, word quickly spread of such an event, by word of mouth and by the publication of several pamphlets: it was claimed that one Martha Taylor, of Bakewell in Derbyshire, a 19-year-old, fairly poor maiden, had survived for several months without food. (She was, ultimately, to live for over a year without food.) Large crowds of all sorts of people came to see her, including the Earl of Devonshire and other members of the Derbyshire gentry who, 'having a great desire to be more fully satisfied in the truth' accordingly 'thought good to make choice of twenty maids to watch and wait with her for seven days and seven nights' (it was 'certified for very truth' by the twenty maids that she received no food). In October 1668, Thomas Robins, a 'wellwisher to the gospel of Jesus Christ', probably a rather ill-educated, but nevertheless educated, nonconformist minister, wrote of the miracle of Martha Taylor in a small cheap pamphlet, *News from Darby-shire; of the Wonder of all Wonders*, which he subtitled 'a perfect and true Relation of the handy work of Almighty God shown upon the body of one Martha Taylor.' For Robins, Taylor was a 'wonder of wonders', 'one of the strangest wondrous works . . . wrought by the handy work of God in love to sinners upon earth.' He wrote that 'she hath not taken any manner of food, bread, drink or water, or anything to preserve mortal life' for over forty weeks, except for her mother anointing her lips 'with a feather and spring water' from time to time. Robins, pointing out that while Moses and Jesus fasted forty days and forty nights each, this maid 'as fasted for every day for a year or more', claimed that

> it is for love that the Lord bears to that poor creature, which makes him to work this wonderful work upon her, for indeed I could wish with all my heart, that I and every poor soul living were but in as good a condition as the soul of that poor Christian is in, for . . . she is fed with Angels food and the power of heaven is with her.

He compares this wondrous work with those miracles worked by Jesus, such as raising Lazarus from the dead, and exhorts his readers 'to consider the Lord hath not shown his handy work upon her only for her own sin.'

But not all those who visited or heard about Martha Taylor saw her as a miraculous wonder. In 1669, the same year in which Robins published a second pamphlet on the subject, John Reynolds published his *A Discourse upon Prodigious Abstinence occasioned by the twelve moneths* [sic] *fasting of Martha Taylor*. Writing explicitly against any explanation of Taylor's survival as a miracle, Reynolds attempted a complex explanation of the phenomenon in medical terms, in a pamphlet which he submitted to the Royal Society. The subtitle of Reynolds' pamphlet clearly states his position:

> Proving That without any miracle, the texture of Humane Bodies may be so altered, that life may be long continued without the supplies of Meat and Drink. With an account of the Heart and how far it is in interested in the Business of Fermentation.

Reynolds' explanation of Taylor's survival without food rested on his use of Thomas Willis' theory of fermentation, published some ten years earlier (*Of Fermentation of the Inorganical Motion of Natural Bodies*, 1659). For Willis, the seminal vessels and genital parts were filled, as were other major organs, with fermentative particles made up of salt, sulphur, earth and water. These bodily elements could ferment within the organs and move in the blood, making it hot. Commenting on the ways in which fermentation could be continued in the blood without new additions of 'chyle', produced by eating and digestion, and pointing out that the natural evacuations of the bowels and saliva glands stopped when eating and drinking stopped, Reynolds concluded that the body actually conserved elements in her blood, and therefore nourished her and allowed her to survive.

He thus directly refutes the notion of Martha Taylor as a miraculous maid. He remarks:

> Some persons as scant in their reading, as they are in their travels, are ready to deem everything strange to be a monster, and every monster a miracle: true it is, the fast of Moses, Elijah, and the Incarnate Word, was miraculous, and possibly of some others; yet why we should make all miracles, I understand not; for what need have we now of miracles.

Reynolds does not distance himself from Christianity – only from the possibility of *current* prodigies and wonders being interpreted as miraculous (a line of argument which would be taken by many contributors to the great intellectual debate on miracles in the early eighteenth century). Besides, this is the correct *theological* line to take, according to Reynolds: in the Preface he says: 'A Just Reverence to Reformed Theologues, asserting a total cessation of miracles, forbad me to immure my self in any such supernatural asylum,' and thus he asserts his Protestant credentials. Indeed, it is his Protestantism and his manliness which enable him to take this reasonable line: at one point in his Preface, he remarks that he might be taken captive by any dogma written by someone he admired 'were I not a Man, and which is more, a Protestant'. This is an interesting statement for many reasons, but especially so given that Robins too is a man and a Protestant; but Robins is a poor man, and an enthusiast at that, while Reynolds is a gentleman.

Reynolds certainly believes that Taylor has survived without food for a year: he is not sceptical about the phenomenon itself, and in fact criticizes those who are. His aim is simply to explain this rationally and scientifically. He is clearly keen to copy and impress the Fellows of the recently founded Royal Society; his text is full of references to important figures in the world of restoration science, most notably Robert Boyle.

Indeed, Reynolds' explanation of the Martha Taylor phenomenon indicates the speed with which the new philosophy made its way to the provinces after the foundation of the Royal Society in 1662, or points to the possibility that the methodology of the new philosophy was being developed in the provinces at the same time that it was being developed at the universities and in London. Very quickly, gentleman scholars not only in London but around the country began to meet together as the Philosophical Society had been meeting sporadically since 1645 in London (which, with a royal charter, became the Royal Society in 1662). They also wrote pamphlets or letters proffering a variety of theories about and explanations of all kinds of apparently natural and unnatural phenomena, sometimes including descriptions of their own experiments, and sent them to the Royal Society for publication in the *Philosophical Transactions* which were first issued in 1665.

Thus competing interpretations began to be offered of apparently unnatural or miraculous events, and phenomena such as Martha Taylor's survival without food began to be the subject of debate, at local and national levels. Miraculous and supernatural events had always been the subject of debate, of course, but within the bounds of religious criteria: that is, people asked whether a miracle was the work of good or evil forces, whether a person was the recipient of divine revelation or possessed by evil spirits. The impact of the new philosophy was such that as more people began to observe and interpret such events, a variety of explanations began to flourish. While some people continued to attribute such events to divine intervention, others began to ask whether such a phenomenon was the result of such divine intervention, or could be explained 'naturally'; yet others began to ask more frequently whether so-called miracles were really hoaxes. In the case of Martha Taylor we see a number of explanations at work.

For Robins, Taylor's body was a public, interpretable sign of a mysterious work of God. In his second pamphlet, *The Wonder of the World*, written in 1669, he suggests that God 'hath made his chosen vessel of this Damsel, for to work this marvelous work upon as a comfortable sign to a sinful and hypocritical nation'. The event of her miraculous body (the vessel of God's work) is not only to be publicly debated, but is also to be given public significance: it is a sign that a sinful and hypocritical nation must repent. In this, Robins mixes an interpretation of Taylor's survival as miraculous with the language of providence. Robins also records for us another interpretation, namely that there were those who scoffed at the whole thing: 'and yet there is some so hard of belief, that they will not stick to say; I mean concerning this maid; that there is some desembleation in it.' And then there was Reynolds' attempt to explain Taylor's apparently unnatural survival in *natural* terms.

The advent of competing interpretations of such events led necessarily to a greater emphasis on proofs and witnesses. One needed to prove one's case. Robins recorded that the Earl of Devonshire, and others of the head of the gentry in the Derbyshire area had 'a great desire to be more fully satisfied in the truth'. Robins adds his own gloss: 'the thing being so wonderful and strange that they scarce know how to believe.' Accordingly, 'they thought good to make choice of twenty maids to watch and wait with her, that they might be satisfied in the truth.' Those twenty maids therefore watched over her for seven days and seven nights, and 'it was certified for very truth' by the twenty maids that she received no food. Robins thus hoped that such a test would 'satisfy every true believing Christian that they may receive this wonderful, strange story as a true story, and not as a fable'. The writing of his second pamphlet was prompted by his own visit to Martha Taylor, and the whole text is peppered with assurances to the reader of his authority as an eye-witness, and therefore of the truth of his interpretation of what he has seen. The accounts of other witnesses to support his relation of the phenomenon are also important: attached to the second pamphlet is another account of Martha Taylor's physical condition and survival by 'a gentleman in Chesterfield, a frequent visitor of Martha Taylor for many months also attested by divers others'.

Thus we have here the (scientific) examination of the apparently miraculous body. In the early days of the Royal Society, it was realized that certain standard criteria had to be established for conducting experiments. Members of the Royal Society asked how claims – especially competing claims – were to be established as knowledge. They asked: What was to count as knowledge or 'science'? How was this to be distinguished from other epistemological categories such as 'belief' or 'opinion'? Robert Boyle was prominent in constructing what Steven Shapin calls 'material, social and literary technologies' for the conduct of experiments and the production of knowledge. Prominent among these technologies were the performance of experiments in a public space (the scientist's lab rather than the alchemist's closet), the testimony of witnesses present at those public events and the means of ensuring that these witnesses were reliable (that is, were of the right educational and social rank, and the right gender), and the development of clear scientific prose for describing those events for people not present (virtual witnessing).

What does this have to do with Martha Taylor? Her case presents an early example of the beginnings of such 'technologies' as they began to be applied to religious experiences and examples of the wondrous. Robins' pamphlets, if not examples of clear scientific prose, nevertheless describe the phenomenon and the events surrounding it for those not present; the twenty maids are witnesses, examining the body of Taylor (and an unusual example of *women* being allowed to be such witnesses; in all other cases such witnesses are usually local, worthy gentlemen – vicars, doctors, gentry and men of letters – people who would make reliable witnesses because of their gender and social rank); and while Taylor survived and stayed within her home, that house became a public place as crowds came to visit her, as Robins reports.

We therefore have in this tale of Martha Taylor a rather more complex picture of events than that usually presented in the traditional story of the rise of rationality. First, events such as this cropped up everywhere in daily life and were *publicly* debated: competing explanations and interpretations began to be offered in printed pamphlets of all sorts, newspapers and other periodicals by people as varied in education and social status as Reynolds and Robins. There were no certain criteria for identifying whether such an incident as this was a miracle (after the apparent aboli-tion of miracles in the Protestant Reformation), so the creation of such criteria was 'up for grabs' so to speak. Anyone who visited Martha Taylor or had the literacy skills to write a pamphlet could voice an interpretation of the event, and the question of being an authentic, experiential witness was one which many people faced. (This is, perhaps, in contrast with France, where the mechanisms of the Roman Catholic Church remained in place to test the existence of a miracle according to certain established religious criteria.) This seems to confirm J. Paul Hunter's thesis that 'Once unleashed, the power of the individual to interpret was impossible to control, and . . . the impulse to "read" all events intensely became very strong'. Hunter, in *Before Novels*, says that 'In times of great anxiety or when a special event dramatically captured the public attention . . . different interpretations competed for acceptance.' We may quite safely take the survival of the fasting Martha Taylor as just such 'a special event'.

This brings us to a second important point about this case; namely, that with a variety of people 'reading' Martha Taylor (far more than the number who wrote about her), there were many points of contact between people of different social and educational status. The phenomenon of Martha Taylor's survival aroused great interest: an earl, members of the gentry, physicians, surgeons, clerics and gentleman scholars came to see her, as well as the 'people' whom we would expect to be interested in an event such as this. All these people jostled and crowded to visit Taylor, confined to bed in a lower room by the fireside in her rather lowly family home, to observe, witness and interpret her for themselves. In *A Discourse Upon Prodigious Abstinence*, Reynolds recorded that Taylor was 'visited so plentifully by the curious from many parts, as also by the Religious of all perswasions'. Thus the existence of a sharp gulf between the elite and people, in approaching religion and the rational self, can be questioned.

Finally, we must note the way in which such educated gentlemen not only mixed with the 'people' to witness this event, but also built certain apparently rational theories on real, apparently miraculous, bodies such as that of Martha Taylor (I am thinking of Reynolds' pamphlet here). This begins to break down, maybe even invert, the assumption that rational ideas necessarily trickled down to erode the popular religious practices of the 'masses' and the further assumption that rational ideas remained untouched by religious practices. Indeed, this case of Martha Taylor is just one of many such miraculous events and religious 'practices' which occurred in the late seventeenth and early eighteenth centuries and stimulated lively, public debates about the possibility of miracles. The early Enlightenment 'rational self' was fashioned in the very act of observing, examining and interpreting such religious and wondrous events as Martha Taylor. Conversely, the act of observing, examining and interpreting these events, claimed (at least by some) to be miraculous, mystical or super- natural, began the process by which such events would be categorized by modern philosophers of religion as 'religious experience'.

The Martha Taylor event may also suggest, or at least illustrate, the ways in which the rational self came to be gendered – the Enlightenment rational self was generally presumed to be masculine. A simple interpre- tation would note that while we have the *words* of the men, we only have the fasting *body* of Martha Taylor; it is the man who is the observing rational self, while the woman is observed – thus the supposedly disembodied, free and autonomous rational self is male. But a slightly more complex interpretation would point to the possibility that the rational self of the Enlightenment period needed such 'irrational' events in order to create his identity, and therefore that apparently abstract, disembodied philosophical discussions about miracles were literally built on the miraculous bodies of women such as Martha Taylor. I would even like to suggest that the existence of such 'embodied' debates formed the necessary backdrop to the far more famous intellectual debate on the possibility of miracles which reached its height in the 1720s and 1730s in England (the most famous text of which is Hume's little treatise, 'Of Miracles'). In the case of Martha Taylor, the story of the rise of rational man – symbolized here by John Reynolds, the gentleman scholar, who attempts to explain an apparently miraculous (literally supra-natural) event according to the operation of observable natural laws – is located in the very embodied and gritty context of a poor and ill-educated young girl's bedchamber.

5

THE EUROPEAN ENLIGHTENMENT AND THE HISTORY OF THE SELF

E. J. Hundert

What am I?

(James Boswell)

When the great anthropologist Marcel Mauss was invited to give the 1938 Huxley Memorial Lecture, he chose for his subject 'A category of the human mind: the notion of person; the notion of self'. Mauss thought that his contemporaries falsely believed that the idea of the self was an innate and stable human property, and that they further subscribed to an historically aberrant and socially divisive cult of the individual. Instead, and as if to combat the detachment of moderns from their own past, Mauss proposed that the seemingly self-evident conception of ourselves as unique individuals is in reality an artefact of a long and varied history stretching back to the earliest human communities. Not only do other peoples hold very different notions of the self, but each is intimately connected to the ethical community they occupy as members of distinct societies. Mauss referred to ethnographic materials from North America, Australia and archaic Greece to show that in cultures where persons are defined by kinship, descent and status, responsibility flows directly from membership in a family or clan, and neither love nor one's conscience alone can serve as justifications for action. Only with the emergence in ancient Rome of a more abstract notion of a person, seen as the locus of general rights and duties, could individuals understand themselves as endowed with a conscience and inner life, chiefly through the medium of Christianity. It is this notion of the person as a sacred being, later articulated as the possessor of a moral consciousness, as the source of autonomous motivation and capable of self-development, that is the foundation of our own self-understanding.

Nearly half a century later, Mauss' readers are sceptical about there being any one grand narrative which could possibly account for self-conceptions of the human subject, and perhaps more attentive than were his contemporaries to the impersonal nature of the coercive and disciplinary forces which shape modern consciousness. Moreover, unlike Mauss, we have good reason to think of human capacities as biologically rooted, emerging at developmentally critical moments in everyone's neurophysiological history. A conception of the self at once necessarily rests upon these processes, and at the same time has generated histories so diverse that the indigenous psychology of other or earlier societies may be nearly incomprehensible to us. Nevertheless, any plausible account of modern self-awareness must acknowledge Mauss' claim that an individualist mode of self-understanding has become distinctive of contemporary Western cultures. These cultures are characterized on the one hand by role distance – the assumption that individuals are in principle able to adopt or abandon roles at will – and on the other by autonomy – the assumption of a capacity and responsibility to decide between actions and plans of life. Boswell's question is answered for few Westerners by exclusive reference to the social positions they occupy, the history they inherit, their place in the kin group and by the moral order established with finality by divine powers. Mauss argued that the assumptions upon which the modern self rests acquired much of their distinctive character during the eighteenth century, perhaps the one claim about which both the Enlightenment's current critics and defenders would agree. In what follows, I want to refine this insight by examining how a now dominant conception of the person emerged, not from the destruction of an already degraded medieval world picture, as is often supposed, but from a form of perplexity about moral agency in modern commercial society. I will argue that in the eighteenth century the actor came to be taken as a representative individual within an altered public sphere, and that, from this perspective, and through a century-long debate about personhood, a distinctive conception of inwardness emerged through which the modern moral subject of Mauss' concern could imagine itself as unique.

Reflection on the nature of personhood during the Enlightenment is a facet of a shift in moral psychology first begun in late seventeenth-century France, largely within a context of theological dispute. This enterprise was part of a subversive tradition of continental philosophy, of which the main representatives were the sceptical doctrines of the Huguenot refugee philosopher Pierre Bayle, whose writings, Voltaire said, formed the Enlightenment's critical armoury, and the Augustinian pessimism of the most prominent Jansenist Catholic divines, particularly Pierre Nicole, whose essays John Locke translated for his own use. In a complementary fashion, both groups sought to anatomize forms of moral behaviour with the object of showing that a person's apparent practice of Christian virtue in no way provided an observer with indubitable information about the underlying motives informing them. Since apparently virtuous acts were rewarded by public esteem, it was in the obvious interest of the vicious to mime the conventional signs of Christian piety in order to win the approval of their fellows. The vast majority of people could be understood as relent-less egoists. They behaved according to the socially prescribed conventions of propriety, not because of their moral content, but in the expectation that such behaviour would win the approbation of others. Moreover, if virtue could be understood as one of the masks available to fallen men in their pursuit of selfish interests, then the difference between virtue and vice would have nothing to do with behaviour. Instead, the distinction between an act which stemmed from selfish desire and one whose source was genuine Christian charity would, of necessity, depend entirely upon the judgement of God as He inspected each human heart.

Two unsettling consequences followed from these influential arguments. First, it was assumed that the great majority of humankind merely feigned Christian commitments while being, in reality, driven by self-love. Yet the fact that their behaviour was in principle indistinguishable from that of true Christians challenged the conventional assumption that believers who feared hell and yearned for salvation were more powerfully motivated towards virtuous action than were pagans, Jews or atheists. Bayle drew the obvious conclusion: anyone, atheist or believer, could make a good subject, since civil conduct required only the outward conformity to standards of propriety produced by social pressure and communal expectations, enforced by law. The rectitude of a citizen required no spiritually enriched conscience. Second, as was famously suggested by Pierre Nicole, just as the selfish wants of individuals could be harnessed to politically beneficial ends, so too could competing social and economic interests be made to obey similar constraints. Social utility and communal benefit could be under-stood as unintended consequences of historically domesticated forms of self-aggrandizement. The seemingly anarchic tendencies of the scramble for wealth, for example, revealed themselves, at a deeper level, to be social regularities attending the common pursuit of material gratification. Thus gross cupidity and insatiable material interest paradoxically created secret social bonds, while expressions of self-regard could best be understood, not simply as examples of the essential propensity of Adam's heirs to sin, but, again paradoxically, as features of the practices by virtue of which egoism had been locally disciplined.

The decisive transposition of these arguments into a secular instrument of social understanding was undertaken by the London-based Dutch physician and satirist Bernard Mandeville in *The Fable of the Bees*, a work which achieved a European-wide reputation as the epitome of immorality, and one praised by Hume and Kant as placing the human sciences on a new footing. 'Private Vices, Publick Benefits', *The Fable*'s notorious maxim, encapsulated Mandeville's thesis that contemporary society is an aggrega-tion of naturally asocial egoists driven by passions for gain and approbation which bind people together by bonds of envy, competition and exploita-tion. Mandeville saw each individual as a compound of various passions, which 'govern him by turns, whether he will or no'. He argued that established systems of ethics served the essentially political and socializing purpose of deflecting critical attention from the irreducibly passionate and self-regarding sources of actual human desires, for only passions can move one to act, and the goal of any passion can be nothing other than one's own perceived interest or pleasure.

Mandeville cared little about court society, whose habits of life absorbed Nicole and his colleagues during the reign of Louis XIV. Instead, he focused on a wider and rapidly expanding domain – the social dynamics of wealth in modern commercial societies, of which Holland and then Britain had become the exemplar. Here, the 'methods of making ourselves acceptable to others' devised by monied commoners had established new rules of civility. Mandeville accorded prominence to the demands made by such a culture in governing the emotions of its members into elements of judgement and passion that could be satisfied only within the established practices of a commercialized public sphere. If the urgings of pride and the need for esteem were constant and universal features of the human constitution, desires themselves were nevertheless realized or thwarted only in socially structured interactions with others. Mandeville celebrated rather than bemoaned the contradictions of modern societies, where the polish and civility that necessarily accompanied commercial opulence had created a secular world in which, he argued, publicly proclaimed standards of propriety paid mere lip-service to the Christian or antique ideals that modernity had rendered vestigial.

Individuals in commercial society were obliged to respond to a revised structure of priorities if they were to satisfy their impulses. These people were driven not merely by universal appetites for authority and esteem. Rather, in the centres of European commerce, outward displays of wealth were now widely accepted as an index of one's identity. 'People, where they are not known,' Mandeville observed, 'are generally honour'd according to their Clothes and other Accoutrements they have about them';

> from the riches of them we judge of their Wealth, and by their ordering of them we guess at their Understanding. It is this which encourages every Body to wear Clothes above his rank, especially in large and populous cities where obscure men may hourly meet with fifty strangers to one acquaintance, and consequently have the pleasure of being esteemed by a vast majority, not as what they are, but what they appear to be.

Mandeville consolidated a revolution in the understanding of the relationship between motives and acts by viewing commerce and sociability as reciprocally decisive features of the modern dynamics of self-regard. He showed that the aggressive pursuit of wealth had now to be understood not as an activity confined to marginalized minorities, but as central to the self-definition of large urban and commercial populations. He sought to comprehend from the perspective of society itself the behaviour of individuals throughout the social spectrum – from lackeys to lords, as he put it – for whom opportunities for consumption and display encouraged forms of self-presentation that were the vehicles through which they established their identities.

Mandeville argued that since moral judgements were in fact nothing other than expressions of feeling (passion), then the operative traditions of Christian moral psychology could not be enlisted to explain the workings of human desire. These judgements had to be set in a different problem-space from the one typically assumed by Mandeville's contemporaries. Moral codes themselves were not expressions of universal principles, but historically inscribed ideological products crafted in the course of the civilizing process, during which ruling elites established a selfless moral ideal in order to manage egoists through shame and guilt. Mandeville argued that the actual workings of desire in any given community could in principle be accounted for by a sociology of its members' emotions. He placed the expression of supposedly moral sentiments in the context of responses to locally generated opportunities for private satisfaction. And once Mandeville was able to demonstrate that a good action (economically or socially considered) need not be the action of a good man, but the un-intended result of his 'private vice', he could then also make the telling point that what constituted happiness for any given individual was independent of officially sanctioned moral standards. Social action could strictly be conceived in terms of one's search for pleasure and the degrees to which individuals managed to satisfy their desires. And since these desires had self-regard as their foundation, which depended upon public esteem and approbation, Mandeville could explain why individuals so often spoke and acted in ways which appeared moral (since in so doing they would be publicly rewarded). Behaviour in public consisted of performances designed to win approval – performances whose success depended upon no genuine moral standard, but on how well social actors could satisfy their desires within established conventions of rewards and punishments.

Mandeville, then, conceived of the scene of moral activity as an arena which was not populated by undivided personalities who enquired into those choices which directly affected their own souls, and the good of their community. The actor anatomized in *The Fable* was, by contrast, an inter-subjectively defined, socially situated participant in a communal drama – a person driven by passions who of necessity competed with those around him in a public market for 'tokens and badges' of esteem. Desires alone formed the premises of practical reasoning, while the rewards of the social order to which persons belonged constituted inescapable features of their identities. Mandeville recognized that actions standardly understood as virtuous can, from this perspective, be redescribed as enacting a drama;

and that once so redescribed, these actions immediately lose their moral character, transformed as they are into features of merely prudential attempts to win the approval of the audiences to whom they are directed. By subsuming the moral codes governing behaviour under the heading of mere 'ceremonies', Mandeville succeeded in placing social practices in a theatrical context, within whose histrionic conventions the negotiations of public life necessarily took place.

The ancient figure of the *theatrum mundi*, the world seen as a stage, had been employed for centuries to expose the artificial boundaries placed upon acceptable public behaviour. Like the popular medieval imagery of 'The Wheel of Fortune' and 'The Ship of Fools', the theatrical metaphor was a rhetorical device employed to unmask worldly ambition and pretence. For Jacques in *As You Like It*, as for Don Quixote, the reminder that 'all the world's a stage' served the traditional function of recalling to individuals the fact that they are subject to the scrutiny of a higher power into whose care their souls were entrusted. Within the conceptual ambit of the theatre, individuals could be viewed as puppets in a drama of which they remained unaware, as unwitting actors who inhabited roles which had an illusory, because merely mundane, importance. For Shakespeare and Cervantes, as for Nicole and Bayle, who referred to the social world as 'a spectacle of marionettes', the metaphor of the world as a stage served as an instrument of social intelligibility in the restricted though important sense that it reasserted the central Christian doctrine of the spiritual role-nakedness of all people, regardless of the stations to which they may have been assigned by birth or fortune.

Mandeville's *Fable* helped to transform Enlightenment moral discourse by injecting a radical dimension into an already heightened appreciation of the theatricality of public life. The stage was seen during the eighteenth century as an ideal site for an actor's 'painting of the passions', as it was then called. Actors performed before audiences made familiar, not only by a raft of treatises which together formed the first systematic body of the theory and practice of acting in the West, but by popular journalism and plays themselves with the public expression of nature's rhetoric of emotional representations. Even before Garrick, the century's greatest actor, gave an account of these practices in *An Essay on Acting*, one of Joseph Addison's main purposes in *The Spectator* was to shape a modern public, seen as a 'fraternity of spectators' composed of his metropolitan audience; that is, 'every one that considers the World as a Theatre, and desires to form a right Judgement of those who are actors in it'. These 'impartial spectators', as Addison called them, would 'consider all the different pursuits and Employments of Men, and . . . will [be able to] find [that] half [of] the[ir] Actions tend to nothing else but Disguise and Imposture; and [realize that] all that is done which proceeds not from a Man's very self is the Action of a Player.' At mid-century, by which time the

London stage had become the most successful commercial entertainment in modern European history – with theatre audiences at a proportionately much higher level than at any time since – Henry Fielding had his narrator remark in *Tom Jones*,

> the comparison between the world and the stage has been carried so far and become so general that some words proper to the theatre and which were at first metaphorically applied to the world are now indiscriminately and literally spoken of both: thus stage and scene are by common use grown as familiar to us, when we speak of life in general, as when we confine ourselves to dramatic performances; and when we mention transactions behind the curtain, St. James's is more likely to occur to our own thoughts than Drury-Lane.

Like Addison, but now with Mandeville's arguments explictly in mind, Fielding, along with virtually every major Enlightenment thinker, had become deeply concerned that public theatricality had a hostile relation ship to intimacy, that individuals would became divided selves as the pressures of commercial society required them to adopt the strategic poses of actors. Boswell, for whom the theatre was the exemplary site for the display of emotional states, claimed that forms of public presentation had been refined into art by the cultivation of 'double feeling' by actors them-selves. When he attended a packed Drury Lane Theatre to see Garrick play Lear, followed by a popular comedy, Boswell testified to the fact that much of public behaviour had come to be understood as a discontinuous series of heightened moments of affective engagement, directed to others prepared by their own expectations and theatrical habits to respond in a similarly discontinuous fashion.

> I kept myself at a distance from all acquaintances, and got into a proper frame. Mr Garrick gave the most satisfaction. I was fully moved, and shed an abundance of tears. The farce was 'Polly Honeycomb', at which I laughed a good deal.

Just as the classical figure of the masked actor, the *hypocrates* who merely impersonates by playing a role, could never be relied upon to treat his fellows as brothers, so a genuine sense of moral duty could not be expected of individuals for whom being and appearing had become two different things, and whose public professions were always mediated by masks of propriety.

Envy and emulative propensities, it was commonly asserted, had become propulsive features of modern life, despite the prevailing moral ortho-doxy's disapproval of self-indulgence. The self-regard which characterized all people in nations shaped by commerce took the form of man as a consuming and, most especially, a displaying animal – a creature whose appetites are governed by the desire for esteem within an expanding arena of marketable goods. An ethos of public display fired an economy of conspicuous consumption, which in turn depended upon the promotion of unstable fashion and social fantasy, of which women – archetypically fickle, seductive and promiscuous – were prominent symbols. Individuals were required to adopt highly stylized public personae as they regularly confronted virtual strangers whose approval and esteem they sought. This was especially so in the widening urban spaces whose rituals became the subjects of popular art – the coffee house, club, square, and, as Voltaire pointedly remarked, the London Stock Exchange, where material interest alone formed a social bond, promoting civilized intercourse among un-related individuals with otherwise incommensurable beliefs. 'In populous cities,' Montesquieu wrote in *The Spirit of The Laws*, the eighteenth century's most influential political treatise, 'men are motivated by an ambition of distinguishing themselves by trifles . . . [;] strangers to one another, their vanity redoubles because there is greater hope of success. . . . The more people communicate with each other the more easily they change their manners, because each becomes to a greater degree a spectacle to the other.' Theatrical relations, Montesquieu understood, expressed the tacit picture of the world inhabited by individuals unavoidably situated in com-munities whose practices stood at some remove from their professed beliefs.

After the controversy about the nature of egoism begun by Mandeville's *Fable*, virtually all socially engaged critics and philosophers were obliged to confront the claim that reason's essential practical role is to answer those questions which the passions provide the only motives for asking. If reason's purpose is merely the instrumental one of prescribing efficient means for the achievement of the ends set by the passions, then any plausible account of morals would have to be undertaken within the context of a hierarchy of indelible desires. Within this conceptual space, all actions may coherently be considered in terms of the divided person-ality's need to establish an outward appearance for the approval of others, while attempting to satisfy its hidden impulses. When Hume asserted that 'reason is, and ought only to be the slave of the passions and can never pretend to any other office than to serve and obey them', he distilled this precept into a philosophical principle, and drew from it an account of the development of morals founded upon the intersubjective, theatrical relationships located at the heart of commercial sociability. 'In general,' Hume said, 'the minds of men are mirrors to one another',

> not only because they reflect each other's emotions, but also because those rays of passions, sentiments and opinions may often be rever-berated, and may decay away by insensible degrees. Thus the pleasure which a rich man receives from his possessions being thrown upon the beholder, causes a pleasure and esteem; which sentiments again, being perceived and sympathized with, encrease the pleasure of the

possessor; and being once more reflected, become a new foundation for pleasure and esteem in the beholder. . . . But the possessor has also a secondary satisfaction in riches arising from the love of esteem he . . . acquires by them. . . . The secondary satisfaction of vanity becomes one of the principal recommendations of riches, and is the chief reason we either desire them for ourselves or esteem . . . them in others.

Beginning from the spectator's point of view, Hume not only viewed the self as a kind of theatre, 'where several perceptions successively make their appearance, pass, repass, glide away, and mingle in an infinite variety of postures and situations'. The individual's limited sympathies for the welfare of others could, he argued, be fully accounted for in terms of a self-interested beholder's responses to the poses and demands of others. Similarly, for Adam Smith, social life of neccessity resembles a masquerade. The approbation and disapprobation of oneself which we call conscience is but a mirror of feeling, a social product which is an effect of each of us as a spectator judging others while finding others as spectators judging ourselves. Smith claimed that unlike the 'indulgent and partial spectator' of Mandevillian provenance who merely seeks applause, a self-disciplined 'impartial spectator' could somehow be governed, not by the need for praise, but by the desire for praiseworthiness itself. Yet most people, he recognized, are moved by the comprehensive ambition to earn the applause of spectators. We expose ourselves to 'the public admiration', either by playing roles or by competing for distinctions through the mediation of things – by the accumulation of wealth or goods which stand as proxies of honour and respect. Such admiration is bestowed only on the condition of visibility. All individuals require mirrors, 'to be observed, to be attended to, to be taken notice of with sympathy, complacency and approbation', for without society, one 'could no more think of his own character . . . than of the beauty or deformity of his own face', and the only mirror in which this person can view his character 'is placed in the countenance and behaviour of those he lives with'.

Smith, along with his Enlightenment contemporaries, not only accepted that the abiding problem posed by commercial sociability was to show how individuals could be thought of as moral if they were irreducibly prideful and vain, and that the dynamics of commerce depended upon the encouragement of these natural propensities. He also confronted the disturbing possibility that

society may subsist among different men, as among different merchants, from a sense of its utility, without any mutual love or affection; and though no man in it should owe any obligation, or be bound in gratitude to any other, it may still be upheld by a mercenary exchange of good offices, according to agreed valuation.

In other words, he confronted the possibility that in commercial society, where social standing and public identity so intensely depended upon the opinion of others, one's moral autonomy threatened always to be compromised. As shown most starkly in *Rameau's Nephew*, in which Diderot's eponymous amoral mime reduces a philosopher attempting to defend virtue to astonished silence, moral reasoning had few defences in a world where beliefs were decisively shaped by economic contingency.

Eighteenth-century thinkers were thus faced with the argument that character itself was in essence a social artefact, a construct existing in an intersubjective space of the demands of others, and within which a person's identity was of necessity devised. Once this problem was addressed in the dominant psychological idiom of the passions, individuals could immediately be understood as players pressured by circumstance and goaded by opportunity to perform in ways designed to elicit that public approbation demanded by their dominant desires. As Kant observed, 'the more civilised men become, the more they become actors. They want to put on a show and fabricate an illusion of their own persons.' As if to address Smith's worry about the connection between modern morals and mercenary exchange, Kant continued, 'all human virtue in circulation is small change. Only a child would take it for real gold. But it is better to have small change in circulation than no means of exchange at all.' Reference to naturalistic acting practices, first crafted in Britain (and then adopted on the Continent in works like Diderot's *Paradox of Acting*, Lessing's *Hamburg Dramaturgy* and Goethe's *Rules for Actors*), ideally suited the purposes of those determined to comprehend a new and culturally transformative society, in which personation was required for public identity. As Rousseau protested in his polemic against the theatre, his contemporaries sought 'to present virtue to us as a theatrical game,' for as modern persons were driven by the 'furor to distinguish themselves' in a market for marks of esteem, mere 'opinion' had become 'the queen of the world'.

Rousseau's anti-theatrical animus was an expression of two incompatible positions. In the first, derived from a long-standing opposition to the stage found in classical authors like Plato and Tacitus, republicans such as Machiavelli, and contemporary moralists both clerical and lay, Rousseau viewed the theatre as a symbol of debilitating luxury, of 'discontent with one's self . . . [and] the neglect of simple and natural tastes'. Theatres were institutions in which the simplicity of manners required of active citizens was threatened by a powerful encouragement of the commercial habits of dissimulation, display and anti-civic egoism. Rousseau was intimately aware of these temptations, and often despised himself when he succumbed to them. During Rousseau's visit to England in 1766, Garrick played two characters especially for Jean-Jacques at a packed Drury Lane Theatre. In response, Garrick's wife reported, Rousseau 'was so very anxious to display himself, and hung so forward over the box,' that she had to 'hold him by the skirt of his coat, that he might not fall over into the pit.' In the theatre, and through the dispersion of its habits, the modern self, so Rousseau thought, had become a heteronomous residue of its reflection in the mirror of strangers, themselves in constant need of public reminders of their own identities. In the Preface to his aptly titled play, *Narcissus*, Rousseau defended his own dramatic efforts by arguing that since the 'dangerous doctrines' of egoism spawned by writers like 'Mandeville had more than succeeded', the theatre should be employed, not for the now impossible resurrection of virtue among a population committed to commerce and bereft of non-dissimulating communication, but by legislators seeking to tame vice by manipulating the public opinion which imparted to deracinated metropolitans the sentiment of their own existence.

Rousseau's other mode of argument conceived of the theatre not so much as a vehicle for the promotion of self-regard as a set of devices for the diminution of individuality. From this perspective, he viewed the playhouse as an arena in which the feelings of individuals were manipulated and normalized, for in the theatre, 'we give our tears only to fictions, while our heart closes itself for fear of being touched at our expense'. In modern societies, relations between individuals replicated histrionic transactions in that social life had become at once alienated because theatrical, and immoral because inauthentic. When writing in this mode, Rousseau took leave of those assumptions about the relationship of the passions to both character and behaviour which standardly informed eighteenth-century reflection on morals and their relationship to theatricality. Instead, he searched for features of an individual's history, exemplified by his own, that could never fully be captured by typifying theatrical conventions, either on the stage or in the street. They were expressions of an inner life that, he claimed, resisted all attempts to encode it as a feature of social practices theatrically conceived, precisely because such a life was singular and self-defining. As he wrote in the first page of *The Confessions*, 'I know my own heart. . . . I am made unlike anyone I have ever met. I will even venture to say that I am like no one in the whole world. I may be no better, but at least I am different'.

This claim to certain knowledge of supposedly singular inner states which at once define and certify one's individuality not only departed from the dominant eighteenth-century conception of personality as theatrically plastic. It soon became a model of Romantic identities, and for the practices of representing the self which would characterize both autobiography and biography, narrative history and the modern novel. Rousseau succeeded in giving philosophical statement to an emergent language of feeling, notably expressed in his own *La Nouvelle Héloïse*, probably the best-selling novel of the eighteenth century. Through this language, the tears of his audience could now be deemed to issue from structures of feeling and judgement which themselves shaped one's passions into a unique conjunction: a solitary self seeking authentic expression in environments resistant to its impress, and within which persons are seen to struggle, not so much to win approval, as above all to realize themselves. So conceived, this individual establishes his authenticity and moral freedom by making contact with an inner voice rather than responding to the wills and expectations of others. Hegel, one the first philosophers to reflect upon this altered conception of personhood, grasped this point with some clarity when he metaphorically located it in the theatre. 'It is manifest,' he wrote, 'that behind the so-called curtain, which is supposed to conceal the inner world, there is nothing to be seen unless *we* go behind it ourselves, as much in order that we may see, as that there may be something behind there which can be seen'. Theatricality's primary zone of metaphorical applicability had shifted from the footlights to backstage, while Rousseau's extraordinarily self-dramatized life became one of the foundational fables of the modern self.

6

THE DEATH AND REBIRTH OF CHARACTER IN THE EIGHTEENTH CENTURY

Sylvana Tomaselli

The following reflections on the eighteenth-century conception of the self are grounded in the view that we are shaped by the spirit of the age in which we live. Whatever its status today, such a view was deemed neither embarrassingly trite, nor highly controversial in the eighteenth century. The reasons for this are complex and rather surprising not least because much was said and written by eighteenth-century men, as well as women, both about the precise nature of the period they inhabited and the true extent to which they could be said to be moulded by it. Pronouncements on what even the small coterie of intellectuals and literate men and women thought of the nature of the human personae are as hazardous to make for this as any other period. Indeed, they are arguably more so, since it is not difficult to find examples of nearly every logical position which can and had been taken on this subject in the history of Western thought. What can be said with some confidence, however, is that the self was not a happy topic in the eighteenth century: it was fraught with anxieties at the theoretical and existential levels. Whatever qualified optimism there might have been about any other consideration, there seemed nothing to be jubilant about in the modern individual.

I

For those whose perceived duty it was to reflect on such matters – say, David Hume, Adam Smith, Denis Diderot, Jean-Jacques Rousseau, Frederick II, Mary Wollstonecraft – and for those who could afford to join them in the endeavour, theirs was a distinctly new age, the age of large modern commercial societies. It was the age of luxury, consumption and the marketplace. Commerce seemed to link the various parts of the world in a way which promised to surpass the achievements of the greatest conquerors of history. It had become a matter of national importance. As Hume remarked, trade, which as a subject had been previously entirely neglected by political theorists, was now high on all European political agendas. Moreover, the small city-state typical of the ancient world had clearly ceased to be the prime political unit and with it went, or so it was argued, the practical relevance of the ideals of republicanism and civic virtue held up as a model to humanity most notably by the Renaissance humanists. The martial spirit seemed to be on the wane. Self-denial in the face of the requirements of the polis was no longer the prevailing ethos, or to put it in its positive version, the public realm no longer seemed to afford the means of the pursuit of human excellence. The ideal of the independent citizen having the leisure and means through the owner-ship of landed property to deliberate with his equals about the good of his community and to bear arms to defend it in the face of external threat continued to be admired by many, but it seemed to most to be a thing of the past.

To be alive in the new era was to be subject to the refinement, the polish, the sophistication of what was deemed to be the most advanced stage of civilization. It was also to live under the umbrella of what is now called consumerism. For those who did not have to struggle to sustain themselves – and even the poor were not left entirely unaffected – there were few areas in modern life which could not be contrasted to the feudal, or the ancient, past. From the abundance of commodities and the growing number of luxury items to the manners and sensibilities of people, everything bespoke of a change, the magnitude of which found no match in history, with the possible exception of the spread of Christianity in the Roman Empire or the barbarian invasions which contributed to the erosion of its dominion.

As a number of historians have argued, even the palates and the noses of eighteenth-century men and women were touched by this process. Increasingly, the preference was for simple elegance in all things, includ-ing meals and scents. Excess was perceived as the mark of a barbaric past, delicacy that of an elegant present. Feasts were giving way to dinner parties. Gorging oneself alone, or in company, was being displaced by the gentle art of conversing over the most exquisite dishes. The sumptuous displays of sixteenth- and seventeenth-century life at court do not readily come to mind when thinking of the eighteenth century. The latter period evokes instead the gatherings of literary and scientific societies and the distinguished guests which leading hosts and hostesses competed to attract to their respective salons.

This was so, not because courts and the kind of persona and consumption associated with them vanished in the eighteenth century, nor because the particular type of intimacy favoured in that period had been hitherto unknown. We have entered the terrain of representations and self-perceptions, and various though the images which the eighteenth century itself bequeathed to posterity most certainly are, they do include some which are undoubtedly striking and have come to epitomize the period: Frederick II dining in the company of Voltaire and other philosophes; Madame de Pompadour seated at a table on which the *Encyclopédie* is conspicuous; Denis Diderot outlining his vision of the future of the Russian empire to Catherine the Great; James Boswell's discussions with Dr Johnson; Adam Smith and the young Duke of Buccleugh on the Grand Tour of Europe; public lectures in London attended by a relatively wide variety of people eager to learn about the latest scientific discoveries, and so forth. The images are of learning, learned conversations, learned correspondences, reading, dissemination of knowledge, and, with it, of manners and civility.

These are not, to be sure, the only pictures which the idea of the eighteenth century evokes, but the political caricatures, the bawdy sketches and the lewd parts of many of the standard autobiographies and novels of the period are as it were in dialectical relation to the preceding images. This is not a comment about the relative importance or place of so-called low or popular culture in comparison with so-called high or elite culture, if only because one need just think about the pornographic writings of the Marquis de Sade to be reminded of the impossibility of wielding the dichotomy between high and low, rich and poor, with any degree of accuracy in what was a very complex cultural and social world. Debauchery was considered an issue by some social and political commentators, not others, just as it was a problem in the lives of some, and not others. In the latter case, some families resorted to means which the French Revolution was to eradicate, as when a *lettre de cachet* was used to imprison Sade, or they rallied round Madame d'Épinay to protect her from her husband, as her in-laws did when he gave her a sexually transmitted disease and stole her jewels, to use another example. At a theoretical level, sexual promiscuity and other excesses were frequently treated in age-old terms and with the contempt they had often, but to varying extent, met with for centuries. What was gaining vigour, however, was the view that in the long run, society, commercial, and hence civilized, society, would provide the conditions under which individuals prone to these excesses would cease to indulge themselves. The onus for self-control ceased to be seen to rest entirely with the individual: history, civilization, enlightenment were the forces which would take on the struggle which individuals, albeit with the aid of faith and religion, had had to engage in single-handed. Although by no means the only image the eighteenth century had of itself, the most distinctive self-perception was of a society embarking on a profound change in manners.

Women featured prominently in many of these self-portrayals of the age. They did so and were seen to do so as more than mere adornments to the new salon culture. They entertained, read, wrote, translated, conducted experiments, travelled, and reported on their travels. More than the accumulated sum of the achievements of individual women, the sex as a whole was thought to have instigated and kindled the civilizing process. Indeed, so much so that nineteenth-century historians, like Jules Michelet and critics like the Goncourt brothers were to refer to the century which had preceded them as *l'âge de la femme.*

To speak of the eighteenth century's perception of itself as a new age – and here it should be stressed that the century did not think of itself as the dawn of this historical stage, but perhaps more as its mid-morning or noon, since it seemed clear to most commentators that the process had begun at least several hundred years earlier – is not to say that it was universally welcomed. Far from it. The most acute observers of modernity in all of its varied manifestations were frequently its most virulent critics. Rousseau is the obvious example here. Many were simply ambivalent. Montesquieu or Adam Smith are but two, albeit far from uncontroversial, cases of those who thought that a truly enviable world was lost as one of very mixed blessings was emerging. Some of civilization's consequences met with less disapproval than others. Others worried nearly every observer. The hope that commerce would render nations interdependent and make for international peace was entertained by a good number of thinkers, including Immanuel Kant. The fear that the increasingly specialized and tedious labour demanded of those involved in the manufacturing of goods would atrophy their minds was widespread and led Adam Smith to stress the duty of governments to provide some form of redress, such as education and public entertainments.

For the sternest critics of the times, the modern commercial age did not even live up to any aspect of its self-description. It was nothing but its own antithesis. Thus it was regarded as an age marked by ever greater material inequality, moral and sexual depravity, and the shameless pursuit of the lowest forms of gratification. It was the triumph of the appetites over reason, of licentiousness over liberty, of earthliness over spirituality. Never had man been so alienated from his true self and destiny, from other men and indeed from nature. Never had he been so much under the dominion of woman. Never had either of the sexes been so taken in by the realm of shadows and appearances, including the greatest delusion of all, namely that theirs was a uniquely civilized age.

Incapable of being whole human beings, of exercising their bodies and minds completely, and of living in complete harmony with themselves and others due to the combined factors of the intensification of the division of labour and the system of luxury which resulted from it, men and women's highest ambition was to acquire and display. They lived outside themselves and existed only in the gaze of others. Greed and vanity ruled unchecked by any sense of shame or sinfulness. On the contrary, the most dazzling show met only with envy and admiration.

In this account, the heroic age had long receded from view. Gone were the Ulysses and Penelopes. Even the desire or possibility of seeking to emulate them had ceased to be. The stage of human action was reduced to a pitiful scale. With few exceptions, even the theatre or opera of the day did not seem able to rise beyond the confine of domesticity or the less edifying aspect of human personality. One need only contrast the story of Lucretia's suicide in the aftermath of her rape by Sextus, son of Tarquinius Superbus, to that of Mozart's *Così Fan Tutte* to grasp something of the eighteenth-century sense of the mediocrity of modernity. Both begin with men boasting of their wives' or betrotheds' faithfulness and steadfast love, but while Lucretia was raped as she clung to her virtue, the two women in *Così*, Fiordiligi and Dorabella, are lured and seduced by their fiancés masquerading as other men, and whereas Sextus' heinous deed was followed by a political insurrection, *Così* ends with a reconciliation (of sorts) of the fiancés. Neither the conduct of the men, nor that of the women, could be deemed edifying, let alone heroic. At most, we can be enjoined to be understanding and forgiving of human frailty (including Mozart's and his librettist, Lorenzo da Ponte for portraying us women in this manner).

This is not to say, however, that the Ancient Greeks and Romans entirely ceased to be inspiring in the eighteenth century. Johann Joachim Winckelmann, for one, urged his contemporaries to study and copy their art in his *Reflections on the Imitation of Greek Works in Painting and Sculpture*. But this was after all mostly confined to part of the aesthetic realm, and even then it was about mere imitation of past grandeur. On the ethical level, many of the great moralists of the period were privately drawn to Stoicism – for example, Adam Smith, Denis Diderot – but they tended to describe the moral feelings or sentiments of the age rather than prescribe high moral standards and self-discipline to it, with some exceptions, most notably that of Immanuel Kant. The prevalent mode was to provide psychological explanations for what socialized human beings were inclined to do rather than to urge them to acquire a given moral character and the dispositions which go with it. Jeremy Bentham, for instance, took human beings as they were, as creatures who seek pleasure and avoid pain, and codified the appropriate legal and political system for such beings. David Hume and Adam Smith both provided accounts of the manner in which men and women internalize rules of propriety and judge their own actions as others or as an ideal observer might do. There was very little prospect of transcending the moral expectations of the day, however unexalted these may have been. This was most definitely not the age of Nietzsche's *Übermensch*, except insofar as it was already the end of tragedy, as the philosopher was to explain it in the following century.

Not everyone saw the time in which they lived in this dismal way, of course. David Hume reacted strongly to those who eulogized the ancient past and argued that the ancients, for all their great dramatic and representational art and architecture, were little more than barbarians, whose cities were constantly at war with one another, dependent on a slave economy and the acquisition and maintenance of empires, and whose violence far from being only directed towards others was more often than not also directed towards their own kinsmen and women. Modernity offered the prospect of peace, both internationally through the dependency which commerce and industry forged between trading nations, and domestically through its victory over superstition and enthusiasm which were the cause of so many bloody civil wars of the past. Commerce civilized. The opulence it brought enabled the arts and sciences to flourish to an unprecedented extent and this affected not only a small elite of academicians, such as Charles-Nicolas Cochin (1715–1790) and his pupils, but all of a nation's people. Men and women throughout society benefited from living in modern commercial society; they were more prosperous, more secure, more enlightened than any of their forebears.

None of this meets what one might call the Nietzschean point. The attraction of Hume's view hangs not only on his demystification of the ancient world, but also on his belief that living one's life in accordance with standard notions of propriety is the best one can hope for for humanity. It falls short of any teleological outlook and was certainly offensive to Christian moralists, such as Mary Wollstonecraft who was not alone in engaging in what might appear now as a rearguard action against the forces of modernity.

II

To gain a clearer sense of the overall shape of the history of Enlightenment accounts of the nature of the self however, it is well to remember some of the ontological and epistemological developments of the period, as well as the phenomenal influence of John Locke's theory of personal identity since its first expression in *An Essay Concerning Human Understanding* (1690). With the establishment of empiricism as the predominant epistemological theory by the end of the seventeenth century and the view that knowledge consisted in the understanding of the laws of cause and effect governing any subject area, certain concepts crucial to the study of human nature and ethical theory came under increasing sceptical scrutiny. These included the idea of the soul, self, mental substance or substratum to which the faculties and other mental properties adhered, freedom of the will, and hence also the idea of individual agency. Not every philosopher tackled the topic from every facet, nor indeed was it the case that everyone engaged in eighteenth-century philosophical debates ceased to resort to the vocabulary previously used in discussions of the nature of the human mind and of personal identity. Yet there is little doubt that the terms employed to converse about both came under increasing scrutiny, and this not least because of Locke's *Essay*.

The difficulty of defining the self, of locating it, of speaking meaningfully about it and so forth, was not a problem of Locke's own making. The elusiveness of what is meant by the 'self' had led Pascal, for instance, to include in his *Pensées* (1670) that one never loves anyone for themselves, but only for some of their qualities. Locke, whose entry into the debate was not prompted by the subject of love, but rather the question of what made for the identity of a being with itself over time, argued that the identity of a man consisted in the participation in the same biological life; in other words, the continued identity of the body, despite the many changes it underwent, made for the identity of the man. The identity of a self or person (the terms were used interchangeably by him), on the other hand, required consciousness. Concern for happiness was the concomitant of consciousness and therefore that concern was evidence of personal identity in the present and future. Memory and the appropriation of past actions remembered provided the link with the past.

Unassuming as this account might seem, it both generated huge debates, especially in theological circles, and was appropriated by almost all of the eighteenth-century thinkers of note from Dr Johnson to Condillac. The *Encyclopédie*'s entry on the subject effectively reproduced Locke's Chapter XXVII on it. The popularity of the Lockean definition did not make the problem of the nature of personal identity wither away however. In France, where a number of prominent thinkers espoused, or toyed with, materialism – the view that man is made of one substance only, namely matter – and determinism, this was partly due to the fact that the Achilles' heel of materialism was that it could not begin to produce an intuitively appealing account of selfhood. As Diderot explained in the *Rêve D'Alembert* (written in 1769; first published in 1830),

> [O]bviously, the fact of the matter is clear, but the reason for the fact isn't in any way, especially for those who hold the hypothesis that there is only one substance and who explain the formation of man or of animals in general by successive opposition of several sensitive molecules.

Nor was this true only within continental philosophical circles. As Hume noted in *A Treatise of Human Nature* (1739/1740) it had become a major question even in England, where the materialist controversy was of lesser interest.

III

The problem of personal identity was not, however, a topic confined to abstruse philosophical disquisitions. Biographical writings of the period are replete with sometimes bemused, sometimes anxious, reflections on the vicissitudes of the self. Rousseau's self-portrait in *Le Persiffleur* (first published in 1781) develops that very theme. *Rien n'est si dissemblable à moi que moi-même* ('Nothing is so unlike myself as myself'), he wrote, adding that a Proteus, a chameleon, a woman, were less changeable beings than he. At best, he thought that after much self-examination he could detect some recurrences, including a weekly alteration between a wisely mad self and madly wise one.

Similar reflections bringing together the Lockean theory of personal identity with its emphasis on memory and the kind of existential self-realization that Rousseau experienced can be found in different literary genres. 'In one and the same man', Diderot wrote in *De la poésie dramatique* (1758),

> everything is in a perpetual vicissitude, whether one considers him as a material or a moral being; pain follows pleasure, pleasure, pain; health, illness, illness, health. It is only through memory that we are the same individual to others and to ourselves. . . . You and I are two distinct beings and I myself am never in one moment what I was in another.

Hume, whose intellectual pursuits in relation to the *Treatise* caused several years of serious psychological disorder, had been more cautious; he had stressed that memory did not 'so much *produce* as *discover* personal identity, by showing us the relation of cause and effect among our different perceptions'.

Such an outlook on the nature of the self, the human mind and character had a number of implications. A significant literary one had been spelled out at the turn of the century in a preface to the 1725 Jean Hofhout Rotterdam edition of François Fénelon de Lamothe Salignac's widely read and translated *Télémaque* (1699). It explains that the unity of an epic is provided by the unity of the action, not that of the hero. Such a unity could not be provided by a true depiction of a self, it continues, because human beings do not admit of such a unity. Their aims constantly change, their passions conflict with one another. The verisimilitude of such a portrayal would entail the rendering of something akin to psychological chaos. For this reason an epic was not in praise of a hero held as a model, but focused rather on an illustrious deed presented as an object of emulation.

In ethics, the focus shifted likewise from the moral agent as a whole to principally action-centred theories. Utilitarianism is the best example of such a theory as it was developed in the eighteenth century and systematized by Bentham. Moral judgements, he argued, should have actions and their consequences as their objects and not character traits, motives or lives taken in their entirety. For whereas the former were tangible and uncontroversial facts which could be readily studied, discussed and evaluated, the latter were subjective, elusive and offered no solid ground for clear-cut moral decisions, let alone just sentencing in the court-rooms, Bentham's primary concern.

Such approaches to moral judgement were very far removed from the Aristotelian ethics which claimed that the best vantage point from which to decide whether a given man was a good man was after his death; for only then could his life be assessed as a whole and gazed upon much as is a work of art fulfilling an intention and potential. Nor could it have been much further from a Christian conception of the good life as one seeking to imitate that of Christ and the saints and martyrs. The idea that the will is free, the belief in the existence of individual human souls and in the transparency, if only to the divine eye, of the intentions behind every action, are necessary to the latter. The notion that there is such a thing as human excellence and that it is the purpose of man to achieve it, even if only a small elite has either the means or the ability to do so, underpins the former. All these were far from being ideas that the Enlightenment took for granted, however much eighteenth-century society continued to be a believing society and one in which classicism predominated in architectural and all other aesthetic representations, in the syllabuses of school and privately educated children. The ancients were read, studied and imitated in art, while political theorists were for the most part agreed that the small, ancient republic animated by the spirit of civic virtue and liberty which required the active participation of citizens in the ruling of the polity was unrealizable in the modern world. The latter being composed of large countries which could at best only be governed through systems of representations; such countries were in turn peopled with individuals who conceived of happiness as the pursuit of private interest, not the public good, however much they unintentionally secured the latter by devoting themselves to the former.

IV

The French Revolution, with its language of citizenship, its attempt to instigate a civic religion, its cult of the Roman republic, its exhortation to self-sacrifice for the new regime and its glorified gore, was a demonstration of the powerfulness of the images and rhetoric of the ancient world. It also attested to the disjunction between the vision that its leaders sought to evoke and political and social reality. Even the most skilful manipulation of republican ideology could not mask for long the true nature of the financial, military and administrative predicament of France to its people. But this is not to deny or even belittle the fact that as the century ended, however, there were various reassertions of the very languages and concepts whose demise or precariousness the preceding sections of this chapter have sought to outline.

It would be tempting, but wholly misguided, to think of these as a reaction or a series of reactions to the Enlightenment. Among the reasons for not doing so is the fact that like most sophisticated movements of ideas, the Enlightenment consisted of many voices, sometimes used by one and the same person. Thus a figure such as Diderot spoke with seemingly unbounded confidence in the Enlightenment project when writing for the *Encyclopédie* (1751–1772), total despondency when composing *Le Neveu de Rameau* (or some of the other works he kept unpublished in his lifetime), but also nostalgia about the ancient moral outlook and real identification with ancient figures, notably Seneca, in *Essai sur Sénèque* (1779), enlarged as *Essai sur les règnes de Claude et de Néron* (1782). The Enlightenment consisted in the tension between these different strands.

As the eighteenth century was for many of its most astute commentators the age of women, it would seem fitting to leave the last words to Mary Wollstonecraft. What makes Wollstonecraft particularly interesting in relation to the subject of the modern self is that she matched her real understanding of its nature with a passionate loathing of it, at least in her *Vindication of the Rights of Men* (1790) and *Vindication of the Rights of Woman* (1792); for true to the spirit of her times, she continued debating within herself as well as with others many of her seemingly most fundamental beliefs.

To the degree that she saw her age as that of women, she both hated the age and the women whose age it could be said to be. Wollstonecraft objected to commercial society because she, like Rousseau and others, did not think it lived up to its purported claims of offering, despite growing inequality between ranks, a better standard of living to even the poorest labourers. Had that been otherwise she would have condemned it none the less, for what she abhorred above all else was the kind of individual, male or female, it generated. Vanity seemed the preponderant quality of the day. All lived to appear and everything was sacrificed to appearances. Women, bred to please and flirt, were condemned to remain nothing other than beautiful playthings, and embraced their fate with unstoppable zeal. After a few years devoted to the cult of the latest fashion and exhibiting themselves in the world, they married. They were then expected to be faithful wives and dutiful mothers. Modern society was thus founded on a farcical anticipation of a domestic bliss which it otherwise strove to undermine from every angle.

Wollstonecraft painstakingly demonstrated the absurdity of this situation and the web of contradictions within which women were caught. She argued that duties could not be exacted from those deprived of rights. Foremost among these was the right, which she conceived of as a duty, namely the duty to develop God's gift to mankind, reason. This required not only provisions for the education of women. Even full civil and political rights would not suffice to enable them to live a Christian life and to seek to become fully-fledged citizens, sacrificing themselves for the greater good of their community and humanity as a whole by dedicating themselves to their family, and creating new generations of true citizens. For women to acquire such notions of what the good life truly consisted in, men had to change. Both the sexes, in fact, had to undergo a moral revolution. Modern commercial society effected a revolution in manners, but that, Wollstonecraft insisted (especially to her main interlocutor, Edmund Burke, against whom she had been prompted to write her *Vindication of the Rights of Men*) was the antithesis of moral progress. True civilization ought to deliver a social stage in which men and women could fulfil themselves as rational, God-fearing and duty-bound creatures. Her age provided only the conditions for the worship of the self in the hall of mirrors which existed not only in Versailles, but throughout society as every pair of eyes sought in others a pleasing image of themselves, as a being whose appearance was deemed enviable and embodied the *dernier cri*. Society, in her view, should not be allowed to drift further along those lines and she entertained a glimmer of hope that the momentous changes in France could be directed by the revolutionary leaders to truly emancipate mankind from the tyranny of appearance.

Added and related to her concern about the moral and spiritual destiny of the species were what might be called aesthetic considerations. For like many leading commentators of the period, Wollstonecraft feared the spread of uniformity and with it, mediocrity. The proliferation of consumable goods did not lead to diversity of taste and desire. Instead, everyone slavishly aspired to mimic their social 'betters'. Even the difference provided by class was under threat as the middle ranks increasingly had the resources to ape the aristocracy. Human excellence, heroism, grandness of spirit and passions were no longer idealized. Like Burke, Wollstonecraft thought a levelling was talking place without any increase in equality; unlike him, however, she did not think it was caused by social and political revolution, but instead pointed to the cult of the golden calf.

Ironically, it was in the course of trying to locate a missing cargo of bullion that Wollstonecraft came to understand herself and probe the strength of her own character. In a three-and-a-half-month journey, from the end of June to the beginning of October 1795, she travelled through Scandinavia – an unusual destination at the time and made all the more difficult for taking place when all of Europe was warring with France. Added to this, Wollstonecraft travelled with her infant daughter, Fanny, and a young French maid in an attempt, as Per Nyström revealed two decades ago, to find a stolen ship whose contents, silver and Bourbon plate, belonged to the American Gilbert Imlay, Fanny's father. His unfaithfulness had led her to one attempted suicide; another was to follow her return home. Imlay had been traficking through the naval blockade imposed against France and, in seeking to find the whereabouts of the ship which its Norwegian captain had secured for himself, Wollstonecraft was guilty by association of acting against the reason of state insterest of her country. In a series of letters to Imlay, published as *A Short Residence in*

Sweden, Norway and Denmark (1796), Wollstonecraft gives not only a very interesting account of her journey, with striking descriptions of the land-scape and towns, as well as detailed portrayal of the peoples and their habits, but consciously reveals herself in the act of violating every principle she held up to her readers of her *Vindications*. With a degree of honesty and self-irony which Rousseau could never achieve, she allows herself to be seen as she had become. The critic of women who were governed by anything but their reason was herself presently being led by her hopeless passion for a wholly unworthy man. She, who had condemned women for their coquetry, was now unashamedly embarked on a last attempt to seduce a man through her prose. She, who had deplored the end of true heroism and patriotism, was involved in a mysterious trip which violated a blockade imposed by her country on its enemy. Most perturbing perhaps, the author of the *Vindication of the Rights of Woman* was now disclosing for the world to read that:

> You know that as a female I am particularly attached to her [Fanny] – I feel more than a mother's fondness and anxiety, when I reflect on the dependent and oppressed state of her sex. *I dread lest she should be forced to sacrifice her heart to her principles, or principles to her heart.* With trembling hand I shall cultivate sensibility, and cherish delicacy of sentiment, lest, whilst I lend fresh blushes to the rose, I sharpen the thorns that will wound the breast I would fain guard – I dread to unfold her mind, lest it should render her unfit for the world she is to inhabit – Hapless woman! what a fate is thine!
>
> (my emphasis, p. 97)

As Wollstonecraft herself sacrificed her principles to her heart and did not know whether to raise Fanny to be a rational or a passionate being, she might have found some consolation in knowing that on the bicentenary of the publication of *A Short Residence in Sweden* her words were as moving as she meant them to be for Imlay and, paradoxically, revealed her to embody more of the heroic qualities she admired in the Ancients than she thought could be acquired in the commerical world of appearances she so deprecated. That she displayed them best in the pursuit of silver and plate for a man who had betrayed her and would do so again rather than in the service of her community or a noble ideal is perhaps not what in itself makes of her story a modern drama. What certainly gives it a tragic quality is her own recognition of her violation, not of taboos or social conventions (that she did – children out of wedlock, attempted suicides, passing for married and so forth – and these and the openness with which William Godwin, her husband from 1797, wrote about them in *Memoirs of the Author of The Rights of Woman* cost her great notoriety well into the twentieth century), but of principles which she had elaborated for herself and other women. What gives her life a modern quality is the almost triumphant exposure she and Godwin gave to what her earlier self would have thought a shameful failure or, to put it differently, it is the endeavour to render moral failure into art by public avowal that makes the later Wollstonecraft a tragic modern heroine.

7

'ANOTHER SELF IN THE CASE'

Gender, marriage and the individual in Augustan literature

Carolyn D. Williams

The seventeenth and eighteenth centuries witnessed a great deal of speculation about the nature of personality. Traditional Christian notions of the soul as an eternal, immaterial spiritual substance were under attack. As the Enlightenment proceeded, the uniqueness and complexity of individual character came under unprecedented scrutiny, and the rights and values of the individual were accorded a new importance. The change is so pronounced that some historians believe this was the age in which 'affective individualism' came to birth, a process which eventually culminated in the 'liberal humanism' which characterizes Western society at the present day. This view has not carried universal conviction: some observers believe that the effects attributed to the Enlightenment really came much later, and that much enlightened thought was deeply conservative; others extend their critique to post-industrial Western society, arguing that 'liberal humanism' and its attendant doctrines are an attempt to create an acceptable face for capitalist oppression. Perhaps the Enlightenment was more a matter of changing rhetoric than of improved conditions for oppressed individuals; nevertheless, the rhetoric is there, and it repays examination.

This chapter will briefly summarize some influential theories about the nature of the self, then offer a detailed examination of one literary response, with particular attention to its implications for questions of gender and marriage. This will be followed by further explorations of these ideas in a wide range of writings, concluding with a study of their treatment in the period's most characteristic literary development: the novel.

THIS PERSONALITY

René Descartes (1569–1650) provoked much controversy with his claim that he had found the seat of the soul – a location which hitherto had been sought chiefly by Plato, Lucretius and other heathen philosophers. In *Passiones Animae* ('The Passions of the Soul') (1649) he described 'a little gland in the brain where the soul exercises its functions more particularly than in the other parts of the body' (Part I, Section 31), presumably the pineal gland. A soul whose activities could be located so precisely was too material for many Christian readers. More still were outraged by the overtly materialistic doctrines of Thomas Hobbes (1588–1674), who believed that 'immaterial substance' was a contradiction in terms, and argued his case industriously in *Leviathan* (1651), Part I, Chapters 5 and 12, Part II, Chapter 29 and Part IV, Chapter 45. His doctrines were later adopted by Anthony Collins (1676–1729). If their view was correct, then the soul must, to a certain extent, be material: an alarming prospect in an age when it was commonly believed that everything material was subject to dissolution, and consequently mortal. Equally contentious was the theory offered by John Locke (1632–1704) in the second edition of his *Essay Concerning Human Understanding* (1694). In Book II, Chapter 27, 'Of Identity and Diversity', he declares that '*self* is not determined by Identity or Diversity of Substance, which it cannot be sure of, but only by identity of consciousness'. By equating the soul with such an evanescent entity as consciousness, Locke seemed on the verge of annihilating it completely. Never had such awesome responsibility been imposed on individual experience:

> *Person*, as I take it, is the name for this *self*. Where-ever a Man finds, what he calls *himself*, there I think another may say is the same *Person*. It is a Forensic Term appropriating Actions and their Merit; and so belongs only to intelligent Agents capable of a Law, and Happiness and Misery. This personality extends it *self* beyond present Existence to what is past, only by consciousness.

To make this revolutionary assertion, Locke pushed his language beyond its existing limits. According to the *Oxford English Dictionary*, he was the first person to use 'consciousness' in the sense of 'totality of the impressions, thoughts, and feelings, which make up a person's conscious being'. In the late twentieth century, it can be difficult to understand why Locke's theory caused so much consternation. As Christopher Fox observes in *Locke and the Scriblerians* (1988), 'That "personality is not a permanent, but a transient thing" and that it has a great deal to do with "consciousness" does not seem strange at all to us, the heirs of Proust and Woolf.' But our inheritance was not entered upon without difficulty: 'What initially strikes a modern reader of his earliest critics . . . is their honest sense of befuddlement over what Locke is saying about the self.'

A NATURAL, AS WELL AS LEGAL ABSURDITY

Some of the most amusing and creative reactions to Descartes, Locke and the materialists appear in *The Memoirs of Martinus Scriblerus* (1741), a satire on false taste in learning. It began as a joint composition by the Scriblerus Club, which met in 1714 and 1726. The bulk of the material was probably provided by the learned physician John Arbuthnot (1667–1735), with additional contributions by Jonathan Swift (1667–1745), John Gay (1685–1732), Thomas Parnell (1679–1718) and Robert Harley, first Earl of Oxford (1661–1724). Alexander Pope (1688–1744) took the editorial role, giving the work its final shape.

The Memoirs is a fictitious narrative, purporting to be the biography of Martin Scriblerus, who devotes his life to the pursuit of knowledge. Chapter 12 describes his 'Enquiry after the *Seat* of the *Soul*'. Combining Descartes' theory with the materialism of Hobbes and Collins,

> At length he grew fond of the *Glandula Pinealis*, dissecting many Subjects to find out the different Figure of this Gland, from whence he might discover the cause of the different Tempers in mankind. He suppos'd that in factious and restless-spirited people he should find it sharp and pointed, allowing no room for the Soul to repose herself; that in quiet Tempers it was flat, smooth, and soft, affording to the Soul as it were an easy cushion. He was confirm'd in this by observing, that Calves and Philosophers, Tygers and Statesmen, Foxes and Sharpers, Peacocks and Fops, Cock-Sparrows and Coquets, Monkeys and Players, Courtiers and Spaniels, Moles and Misers, exactly resemble one another in the conformation of the *Pineal Gland*.

Martin receives a letter on this subject from 'The Society of Free-Thinkers' – a sinister development, since the Scriblerians shared a common tendency to equate free-thinking with atheism. The free-thinkers dismiss the soul as a 'Theological Nonentity' and offer Martin 'an easy *mechanical Explication* of *Perception* or *Thinking*'. They defend their views against advocates of Locke's identification of selfhood with consciousness:

> They make a great noise about this Individuality: how a man is conscious to himself that he is the same Individual he was twenty years ago; notwithstanding the flux state of the Particles of matter that compose his body. We think this is capable of a very plain answer, and may easily be illustrated by a familiar example.
>
> Sir John Cutler had a pair of black worsted stockings, which his maid darn'd so often with silk, that they became at last a pair of silk stockings. Now supposing those stockings of Sir John's endued with some degree of Consciousness at every particular darning, they would have been sensible, that they were the same individual pair of

stockings both before and after the darning; and this sensation would have continued in them through all the succession of darnings; and yet after the last of all, there was not perhaps one thread left of the first pair of stockings, but they were grown to be silk stockings, as was said before.

The above defence shows the Scriblerians solving a ticklish problem: wishing to attack atheistic materialism without making concessions to Locke, they make the free-thinkers offer an objection which leaves Locke's argument intact, yet, for that very reason, makes it look silly. The gradual transformation of the stockings is merely an additional example of that 'Diversity of Substance' which Locke has declared irrelevant to the continuity of consciousness. Yet the common-sense reaction to a theory which equates wool with silk is a conviction that something must be wrong. The Scriblerians tacitly reject both Locke and the free-thinkers, encouraging the readers to adopt the view that the soul is 'a spiritual substance', existing eternally, equally independent of body and consciousness.

These debates become questions of practical urgency in Chapter 14, when Martin falls in love with a girl he sees in a freak show. His beloved is Lindamira, one of 'the two Bohemian Sisters, whose common parts of Generation, had so closely allied them, that Nature seem'd to have conspir'd with Fortune that their lives should run in an eternal Parallel'. Lindamira falls in love with Martin. So does her inseparable twin Indamora, who at first suffers torments of jealousy, but finally decides to 'advance her Sister's Amour, and in that her own', moved by the reflection that

> The pangs that others feel in Absence, from the thought of those Joys that bless their Rivals, can never sting thy bosom; nor can they mortify thee by making thee a Witness, without giving thee at the same time a share, of their Endearments.

Martin elopes with Lindamira, but his marriage is instantly followed by further complications, as Mr Randal, owner of the freak show, 'seiz'd on the Bohemian Ladies by a *Warrant*, and not content with having recover'd the Possession of them, resolved to open all the Sluices of the *Law* upon Martin'. He accuses Martin of rape, adultery, bigamy and incest, and alienates Indamora's affection from him, causing her to marry the black prince, Ebn-Hai-Paw-Waw, 'while her Sister was *asleep*'.

Martin commences a suit in the spiritual court against his brother-in-law, insisting that 'Lindamira and Indamora *together* made up but *one* lawful wife'. His lawyer, Dr Penny-feather, offers three arguments: first, Lindamira and Indamora (whom he refers to, at this juncture, as 'Lindamira-Indamora') are only one person, because the 'organ of Generation is the Seat of the Soul'; second, even if they are two individuals, they form only one wife, 'For, from whence can the *Unity* of any thing be denominated, but from that which *constitutes* the *Essence* or principal *Use* of it?'; finally,

100

by marrying Lindamira, Martin has 'acquir'd a property' in her, not to mention '*all other Matter inseparably annex'd unto her*', so Indamora's husband has no right to detain her.

Penny-feather's pleadings are not dignified with a logical reply. The defendant's lawyer, Dr Leatherhead, begins with emotional rhetoric, protesting that it is 'impudence to degrade this Queen, the Rational Soul, to the very lowest and vilest Apartment, or rather Sink of her whole Palace' – an outburst calculated to carry no weight with educated eighteenth-century readers, who believed metaphor was an unfit vehicle for ratiocination. Leatherhead then claims it is possible for human personality to exist independently of reproductive organs, because Adam and Eve developed them only after the Fall – an argument designed as a farrago of inaccuracy, nonsense and heretical mysticism. The case is presented as a matter of fools on both sides. The only rational solution is reached when 'the Lords, with great Wisdom, dissolv'd both Marriages, as proceeding upon a natural, as well as legal Absurdity.'

There is, however, much to be learned from closer inspection of Penny-feather's plea, especially where contemporary attitudes to gender are concerned. Feminist reading highlights the gendered asymmetry in Penny-feather's references to sexuality. He draws an exalted picture of reproduction, depicting it as a spiritual, even holy, process, and considers it as a male activity. For the doctrine that the soul is produced *ex traduce*, which he asserts, always attributes soul-making power to the father:

> It is to the Organs of Generation that we owe Man himself; there the Soul is employed in works suitable to the Dignity of her Nature, and (as we may say) sits brooding over ages yet unborn.
>
> We need not tell your Honour, that it has been the opinion of many most learned Divines and Philosophers, that the Soul, as well as Body, is produced *ex traduce*. . . . For since the whole man, both Soul and body, is *here* form'd, and since nothing can operate but where it *is*, it follows, that the soul must reside in that individual place, where she exerts her generative and plastic Powers.

The Scriblerians probably employed gendered language here in a spirit of mockery. Nevertheless, there was much eighteenth-century support for the idea that fathers provided their children with their personalities, if not their entire physical conformation; in 1776 James Boswell (1740–1795) was still trying to persuade his father to disinherit all his female relatives, on the grounds that 'our species is transmitted through males only, the females being all along no more than a *nidus*, or nurse, as Mother Earth is to plants of every sort'.

However insignificant the part women play in reproduction, they take the lead in lust. They are cited as the illustration for Penny-feather's next argument:

This our Doctrine is confirm'd by all those Experiments, which conspire to prove the absolute Dominion which that part hath over the whole body. We see how many Women, who are deaf to the persuasions of the Eloquent, the insinuations of the Crafty, and the threats of the Imperious, are easily governed by some poor Loggerhead, unfurnish'd with the least art, but that of making immediate application to this *Seat of the Soul.*

Again, there may be an element of deliberate distortion. In 'Sober Advice from Horace, to the Young Gentlemen about Town' (1734), Pope described the penis as 'that honest Part that rules us all' (l. 87). Nevertheless, there was still a prevalent belief, based on centuries of tradition, that women were the more lustful sex. It was beginning to lose its hold in the middle of the eighteenth century – a trend which probably had some connection with the increasing influence of women as consumers, and producers, of literature.

A feminist reading would also stress Penny-feather's assaults on the psychic integrity of Lindamira and Indamora. He attempts to merge Lindamira's personality with Indamora's, he reduces a wife's identity to her sexual availability to her husband, and he argues that a married woman not only loses all rights to property of her own, but becomes her husband's possession. These are chillingly slight exaggerations of the early modern female predicament in general. The conflict of interests between Lindamira and Indamora, which proves that they are separate personalities, is dismissed in a masculist gibe at female inconsistency:

if a multiplicity of Wills implied multiplicity of Persons, there are few Husbands but what are guilty of *Polygamy*, there being in the same Woman great and notorious diversity of Wills: A Point which we shall not need to insist upon before any married person.

Pope himself, in his 'Epistle to a Lady' (1735), makes a similar assertion that female identity is a very scarce commodity:

> Nothing so true as what you once let fall,
> 'Most Women have no Character at all'.
> Matter too soft a lasting mark to bear,
> And best distinguish'd by black, brown, or fair.
> . . .
> Chuse a firm cloud, before it fall, and in it
> Catch, ere she change, the Cynthia of this minute.
> Rufa, whose eye quick-glancing o'er the Park,
> Attracts each light gay meteor of a Spark,
> Agrees as ill with Rufa studying Locke,
> As Sappho's diamonds with her greasy smock.
> (ll. 1–4, 19–24)

Pope's allusion to Locke seems to be a deliberate recollection of his theory that identity inheres in consciousness, and an implied acknowledgement that, where women are concerned, this may well be true – a concession which reflects little credit on either Locke or women.

Marriage raised further problems for eighteenth-century women who wished to be recognized as possessors of separate, stable, autonomous identities. Today, feminists often complain about language that fragments women, or reduces them to objects, but seldom with as much justification as they would find in Penny-feather's grossly materialistic statement of Martin's case:

> if a knife or hatchet have but one blade, though two handles, it will properly be denominated but one knife, or one hatchet; inasmuch as it hath but one of that which constitutes the Essence or principal Use of a knife or hatchet. So if there were not only one, but twenty *Supposita Rationalia* with one common Organ of Generation, that one system would make but one Wife. Upon the whole, let not a few Heads, Legs, or Arms extraordinary, biass your Honour's Judgment, and deprive the Plaintiff of his legal Property.

What Penny-feather proposes is nothing less than the rape of Indamora. Furthermore, by his reckoning, if Martin were to rape eighteen other women in the process, he would still only be exercising his legal rights over his 'Property', Lindamira.

Again, it must be remembered that Penny-feather is not intended to be taken seriously. Although Pope might not have a high opinion of women in general, he was well aware of the inhumanity which could arise from a woman's loss of self-determination in marriage. He tells his friend, Martha Blount, that she is lucky because lack of money has protected her from the rigours of the marriage market. Her guardian god 'gave you beauty, but deny'd the Pelf/Which buys your sex a Tyrant o'er itself' ('Epistle to a Lady', ll. 287–88) . A year before the publication of the *Memoirs*, Henry Fielding (1707–1754) launched a more direct attack on the injustice of English marriage law in *The Champion*, No. 106, for Thursday, 17 July 1740:

> As to their Women COVERED, the Law seems to consider them as Women buried: Indeed they have no Reason to rejoice in its Lenity; for, besides stripping them of their Entity, it likewise puts it in the Power of their Husbands to strip them of all they have.

Despite these expressions of sympathy, however, nothing was done to increase wives' control over their property, or their bodies. In *Masquerade and Gender* (1993), Catherine Craft-Fairchild argues that 'Cultural constraints make it impossible for a woman to achieve a full "identity"; whatever identity she can negotiate is always in a complex and complicitous relationship to the identity (identities) her society constructs for her.' The plight of Mrs Lindamira and/or Indamora Scriblerus-Ebn-Hai-Paw-Waw illustrates this point all too well.

LOST IN WOMAN

It was not only women whose 'Entity' might be threatened by marriage. A more broadly gender-based reading of the *Memoirs* reveals an underlying concern with the ways in which the nature and employment of the reproductive organs can define, change and even obliterate the identity of all human beings. In his citation of classical and biblical precedents, Penny-feather comes close to saying that the penis is the man:

> Let us search Profane History, and we shall find Geryon with three heads, and Briareus with an hundred hands. Let us search Sacred History, and we meet with one of the sons of the Giants with six Fingers to each Hand, and six Toes to each Foot: yet none ever accounted Geryon or Briareus more than one Person: and give us leave to say, the wife of the said Geryon would have had a good Action against any women who should have espous'd themselves to the two other heads of that Monarch. The Reason is plain; because each of these having but one simple [sic] αἰσοιον, or one Member of Generation, could be look'd upon as but one single person.

The following paragraph suggests that personal identity must be very insecure, if it is lodged in an organ whose chief function is to make intimate contact with another body:

> In conformity to this, when we behold this one member, we distinguish the Sex, and pronounce it a *Man*, or a *Woman*; or, as the Latins express it, *unus Vir, una Mulier; un Homme, une Femme; One Man, One Woman*. For the same Reason Man and Wife are said to be one Flesh, because united in that part which constitutes the Sameness and Individuality of each sex.

Penny-feather's doctrines are obviously designed to be ridiculous, but they contain some grains of what would have passed for truth in the eighteenth century, and perhaps even today. They raise questions about marriage and identity, especially male identity, that can best be answered by exploring other contexts.

The idea of marriage as the coalescence of man and woman, in which they became 'one flesh', became increasingly alarming in the eighteenth century. One sign of this development is the growing unpopularity of the metaphorical hermaphrodite, a double-sexed being which had often been used in Renaissance art and literature as the symbol of a happy marriage. A mounting uneasiness is apparent as early as 1647, with the publication of a wittily paradoxical poem by John Cleveland (1613–1658), 'Upon an

Hermaphrodite'. Beginning 'Sir, or Madame' (l. 1), it states that 'man and wife make up one right / Canonicall Hermophrodite' (ll. 17–18). This poem was familiar to many eighteenth-century readers, but they regarded the prospect with little enthusiasm.

From classical times, there has always been a strong element of ambiguity in the use of the hermaphrodite as a symbol of sexual union. First, there was the benign version attributed to the comic dramatist Aristophanes by Plato (*c.* 428–*c.* 348 BC) in the *Symposium*: human beings were originally created as self-sufficient entities, with four arms, four legs and other organs accordingly; split apart by the gods for presumptuous arrogance, they seek sexual union as a means of reuniting themselves with their missing halves. In Plato's text, some of Aristophanes' primal humans were composed of two male halves, some of two female halves, and some of a male and female half, but most commentators ignore the male homosexual and lesbian options, concentrating on the myth's implications for heterosexuality. Viewed in this light, every marriage is a fulfilment of potential, a replacement of missing parts in which man and woman become whole. Christians sometimes depict the marriage of Adam and Eve as the true precedent for this type of union: after all, Eve was made from Adam's rib. One example appears in *The Divine Weeks* by Guillame de Saluste, Sieur du Bartas (1544–1590), as translated by Josuah [sic] Sylvester (*c.* 1562–1618) in 1605:

> No sooner Adams ravisht eyes did glaunce
> On the rare beauties of his new-come Halfe,
> But in his heart began to leape and laugh,
> Kissing her kindly, calling her his Life,
> His Love, his Stay, his Rest, his Weale, his Wife,
> His other-Selfe, his Helpe (him to refresh)
> Bone of his Bone, Flesh of his very Flesh.
>   Source of all joyes! sweet *Hee* – *Shee* – Coupled – One
> Thy sacred Birth I never think upon,
> But (ravisht) I admire how God did then
> Make Two of One, and One of Two againe.
>   ('The Sixth Day of the First Weeke', ll. 1044–54)

A less appealing hermaphrodite myth reads more like the death of two individuals than the birth of a happy partnership. In this version, masculinity and femininity are pre-existing, separate states, whose combination brings together elements which ought to have been kept asunder. This is the story of Salmacis and Hermaphroditus; the earliest known text is *Metamorphoses* IV, ll. 285–388, by the Roman poet Ovid (43 BC–AD 17). Hermaphroditus' name suggests that he was originally a double-sexed being from birth, and proud of it, but Ovid makes him a normal boy, the son of Hermes/Mercury, a god often associated with masculine virility, and Aphrodite/Venus, goddess of love. His wanderings bring him to Caria, where he meets the beautiful water nymph Salmacis. He spurns her advances, but the heat of the day induces him to bathe in the pool which bears her name. She follows him into the water, clasps him like an octopus, and prays that they may never again be divided:

> *nec duo sunt et forma duplex, nec femina dici*
> *nec puer ut possit, neutrumque et utrumque videntur.*
>
> (ll. 378–9)

(There are no longer two of them, and a double shape appears that cannot be called a woman or a boy; they seem both neither and either.)

This event is presented as an unmitigated disaster, whose sole victim is Hermaphroditus, now 'semimarem' (half a man) (l. 381). Salmacis is not mentioned again; presumably, she had nothing to lose. Hermaphroditus begs his parents that any man who bathes in this pool may lose half his manhood, and they answer the prayer of their 'nati . . . biformis' (double-shaped son) (l. 387).

Ovid, being a poet, is keenly aware of the paradoxes inherent in his subject, and expects his readers to admire the skill with which he makes confusion worse confounded. His Renaissance English translators and imitators grapple gleefully with their ambiguous heritage. According to the 1567 version of Arthur Golding (*c.* 1536–*c.* 1605), 'Ye could not say it was a perfect boy, / Nor perfect wench: it seemed both and none of both to beene' (ll. 469–70). Francis Beaumont (1584–1616) freely adapts this episode at the climax of his erotic romance, *Salmacis and Hermaphroditus* (1604). It culminates with Hermaphroditus' prayer:

> Grant that whoe're, heated by Phoebus' beams,
> Shall come to coole him in these silver streams,
> May never more a manly shape retaine,
> But halfe a virgin may return againe.
>
> (IV, ll. 915–18)

Doubtless feeling that 'half a virgin' is too ambiguous even for this equivocal being, George Sandys (1578–1664) renders the request as follows in his 1632 translation of Ovid's *Metamorphoses*:

> May every man, that in this water swims,
> Return halfe-woman, with infeebled lims.
>
> (IV, ll. 432)

Sandys lays more stress than Ovid on the fact that Hermaphroditus has not simply lost masculinity, but acquired femininity:

> No longer he a Boy, nor she a maid,
> But neither, and yet either, might be said.

106

Hermaphroditus at himself admires:
Who halfe a female from the spring retires.
(IV, ll. 423–6)

'Admires' at this period still has its root meaning of 'wonders', and does not necessarily connote approval; still, Sandys is at least prepared to consider that Hermaphroditus' double form is a phenomenon worthy of attention.

No wondering pause is allowed by the Augustan Joseph Addison (1672–1719), in his translation of *The Story of Salmacis and Hermaphroditus* (1694). Nor is there any dalliance with the 'neither-yet-either' trope. We are simply told that

> Both bodies in a single body mix,
> A single body with a double sex.
> (ll. 113–14)

Femininity is portrayed as sheer negation; Hermaphroditus becomes 'The boy, thus lost in woman'. The difference between Addison and his predecessors illustrates Pat Rogers' contention in *The Augustan Vision* (1978) that 'the Jacobean malady was a consuming fear that things would fall apart. From this Renaissance nightmare, we pass to a psychic situation exactly the converse. The primal Augustan terror is that things will merge.' Away from the marginal territories of mystical dissent (which will be considered in the next section) the marriage hermaphrodite fades into undignified obscurity. It is invoked by an anonymous 'Lady' in 'An Epithalamium' (1731), where its monstrosity and sterility reflect the antaphrodisiac effect of marriage on previously ardent young couples:

> In wife and husband, girl and boy are lost,
> And make one poor *Hermaphrodite* at most.
> (ll. 71–2)

On the whole, the hermaphrodite was even more threatening to men. According to traditional constructions of sexuality, it was not masculinity but effeminacy that made men vulnerable to female charm. If they yielded to desire, they would be softened up even further. One danger was physical debility caused by the expenditure of precious semen: the 1782 edition of *Aristotle's Last Legacy* was still warning its readers that 'the whole body is thereby deprived of its best and purest blood, and also of the vital spirits; insomuch that many who have been too much addicted to that pleasure have killed themselves in the very act'. An even graver problem was ebbing self-control. In *Paradise Lost* (1667), John Milton (1608–1674) allows the unfallen Adam to wonder whether, at the creation of Eve, God had been over-generous with the raw materials. He fears

> that
> nature failed in me, and left some part

107

Not proof enough such object to sustain,
Or from my side subducting, took perhaps
More than enough.

(VIII, ll. 534–7)

The Archangel Raphael denies that this is the case: if Adam fails to maintain masculine authority, it will be his own fault. Later on the Archangel Michael points out that Adam is wrong to blame women's blandishments for men's sin:

From man's effeminate slackness it begins,
Said the angel, who should better hold his place
By wisdom, and superior gifts received.

(IX, ll. 634–6)

Although Milton does not support the contention that women's very existence makes men effeminate, he still believes that their seductive presence occasions regrettable lapses.

Even those who advocated marriage believed that close contact with women would inevitably compromise masculinity. Husbands must exert self-control and vigilance to strike a proper balance. An article in the *Daily Courant* of 25 November 1731 observes that

Tho' the Beauty of the fair Sex was not made to effeminate, it was certainly designed to soften Ours; and without adoring their Charms, we may reasonably admire them. If Men of Sense would so far admit Love, as not to exclude their necessary and important Duties, they need not be ashamed to indulge one of the most valuable Blessings of an innocent Life.

Addison warned, in the *Spectator* of 27 July 1711, 'the Passion of an ordinary Woman for a Man, is nothing but Self-Love diverted upon another Object: She would have the Lover a Woman in every thing but the Sex.' Should every bride be seen as a potential Salmacis? In the *Memoirs*, the image is employed when Lindamira and Indamora are first brought to Martin's attention: in Chapter 14, outside the freak show, he sees 'the pourtrait of two Bohemian Damsels, whom Nature had as closely united as the ancient Hermaphroditus and Salmacis'. The simile is not entirely apt, since the picture shows the conjunction of two females, but it foreshadows, on a symbolic level, the attempted conjunction of Martin with Lindamora. Furthermore, the eighteenth-century reader would detect enough ominous undertones to start wondering whether this picture was an invitation or a threat.

UNITED CONTRADICTIONS

In the last analysis, however, writers find most fault with marriage when the union is not close enough. Ideally, it should be a complete coalescence of body, mind and spirit, in which the wife's identity becomes an extension of her husband's. Robert Burton (1577–1640), in his *Anatomy of Melancholy* (1621–1651), cites classical precedents for this type of relationship:

> A good wife, according to Plutarch, should be as a looking-glass to represent her husband's face and passion: if he be pleasant, she should be merry; if he laugh, she should smile; if he look sad, she should participate of his sorrow, and bear a part with him; and so they should continue in mutual love one toward another. . . . And she again to him, as the bride saluted the bridegroom of old in Rome, *Ubi tu Caius ego semper Caia*, Be thou still Caius, I'll be Caia.
>
> (Part 3. Section 2. Member 1. Subsection 2)

This attitude could lead to high hopes, and proportionately bitter disappointments. Milton argued that mental and spiritual incompatibility should be grounds for divorce. In *The Doctrine and Discipline of Divorce* (1643) he says the biblical decree that man and wife should be one flesh

> wil be found to import no more but only to make legitimate and good the carnal act, whch els might seem to have somthing of pollution in it: And inferrs thus much over, that the fit union of their souls be such as may even incorporate them to love and amity; but that can never be where no correspondence is of the minde; nay instead of beeing one flesh, they will be rather two carkasses chain'd unnaturally together; or as it may happ'n, a living soule bound to a dead corps, a punishment too like that inflicted by the tyrant *Mezentius*; so little worthy to be receav'd as that remedy of lonelines which God meant us.

The full horror of Milton's analogy emerges when reference is made to Virgil's *Æneid*, VIII, ll. 485–8. In *Virgil's Æneis* (1697), John Dryden (1631–1700) translates as follows:

> The living, and the Dead, at his Command
> Were coupled, Face to Face, and Hand to Hand:
> 'Till choak'd with Stench, in loath'd Embraces ty'd,
> The ling'ring Wretches pin'd away, and dy'd.
>
> (ll. 636–9)

Milton's vehemence has given rise to the view that he is expressing a new sensibility, which seeks the fulfilment of romantic love within marriage. As James G. Turner says in *One Flesh* (1987),

> The divorce tracts are heavy with the accumulated longing of this quest for a perfect mistress, and suffused with a vision of Eros that is both neo-Platonic and intensely practical . . . Every proposal in these tracts is weighed by the standard of love, and every complaint issues from a wounded expectation of love.

109

In early modern England, such proposals met with great hostility. The religious objection was devastatingly simple: whatever Milton's ingenious straining of texts might claim, there was no explicit provision for divorce on these grounds in the Bible. There was also opposition on moral and political principles; easy divorce was condemned as the prelude to sexual promiscuity and social chaos. Marriage was supposedly the basis of society; it was better for the state that unhappily married individuals should suffer than that marriage itself should become unstable. In the circumstances, it is quite likely (though almost impossible to prove) that pleas for divorce on grounds of incompatibility struck a sympathetic chord in many readers who dared not voice their approval, for fear of incurring public condemnation. In retrospect, the few who dared to make this plea do not seem impious, lewd or irresponsible: they placed an exceptionally high value on the individual, on love and on marriage itself – which was too good to waste on incompatible couples.

The most celebrated eighteenth century advocate of divorce for incompatibility was the Restoration dramatist, George Farquhar (c. 1677–1707), who introduces it into his comedy, *The Beaux Stratagem* (1707). Mrs Sullen, a fine lady accustomed to town life, has married a boorish country squire, and both are miserable in consequence. They have no common ground in tastes or character; as she says, 'we are united Contradictions, Fire and Water' (II, ll. 144–5). Unfortunately, these contradictions have *not* united, but remained in uneasy confrontation. Their bickering recalls Milton:

Sullen. You're impertinent.
Mrs Sullen. I was ever so, since I became one Flesh with you.
Sullen. One Flesh! rather two Carcases, join'd unnaturally together.
Mrs Sullen. Or rather a living Soul coupled to a dead Body.
(III, iii, ll. 283–6)

Mrs Sullen's situation becomes unbearable when she falls in love with Archer, an accomplished gallant who is her equal in breeding and wit. The interaction between this couple, who experience both sexual passion and a meeting of minds, shows exactly what is lacking in Mrs Sullen's marriage, which was arranged for social, financial and dynastic convenience. In a final scene based on pure wishful thinking, the Sullens divorce each other, and Archer triumphantly declares,

Consent, if mutual, saves the Lawyer's Fee,
Consent is Law enough to set you free.
(V, iv, ll. 295–6)

By the standards of romantic love, the Sullens have never been married at all.

Romantic aspirations to spiritual union within marriage reach a strangely logical conclusion in the faith of the visionary mystic, Emanuel Swedenborg (1688–1772). He promotes the marriage hermaphrodite from metaphorical status on earth to actual existence in heaven. He drives a coach and horses through Matthew, 22:30, where Jesus said there was no marrying in heaven. Apparently, Jesus was speaking figuratively. 'Marriage' meant the union between the human soul and God, which took place during life on earth, and, being eternal, was not repeated after death. Virtuous couples who have been happily married on earth are reunited in heaven, where they proceed much as before, except that they experience more pleasure and do not have children. They continue a process which has begun on earth, where they first desired to become a unit. In *Delitiae Sapientiae de Amore Conjugali* ['The Delights of Wisdom Relating to Conjugal Love'] (1768), Swedenborg gives woman the credit for taking the initiative: 'the inclination to unite the man to herself is constant and perpetual with the wife, but inconstant and alternate with the man' (Section 169). It has been divinely ordained that the woman should use her prudence to conceal from the man the effort she is devoting to this purpose.

Their melding is progressive and continuous; death is a minor interruption, not worth mentioning:

> Conjunction is effected from the first days of marriage successively, and . . . with those who are principled in love truly conjugal, it is wrought more and more thoroughly to eternity. . . . They become one man according to the increments of conjugal love; and as this love in the heavens is genuine by virtue of the celestial and spiritual life of the celestial and spiritual life of the angels, therefore two married partners are there called two, when they are named husband and wife, but one when they are named angels.
>
> (Section 177)

Swedenborg adds much helpful detail, including the reassuring information that suitable partners will be found for newly arrived spirits without celestial pre-engagements. The overwhelming impression conveyed by his vision is a combination of bureaucratic efficiency with bourgeois respectability. Nevertheless, with her prudently concealed encroachments on her husband's identity, the wife still has a touch of Salmacis.

YOUR OWN FANCY

As the eighteenth century progressed, fears that marriage might lead to emasculation were expressed less frequently: this danger was commonly perceived in less orthodox sexual activities. Instead of a blending of two into one, marriage was now presented as a system of complementary co-operation. Greater stress was laid on the idea that the chief binding force in a heterosexual relationship was not similarity but difference.

In *The Religion of Nature* (1724), William Wollaston (1660–1724) describes such marriages in practical terms:

> many things there are, which may be useful, perhaps necessary to the *man*, and yet require the delicate hand or nicer management and genius of the *woman*: and so, *vicissim* ['in turn'], the *woman* cannot but want many things, which require the more robust and active powers or greater capacity of the *man*.

The image of the wife as her husband's emotional counterpart still persists, but now, instead of passively reflecting his moods, she contributes qualities she has already developed on her own account. George Lyttelton (1709–1773) recommends a union of this type in 'To Mr. Poyntz, Ambassador at the Congress of Soissons, in 1728':

> A chosen bride shall in thy arms be plac'd,
> With all th'attractive charms of beauty grac'd,
> Whose wit and virtue shall thy own express,
> Only distinguish'd by their softer dress.
> (ll. 77–80)

Within marriages of this kind, men and women might experience change in their outward circumstances, perhaps even their inward nature, but their existence as individual entities was secure until death – and after. This belief could be taken very seriously by devout Anglicans. On 4 November 1749, Catherine Talbot (1721–1770) writes to her friend, Elizabeth Carter (1717–1806), advising her to marry:

> Happy you doubtless are at home, but happier would you be were you to change it for a home, more properly your own, with one well chosen friend for life; for though one is apt to attach oneself fondly to scenes one has been any time fixed in, yet certainly that is not the kind of happiness intended for us, in this changeable state, where action, improvement, and a continual progress is our allotted part. In this our short travelling day we should go as far, and take in as great a variety of prospects, and diffuse any good influence we may have as wide as we can. The more connections we make here, the more friends we shall have to rejoice with hereafter in a permanent state of felicity, looking back with them to those perplexed scenes of human life, in which we have assisted and comforted each other. Human creatures are not like plants to grow only in one spot, but flourish the better for every proper change of place.

The reader can only marvel at this conception of a selfhood so rigidly bounded, so indomitably enduring, that its circle of heavenly friendship will be confined to those it was introduced to on earth.

Less emphasis was laid on the compatibility of men and women in general, more on the suitability of particular types for each other. This resulted from an increased readiness to acknowledge that there *were* different types of man and woman, and that this was the effect of a healthy natural variety, rather than of deplorable failures to conform to uniform standards of mental, moral and physical perfection. One consequence could be a gesture towards sexual egalitarianism, in cases where couples were matched according to their qualities as individuals, rather than on the assumption that certain characteristics (such as judgement and strength) would predominate in the man, and others (such as timidity or excessive emotionalism) in the woman. This happens in the sentimental comedy, *The West Indian* (1771) by Richard Cumberland (1732–1811). The naive and impulsive hero, Belcour, realizes that he needs an exceptionally prudent wife:

> If ever I marry, it must be a staid, sober, considerate damsel, with blood in her veins as cold as a turtle's, quick of scent as a vulture when danger's in the wind; wary and sharp-sighted as a hawk when treachery is on foot: with such a companion at my elbow, forever whispering in my ear – have a care of this man, he's a cheat; don't go near that woman, she's a jilt; overhead there's a scaffold, underfoot there's a well: Oh! sir, such a woman might lead me up and down this great city without difficulty and danger.
>
> (III, i)

Acceptance of individual quirks of taste could, however, have far less egalitarian implications. Lawrence Sterne (1713–1768) exploits the variety of taste in Vol. VI, Chapter 38 of *Tristram Shandy* (1759–1767), where he flatly refuses to give a description of the luscious Widow Wadman. Instead, he leaves a sheet blank, with instructions for readers to design her according to their own specifications:

> To conceive this right, – call for pen and ink – here's paper ready to your hand. – Sit down, Sir, paint her to your own mind – as like your mistress as you can – as unlike your wife as your conscience will let you – 'tis all one to me – please but your own fancy in it.

This passage neatly exemplifies some important limitations of liberal humanism in the Enlightenment, and afterwards. The authorial persona offers a freedom of choice to his male readers that is not balanced by a corresponding invitation for each lady to depict her ideal lover: he is so firmly convinced that all women want sexually active men with generously proportioned genitalia that he never considers the possibility that they might take an interest in other features. He also takes it for granted that only men would find a woman sexually attractive. Worst of all, he totally sacrifices Widow Wadman's individuality. It seems that, where sexual preferences are concerned, there is only a limited amount of individualism

113

to go round, and the male readers of *Tristram Shandy* have been permitted to hog the lot. At least Pope, in his 'Epistle to a Lady', declared that women were 'black, brown, or fair' (l. 4); Sterne has obliterated even this distinction.

THE BEAUTIES OF HER MIND

Despite its occasional masculist lapses – or because of them? – the novel provides a wealth of insights into contemporary ideas about the impact of love, desire and marriage on human identity. The transforming power of passion is the subject of *La Princesse de Clèves* (1678), attributed to Madame de Lafayette (1634–1693). The heroine's mother 'was troubled by no fear that she was giving her daughter, in the Prince de Clèves, a husband whom she could not love'. The ambiguity of this sentence leaves the reader uncertain whether the mother did not know her daughter's true feelings or simply did not care about them. The prince, passionately in love, complains to the heroine: '"All you feel for me is a sort of kindness that cannot satisfy me. You are neither impatient, nor restless, nor troubled."' As an old-fashioned husband of the authoritarian type, the prince would have been contented with his wife's total obedience: as her romantic lover within marriage, he makes demands of her inner self – demands which she cannot meet. A profound change occurs when the princess meets the Duc de Nemours: 'She saw then that the feelings she had for him were those that M. de Clèves had so often asked of her; she realized how shameful it was to have such feelings for a man other than a husband who deserved them.' Nemours feels similar effects: '"I hardly recognize myself since my return from Flanders."' The prince's death makes it possible for the princess to marry Nemours, but she is deterred by fear of further changes: 'The eventual cooling of Nemours's passion, together with the ills of jealousy, which she believed to be inevitable in marriage, presented an image of the certain misery that awaited her if she took that step.' The author endorses the heroine's painfully won perception that marriage cannot accommodate the stormy subjectivities of romantic love: her mother had been right all the time.

Similar conclusions are reached by François de Salignac de la Mothe-Fénelon (1651–1715), in his didactic romance, *Télémaque* (1699). As preceptor to the Duc de Bourgogne (1682–1711), a possible heir to the French throne, Fénelon was aware of strong political reasons for advocating marriages of convenience. The young prince Telemachus falls in love with Eucharis, a beautiful nymph, an unfortunate liaison which interrupts his quest for his long-lost father, and causes mental, moral and physical degeneration: 'he was pale and dejected, and in every respect so much altered, as scarcely to be known.' All self-control abandoned, he is incapable of leaving her under his own power; his guardian goddess finally gets him away by pushing him off a cliff into the sea. Telemachus' subsequent choice, the princess Antiope, is far more appropriate: he declares

> it is not the tumultuous desire of passion; it is the calm complacency of reason, a tender approbation and esteem. I desire her, as the sister of my soul, my friend and companion for life; and, if the Gods shall ever restore my father to me, and I am permitted to chuse, my fate and the fate of Antiope shall be one.

This attachment threatens neither his psychic integrity nor his regard for his father: its very weakness guarantees its suitability. Some readers may suspect that Fénelon has sacrificed verisimilitude to didactic purpose: it is hard to believe that such a spirited young prince would be content with a marriage based on 'calm complacency' after his intoxicating affair with Eucharis. But Telemachus' attitude nevertheless reflects an important development which leaves its mark on life and literature for the next two hundred years: the ideal of the egalitarian, companionate marriage, where husband and wife are joined in friendship.

In fiction as in real life, it is a difficult and complex task for couples to strike the right balance between the coldness of businesslike separateness and the mutual suffocation of obsessive, romantic passion. It is often considered natural and right that the man should be less fully absorbed in marriage than the wife. In *The Life and Adventures of Robinson Crusoe* (1719), Daniel Defoe (1660–1731) creates a hero who faces the reader foursquare, for whom marriage is a comparatively minor consideration, largely considered in terms of reproduction. After his sojourn on the famous desert island, 'I marry'd, and that not either to my disadvantage or dissatisfaction, and had three children, two sons and one daughter.' When his wife dies, he visits his 'new collony in the island' and discovers that some of the inhabitants 'made an attempt upon the main land, and brought away eleven men and five women prisoners, by which, at my coming, I found about twenty young children on the island.' Nobody could claim that this was the language of love, but that is not expected from a briskly efficient adventurer like Crusoe.

When Defoe adopts a female persona, however, the idea of a married woman who maintains individual interests causes problems. The much-wedded (and even more frequently bedded) heroine of *The Fortunes and Misfortunes of the Famous Moll Flanders* (1722) negotiates the bumpy terrain between romance and convenience with appalling agility. The great love of her life is the highwayman Jemy, her Lancashire husband. They are so close that they can communicate by extrasensory perception: he leaves her, but returns when he hears her calling, from miles away, '"O Jemy! O Jemy! come back, come back."' They part a month later, and the next time she sees him she avoids letting him see her: she has just married a previous suitor, a respectable tradesman. This supremely convenient marriage begins with a honeymoon in the best romantic tradition: 'I was a meer Bride al this while, and my new Spouse strove to make me entirely easie in every thing; O could this State of Life have continued!' The happy couple enjoy 'an uninterrupted course of Ease and Content for Five Years', with no suggestion that Moll is secretly hankering for her dashing highwayman. Later on, Moll and Jemy are reunited, and they go to America. Another obstacle to marital union appears when Moll has a secret meeting with her son, a wealthy Virginia planter:

> I was as if I had been in a new World, and began secretly now to wish that I had not brought my *Lancashire* Husband from *England* at all.
>
> However, that wish was not Hearty neither, for I lov'd my *Lancashire* Husband entirely, as indeed I had ever done from the beginning; and he merited from me as much as it was possible for a Man to do, but that by the way.

Moll's reservations may be assertions of her independent selfhood, but they compromise the integrity of that self: can she feel anything 'entirely'?

Samuel Richardson (1689–1761) and Henry Fielding are much concerned with the claims and concessions required to make a successful marriage. In *Pamela* (1740–1741), Richardson tells the story of a servant girl who resists her master's attempts at seduction; against all odds, she marries Mr B. She combines unimpeachable virtue with an indomitable sense of her own value as an individual. Mr B. says, '"It was indeed her person that first attracted me and made me her *lover*: but they were the beauties of her mind, that made me her *husband*."' He was also won by her mind's strength. Fielding, too, shows situations where the man must yield to, and learn from, the woman. Sophia, the heroine of *Tom Jones* (1749), refuses the odious Blifil, who takes no interest in winning her heart: 'Her Fortune and her Person were the sole Objects of his Wishes, of which he made no Doubt soon to obtain the absolute Property.' He is so blinkered by vanity that he does not realize Sophia is in love with Tom: 'he was well assured that there was not another Self in the Case' (Book VI, Chapter 7). Yet even if Tom did not exist, Blifil would still have Sophia's self to reckon with. When she runs away from home, it is not to find Tom but to avoid Blifil. Tom, on the other hand, respects Sophia's opinions. She declares she will never marry a man whose concept of chastity does not match her own; Tom replies, '"I have learnt it already. The first Moment of Hope that my Sophia might be my Wife taught it me at once."' Tom's notions of marital bliss are diametrically opposed to Blifil's: he wants to know '"when I shall have that dear, that vast, that exquisite, extatic Delight of making my *Sophia* happy?"' (Book XVIII, Chapter 12). As Angela Smallwood says, in *Fielding and the Woman Question* (1989), 'The good marriage, with its literal fruitfulness, is the paradigm of the ideally equal human relationship, undistorted by self-interested behaviour. The bad marriage is the image of all selfish power-struggles between individuals.'

Women novelists tackle the topic of marriage with understandable enthusiasm. The writings of early modern women on this or any other subject merit careful attention because female self-expression at this period was still a controversial and difficult matter. According to Catherine Belsey, in *The Subject of Tragedy* (1985), women of the Renaissance were not able to speak, much less write, with independent authority:

> The subject of liberal humanism claims to be the unified, autonomous author of his or her own choices (moral, electoral and consumer), and the source and origin of speech. Women in Britain for most of the sixteenth and seventeenth centuries were not fully any of these things. Able to speak, to take up a subject-position in discourse, to identify with the 'I' of utterance and the uttering 'I' which always exceeds it, they were none the less enjoined to silence, discouraged from any form of speech which was not an act of submission to the authority of fathers and husbands. Permitted to break their silence in order to acquiesce in the utterances of others, women were denied any single place from which to speak for themselves.

This 'single place' has been hard to find; many women believe it has yet to be located; but at least in the period between 1680 and 1820 the search was on.

Aphra Behn (*c*.1640–1689) surveys many of the predicaments in which wives could be placed by an unjust society, and their more or less resourceful reactions. None can match, for sheer thoroughness, Isabella, heroine of *The History of the Nun; or, the Fair Vow-Breaker* (1688), who discovers she has inadvertently committed bigamy, and responds by murdering both her husbands with deft efficiency. The most lavish praise, however, is bestowed on Imoinda, the wife of the royal slave Oroonoko, who resists all other suitors, joins him in armed rebellion and lets him kill her to prevent their child being born into slavery. At the conclusion of *Oroonoko* (1688), Behn expresses both diffidence and pride in her authorial role, in a way that matches the ambiguous status of her hero and heroine. She is a great writer, though a woman; they were a noble couple, though slaves. Well-matched in marginality, they somehow authenticate each other:

> Thus died this great man, worthy of a better fate, and a more sublime wit than mine to write his praise. Yet, I hope, the reputation of my pen is considerable enough to make his glorious name to survive to all ages, with that of the brave, the beautiful, and the constant Imoinda.

Although the story is nominally Oroonoko's, Behn ensures that Imoinda, his wife, not only has, but is, the last word: even her destruction can be seen as a statement of independence and strength, because she consented to it willingly.

Catherine Craft-Fairchild is one of many critics who detect subversion and resistance in women's novels:

> Early female authors, by portraying female economic and sexual victimization, by exiling their heroines or submerging them in marriage, helped to form and define the codes and institutions of society that persist into the present. At the same time, they questioned the foundation of those systems, exposed their injustice and violence, and emphasized that the 'domestic woman' was a culturally produced category.

Towards the end of the eighteenth century, female novelists began to protest against Pope's depiction of women as creatures without character. They either flatly denied the charge, or claimed that it did not apply to really good women (like the heroines of their novels), or argued that lack of character was encouraged by men, who found women easier to manage if they had no will of their own. In this respect, as in many others, Jane Austen (1775–1817) created new refinements, with heroines who combined wit, intelligence and virtue in equal proportions, and whose moral and psychological perceptions promised to keep them one jump ahead of their husbands. *Pride and Prejudice* (1813) places a high value on individuality: it is not enough that the right people should marry; they must reach the right phase of development. The Darcy who proposes to Elizabeth against his better judgement and the Elizabeth who believes him capable of deliberate injustice towards Wickham would be an ill-matched couple; only after they have learned to value each other fairly – and done some growing up in the process – will their union be equally romantic and rational. In Chapter 58, shortly after his successful proposal, she exercises unprecedented self-restraint in conversation with Darcy: 'Elizabeth longed to observe that Mr Bingley had been a most delightful friend; so easily guided that his worth was invaluable; but she checked herself.' Is this a sign that marriage will destroy her power? Hardly: she is only choosing the right time for Darcy's advanced training. 'She remembered that he had yet to learn to be laughed at, and it was rather too early to begin.' Like one of Swedenborg's prudent wives, Elizabeth is tactfully holding back, keeping something of herself in reserve, so that she and her husband may become even more closely united in future. The marriage hermaphrodite has the last laugh.

8

FEELINGS AND NOVELS

John Mullan

Do feelings vary between different times, or different cultures? How are feelings learned? Would it be possible to write a history of the development of feelings, or have they always had some basic vocabulary which does not change? Such questions occur when one reads something like the following letter, written to the novelist Samuel Richardson by one of his regular correspondents, Lady Dorothy Bradshaigh. Lady Bradshaigh had already read, several months earlier, the first four volumes of Richardson's *Clarissa*, and, like all Richardson's other readers, had been waiting for him to complete the novel. At the end of Volume IV, Clarissa had escaped the clutches of her would-be seducer, Lovelace, but he had found her hiding place and, on the last page, was keenly and exultingly in pursuit of her. For eight months, readers had had to wait for the final instalment of the huge novel – many of them writing to Richardson with pleas or suggestions about its ending. Now Lady Bradshaigh had received the final three volumes, sent to her by the author himself, and was obeying her promise to him that she would read to the end of the book and write to him with her opinions on it. Here is what she told Richardson, in a letter of January 1749:

> I verily believe I have shed a pint of tears. . . . When alone in agonies would I lay down the Book, take it up again, walk about the Room, let fall a Flood of Tears, wipe my Eyes, read again, perhaps not three Lines, throw away the Book crying out excuse me good Mr. Richardson, I cannot go on. It is your Fault you have done more than I can bear. . . . [I] threw myself upon my Couch to compose, recollecting my Promise (which a thousand times I wished had not been made) again I read, again acted the same Part. Sometimes agreeably interrupted by my dear [husband], who was at that Time labouring through the Sixth Volume with a Heart capable of Impressions equal to my own, tho' the effects shewn in a more justifiable Manner, which I believe may be compared to what Mr. Belford felt when he found the beauteous Sufferer in her Prison Room. 'Something rose in my

119

throat, I know not what; which made me gurggle as it were for Speech' – Seeing me so moved, he begg'd for God's sake I would read no more, kindly threatened to take the book from me, but upon my pleading my Promise, suffered me to go on. That Promise is now fulfilled, and [I] am thankful the heavy Task is over, tho' the effects are not. . . . My Spirits are strangely seized, my Sleep is disturbed, waking in the Night I burst into a Passion of crying, so I did at Breakfast this Morning, and just now again. God be merciful to me, what can it mean? . . . I must lock up such a History from my Sight.

Do we recognize *these* feelings? Some kinds of popular fiction are still supposed to exert a strange power over readers' emotions, but it is difficult to imagine that a novel could do to us what *Clarissa* seems to have done to Lady Bradshaigh. Despite this, it may be that her tears and insomnia are not so far from feelings that we do recognize. The *Oxford English Dictionary* suggests not only that 'feelings' do have a history – that a culture might well fabricate them to meet new needs or provide new satisfactions – but that novels might have been where those feelings were explored. The very word *feelings* – used in its now most common sense to mean *emotions* – has its first recorded use in the 1770s. The two earliest examples cited are both taken from novels: by Elizabeth Griffith and Ann Radcliffe. (By 1804, the *OED* has managed to detect an example of a phrase from which it is now difficult to disentangle the word *feelings*: 'Do not hurt my feelings . . . '.) *Feeling* (singular) dates from at least the fourteenth century; *feelings* (plural) is an eighteenth-century coinage: a new concern or possession of the privileged. We might say that the polite culture of novel-consumers that Richardson helped to make was one whose members were learning to do what we do so readily – to have 'feelings' and to value them. And novels were where you went to have those feelings.

The odd thing about all this was that finding your feelings through novels was supposed to be a *moral* activity. This is why Lady Bradshaigh's letter, precisely because it does not seem disingenuous, does seem rather ridiculous. The feelings of which she writes may be painful, but she cannot help but suppose that they are also admirable. Of course, the language of moral influence has rarely been absent from literary criticism and literary justification. However, in eighteenth-century discussions of 'the rise of the novel', including those that take place within the novels themselves, moralism takes on a special intensity. Novelists, and Richardson especially, were sensitive to the criticism of novels as 'low' or 'vulgar' – a criticism sharpened by the success of Richardson's *Pamela*: the story, in her own words, of a servant girl whom virtue makes a lady. Fine feelings, not only depicted in novels but also, as it were, experienced by their readers as they read, were the guarantee that novel-reading could be morally elevating.

When a popular anthology of extracts from the writings of Laurence Sterne was published as *The Beauties of Sterne* (the first of many editions appeared in 1782) it was subtitled, 'Selected for the Heart of Sensibility'. This 'Heart' was what the best reader possessed.

The process of learning to have feelings was allowed to be morally ennobling because 'sensibility' was not something that everyone possessed. It was a special kind of susceptibility. So special, in fact, that, while a privilege, it could also be a kind of affliction. Those with 'sensibility' had finer nerves than others, and were more easily discomposed or disturbed by their own feelings. In the second half of the eighteenth century, people spoke and wrote about 'sensibility' – as we might speak and write of, say, 'stress' – as if it were palpable and real, and no metaphor (though the word was adapted from its original reference to specifically physical sensitivity). At the same time – and here again one might think of how we have learned to talk of 'stress' – those who wrote of 'sensibility' were aware that they were using the word in a new way. The whole force of the word came from its explicit designation of a phenomenon that was peculiar to a certain culture and a certain time. (A sense of the modishness of 'sensibility' is still present in Jane Austen's *Sense and Sensibility*, published in 1811, though first drafted in the 1790s.) 'Sensibility' was natural and yet newly discovered. The paradox is nicely caught in a passage in Mary Wollstonecraft's *Letters Written during a Short Residence in Sweden, Norway, and Denmark* (1796):

> The more I see of the world, the more I am convinced that civilization is a blessing not sufficiently estimated by those who have not traced its progress, for it not only refines our enjoyments, but produces a variety which enables us to retain the primitive delicacy of our sensations . . . in that state of society in which the judgment and taste are not called forth, and formed by the cultivation of the arts and sciences, little of that delicacy of feeling and thinking is to be found characterized by the word sentiment.

Wollstonecraft's faith in 'civilization' and 'progress' is, by 1796, unconventional enough for us to call it defiant (she writes with the failed ideals of the French Revolution constantly in mind); however, her belief that 'delicacy of feeling' is to be found only in an advanced society is common. Only in such a society was it possible to cultivate that natural capacity for feelings that was usually called 'sensibility'.

Later in the *Letters*, Wollstonecraft, writing about bringing up her own daughter, suggests how this capacity also involves vulnerability. 'With trembling hand I shall cultivate sensibility, and cherish delicacy of sentiment, lest, whilst I lend flesh blushes to the rose, I sharpen the thorns that will wound the breast I would fain guard.' The awkwardness of syntax and metaphor here reflect the author's difficulties with

121

'sensibility', which, in her earlier *Vindication of the Rights of Woman*, she had described as a means of subjugating women (see below). Wollstonecraft's sexual politics were unusual, but some equivocation about the benefits of 'sensibility' was standard in the eighteenth century. With feelings come pain and illness. Lady Bradshaigh's letter records the afflictions of a sensitive reader and a sensitive individual. She compares herself in her suffering to Clarissa – in another letter about the effects of reading the novel she writes, 'My hand trembles, for I can scarce hold my pen. I am as mad as the poor injured Clarissa'. Her comparison is appropriate, for Richardson's heroines, like many who follow in their wake, have sensibilities keen enough to make them ill. They are always trembling, fainting, turning sick with feeling. The best people are so attuned to their own feelings that they can be weakened by them. As they are also laudably responsive to others' feelings, especially of distress, they can be sure that this susceptibility is virtuous. The sensitive hero of Henry Mackenzie's hugely successful novel *The Man of Feeling* (1771) feels and weeps for others so much that, enfeebled by his sympathies, he wastes away and dies – a man too good for an unfeeling world. In *A Vindication of the Rights of Woman* (1794), Mary Wollstonecraft was to blame the cult of sensibility in general, and novel reading in particular, for teaching women habits of weakness and passivity. Ignoring the prominence of this '*man* of feeling' in the period, she assumed that female readers imitated the models of debilitating sensitivity offered them in novels and depicted a class of women reduced by their much-prized feelings to the vapours and a love of lying on sofas. She would have recognized Jane Austen's sardonic account of Marianne Dashwood's ill-making feelings in *Sense and Sensibility* when the man she loves abruptly departs.

> Marianne would have thought herself very inexcusable had she been able to sleep at all the first night after parting from Willoughby. She would have been ashamed to look her family in the face the next morning, had she not risen from her bed in more need of repose than when she lay down in it. . . . She got up with an headache, was unable to talk, and unwilling to take any nourishment; giving pain every moment to her mother and sisters, and forbidding all attempt at consolation from either. Her sensibility was potent enough!

Austen's dry commentary on her character's sufferings, mounting to the acid exclamation that ends the paragraph, sees the combinations of self-indulgence and real pain that sensibility might produce. Belief in its effects is accompanied by illness – indeed, later in the novel Marianne comes close to death when she catches a chill whose powers seem a consequence of all her disappointed hopes and overdeveloped feelings. From the mid-eighteenth century, medical literature reflects – in some cases, fosters – this belief that refined and sensitive people are made ill by their feelings.

It is a belief most famously promoted in *The English Malady* (1st edn, 1733) by George Cheyne, physician to many refined sufferers from 'nervous' complaints, including Samuel Richardson. (Cheyne diagnosed Richardson as having 'Scurbutico Nervose from a sedentary studious Life'.) Cheyne wrote his book for 'my Fellow-Sufferers under these Complaints' and included his own brief autobiography of nervous suffering, 'The Case of the Author'. His copious correspondence with Richardson is full of assurances that he knows from his own experience the effects of 'Grief, Anguish, and Anxiety such a Distemper must have on a Mind of any Degree of Sensibility'. In the age of sensibility, the physician who treats 'the English Malady' (the prevalence of nervous complaints being a symptom of the nation's refinement) is qualified by his own sufferings. If he is to be trusted, he too must know how to feel.

It is hardly surprising, then, that Richardson was highly flattered by Lady Bradshaigh's pained, insomniac reading of *Clarissa*. She was indeed his favourite reader and correspondent. These two roles belonged together, for much of Richardson's voluminous correspondence was taken up with the discussion of his fiction, his correspondents being those on whom he tested his novels (who were also, one might say, those who passed the test of reacting properly to that fiction). Lady Bradshaigh's responses were only the peculiarly heightened expression of what one finds throughout the letters that Richardson received from his circle of avid, mostly female, readers. This circle practised what a wider public was also learning: a delight in reading with a 'Heart of Sensibility'; a delight in learning of feelings through fiction. Novels were the age's laboratories of emotion (and, in part, we know this because they were often mocked for being so). When a book proclaimed itself to be 'A Sentimental Novel', as many did in the wake of Sterne's (posthumously) triumphant *A Sentimental Journey* of 1768, it was not just advertising its content – plenty of tearful scenes – it was also promising something about the experience of reading. People were supposed to cry over books, as well as in them.

In the eighteenth century, the experience of novel-reading was characteristically described as an exercise of sympathy. It was an exercise of sympathy that was a private, exceptional and even covert experience, for sensibility was unworldly. In a sense, a novel was the natural place to find this experience because novels concerned themselves with the private individual. This was partly a matter of their content: in *Tom Jones* (1749), Henry Fielding's narrator describes himself as one of those 'who deal in private Character, who search into the most retired Recesses, and draw forth Examples of Virtue and Vice, from Holes and Corners of the World'. The self-confessed and entirely mischievous 'lowness' of Fielding's novel is premised on its interest in the 'history' of a 'foundling'. (The book's full, ironical title was *The History of Tom Jones, a Foundling*.) The new kind of hero is not even the foundling of what Fielding calls 'idle Romances' – who would be a prince or princess in some imaginary land. The 'private Character' whom Fielding brings to life is, like Pamela Andrews and Clarissa Harlowe, a particular inhabitant of Hanoverian England. As Ian Watt long ago emphasized, it was a novelty of novels to have plots 'acted by particular people in particular circumstances'. The provision of 'such details of the story as the individuality of the actors concerned, the particulars of the times and places of their actions' set novels off from other genres. Those two paragons, the man of feeling and the woman of sensibility, belonged to a genre which was new because it took as significant the story of the private individual – the self as a private person.

This meant that novels were concerned with the private individual in another way. Most vividly in the warnings of those hostile to 'the rise of the novel', novel-reading was depicted as intensely, even surreptitiously, private, and therefore incendiary. So the critic and moralist Vicesimus Knox conceded that Richardson's novels were 'written with the purest intentions of promoting virtue', but imagined the inflaming effects on solitary young (female) readers as 'scenes are laid open, which it would be safer to conceal, and sentiments excited, which it would be more advantageous to early virtue not to admit'. 'It is to be feared, the moral view is rarely regarded by youthful and inexperienced readers,' he said, who 'while they read, eagerly wish to be actors in the scenes which they admire.' The playwright Richard Cumberland, writing in the 1780s, also imagined (although in his case satirically) that the official moralism of *Clarissa* would be undone by actual influence of fiction on a typical reader.

> Few female hearts in early youth can bear being softened by pathetic and affecting stories without prejudice. Young people are all imitation, and when a girl assumes the pathos of Clarissa without experiencing the same afflictions, or being put to the same trials, the result will be a most insufferable affectation and pedantry.

Novels made sympathy most intense in the solitary activity of reading. The image of the easily beguiled young female reader of novels might therefore be taken to tell us something not about the actual readers of these books, but about what many thought of the special powers of this genre. Novels supposedly relied on the intensity of private response. This is why you could read novels to test your feelings, and why the now pejorative adjective 'sentimental' – frequently applied to novels in the late eighteenth century – was a term of approbation from the 1740s or 1750s. (It is telling not only that the *OED* records the first use of 'sentimental', in 1749, in a letter from the same Lady Bradshaigh to Samuel Richardson, but also that, in the passage cited, she senses that 'Everything clever and agreeable is comprehended in that word'.) Other kinds of book could be 'sentimental' – for instance, there was a small fashion for sentimental 'tours' in the 1770s and 1780s – but novels seemed best designed to provide the pleasures and pains, or pleasurable pains, of private feelings. Cultivating sensibility involved turning from an unfeeling world. 'Feelings' were the benefit of refinement and reflection (every sentimental novel includes a successful man of business, who will never possess sensibility).

It is tempting to see this concern of novels with the private individual in the context of the Enlightenment more generally. The most influential accounts of this literary genre, Watt's *The Rise of the Novel* or McKeon's *The Origins of the English Novel*, indeed take its development to be intimate with the rise of both empiricism and what Watt calls 'economic individualism'. It is also possible to see the special emphasis, from *Pamela* onwards, on sentiment and the arousal of feelings as being in the stream of British Enlightenment thought. Read the first sentence of Adam Smith's *The Theory of Moral Sentiments*, first published in 1759, and we might, if we did not know otherwise, be being referred to the perplexing pleasures of novel-reading.

> How selfish soever man may be supposed, there are evidently some principles in his nature, which interest him in the fortunes of others, and render their happiness necessary to him, though he derives nothing from it except the pleasure of seeing it.

The pressing interest in 'the fortunes of others' sounds like one of the characteristics of mid-century fiction: the lachrymose heroes of sentimental novels like Sarah Fielding's *David Simple* (1744) or Henry Brooke's *The Fool of Quality* (1765–1770) are constantly relieving the distresses of those with affecting tales of misfortune. Readers of novels are presented with these tearful sympathizers as if they are obvious paragons. Surely it is no accident that, contemporary with the sentimentalism of such fiction, we find everywhere in philosophy and aesthetics the vocabulary of sentiment and sympathy, and that Adam Smith and David Hume try to found a moral philosophy on the 'natural' capacity for fellow-feeling.

The first chapter of Smith's *Theory of Moral Sentiments* is entitled 'Of Sympathy', and the workings of this principle (what Smith calls 'our fellow-feeling with any passion whatever') is at the heart – as well as at the beginning – of his moral theory. As Edmund Burke recognized when he came to review Smith's work in the *Annual Register*, Smith's theoretical ambition rested on 'sympathy': 'making approbation and disapprobation the tests of virtue and vice, and shewing that those are founded on sympathy, he raises from this simple truth, one of the most beautiful fabrics of moral theory, that has perhaps ever appeared.' Smith's own opening chapter lets us see why empiricism led to this emphasis on 'sympathy'. 'As we have no immediate experience of what other men feel, we can form no idea of the manner in which they are affected, but by conceiving what we ourselves should feel in the like situation.' Sympathy rescues us from solipsism and self-interest. Sympathy means not so much that one individual's experiences *can* become another's, as that they *must* be so translated. Sympathy explains how our expressions of approval and disapproval need not be the reflexes of mere habit or prejudice, but can be understood as the offspring of 'human nature' – and therefore not *mine* or *yours*, but *ours*.

In his anatomy of the arousal of sympathetic feelings, Adam Smith does mention Richardson's novels in passing. The novelist is among those 'poets and romance writers, who best paint the refinement and delicacies of love and friendship, and of all other private and domestic affections'. These best 'poets and romance writers' are good 'instructors' because they celebrate 'that extraordinary sensibility, which we naturally feel for the misfortunes of our nearest connections'. Smith's comment is the exception to a rule: despite the labours of literary historians like Watt and McKeon, novels are not part of the Enlightenment (indeed, 'Enlightenment' is a term that is hardly ever to be found in discussions of eighteenth-century English literature). One important reason for this is that while Enlightenment writers in Britain may have included aesthetics, *belles-lettres* or criticism among the proper pursuits of men of taste, these kinds of literary discussion never included novels. Although it seems to us characteristic of the period that a philosopher like Hume should describe himself as having led a life of 'literary Pursuits and Occupations', 'literature' still meant what Samuel Johnson's 1755 *Dictionary* called 'learning; skill in letters'. 'Literary' enthusiasms might embrace some poetry and drama (although not necessarily in English), but novels were below the horizon of the polite intellectual.

So, while novels and novel-reading are controversial in the eighteenth century, they are scarcely mentioned in elevated discussions of 'Taste' – the heading under which what we might call 'literary criticism' most often took place. There was certainly a traffic between philosophy and the many essays on 'Taste' published in the period, but novels were not objects of 'Taste'. The theory of 'sympathy' in Smith's *Theory of Moral Sentiments* may have been directly influential on the critical and aesthetic arguments of the last decades of the eighteenth century, but these arguments do not comprehend novels. Writers on 'Taste' do turn to 'sympathy' in order to explain how texts affect readers of refined sensibility. Theorists like Edmund Burke, Alexander Gerard and Lord Kames – and, later, James Beattie and Archibald Alison – conflate aesthetic pleasure with the experience of sympathy. In the works of all these writers on 'Taste', published through the second half of the eighteenth century, sympathy is a response to the best painting, poetry and drama. Although notionally universal, it is interpreted as a fellow-feeling available most to those with sharpened sensibilities. James Beattie is representative when he declares in his chapter 'Of Sympathy' in *An Essay on Poetry and Music* that it is a faculty operated by those 'who have a lively imagination, keen feelings, and what we call a tender heart'. For him and for others, 'sympathy' allows moral and aesthetic sensitivities to be equated. Feeling for others becomes the essential experience of literature and art. Alexander Gerard, in *An Essay on Taste* (1759), describes how a man of taste requires 'such a *sensibility of heart*, as fits a man for being easily moved, and for readily catching, as by infection, any passion, that a work is fitted to excite'. A tasteful reader is one whose sympathies are properly prepared. Critics of the second half of the eighteenth century are therefore often preoccupied, like novelists of the time, with the representation of and response to suffering. With suffering comes pathos, the proper relish of the discriminating gentleman. Gerard is conventional when he declares, 'the pathetic is a quality of so great moment in works of taste, a man, who is destitute of sensibility of heart, must be a very imperfect judge of them'.

One might say that novels are left out of Enlightenment aesthetics simply because they are still considered 'vulgar'. But this truism deserves to be probed. It tells us that the kinds of 'text' that comfortably belonged to 'the Enlightenment' – those on which the philosophers could try their experiments of sympathy – were those that were either experienced collectively (tragedy is the outstanding example, the subject of theoretical essays by Addison, Hume and Burke, among others), or as the shared objects of 'Taste' (a social as well as a critical standard). 'Taste' described aesthetic pleasures that might be shared by a self-conscious community of the polite and educated. 'Sensibility' could be imagined as an experience of reading, but only in order to explain the tasteful sampling of tragedy, sublimity and so on. The great contemporary activity of 'sympathetic' literary consumption – novel-reading – was hardly noticed by the writers on taste. Instead, it was a topic of concern to rival novelists (offering their fiction as an antidote to the dangerous effects of other novels) or to didactic moralists (whose descendant is Mr Collins in *Pride and Prejudice*, ludicrously shocked to discover that the Bennet daughters might be permitted to read novels at all).

The Enlightenment did not have room for 'the novel', yet the novel was its true imaginative enactment. In the eighteenth century, it was in novels that the individual self – the experience of the self as individual – was most affectingly represented. Novels as different as those of Defoe and Fielding might equally be called 'empiricist': texts that tell the 'low' yet representative story of an individual who discovers his or her own resources, and thereby makes him- or herself. Comic conclusions sometimes require narratives with the contours of fairy-tale (foundlings turn out to be heirs to fortunes) and official piety requires protagonists to recognize the workings of providence in their histories. None the less, eighteenth-century novels do show how particular undaunted individuals make themselves from their experiences. This is one of the reasons why, whatever the reservations of literary historians, Defoe's *Robinson Crusoe* will go on seeming like 'the first novel': how appropriate that the genre should seem to have its origins in the 'Strange Surprizing Adventures' of a man who fashions himself, as he also fashions pots and religion, from the elements of his experience – a narrator who makes sense of his life by presenting his particular and extraordinary experiences as if they were universally significant. The history of the novel will always seem to have at its beginning the narration of a man who tries to record what 'the Nature and Experience of things dictated to me'.

The very word most frequently used at the time to characterize the ambitions of the new genre indicates why we might think of novels as empiricist texts. 'Probability' is what mattered to novelists and novel-readers. 'Nor is Possibility alone sufficient to justify us, we must likewise within the Rules of Probability', declares the narrator of *Tom Jones*. There is mock solemnity in Fielding's tone, but also a keen sense of what will allow his readers to enjoy his novel. 'Probability' was the genre's appeal to experience. This appeal, so uncontroversial to the modern reader, was exactly what brought critical hostility. This was often not just hostility to the morally troubling effects of 'probability' in successful works of fiction: the apparent permissiveness of Fielding's fiction; Richardson's attention to sexual perils. It was also an antagonism to the vulgarity of detail, the descent to particularity. This, as much as the candour of novels, was what Samuel Johnson had in mind when he wrote an essay for *The Rambler* on the beguiling effects of fiction.

> The works of fiction, with which the present generation seems more particularly delighted, are such as exhibit life in its true state, diversified only by accidents that daily happen in the world, and influenced by passions and qualities that are really to be found in conversing with mankind.

Accident, as much as passion, was the unfortunate preoccupation of this type of book.

> It is justly considered as the greatest excellency of art, to imitate nature; but it is necessary to distinguish those parts of nature, which are most proper for imitation: greater care is still required in representing life, which is so often discoloured by passion, or deformed by wickedness.

It must also have been what Johnson's great admirer Fanny Burney had in mind when she promised in her Preface to *Evelina* (1778) that her novel would 'draw characters from nature, though not from life'. 'Nature' was the generality that dignified a writer's inventions; 'life' was distracting particularity. This thought was still so powerful that novelists themselves would go on claiming 'nature' as the true standard of their narratives.

The appeal of novels to 'experience' was, and is, not just a matter of their 'probable' content. It was also a matter of formal innovation. One of the ways in which novels mapped the particularity of an individual's experience, and sense of self, is caught by a phrase used by the novelist Samuel Richardson to describe his own fiction: *'writing to the moment'*. Richardson used it to explain why he wrote his novels in letters – a form much followed in the second half of the eighteenth century, most famously by Rousseau and Goethe, but entirely abandoned by novelists at the beginning of the nineteenth century. Letters aspired to the present tense. Sometimes this is the present tense of 'life' itself, as letters are actually broken in upon by the events that they must go on to document. The effect is brilliantly parodied in Fielding's *Shamela*, whose calculating heroine (a cynic's redaction of Richardson's Pamela) takes to its logical extreme Richardson's method and scribbles away even as her would-be seducer makes his attack.

> Odsbobs! I hear him just coming in at the Door. You see I write in the present Tense, as Parson *Williams* says. Well, he is in bed between us, we both shamming a Sleep, he steals his Hand into my Bosom, which I, as if in my Sleep, press close to me with mine, and then pretend to awake – I no sooner see him, but I scream out to Mrs. *Jervis*, she feigns likewise but just to come to herself.

Richardson's original, credibly and vividly, offered the present tense of fear, hope and self-examination as the very chart of individual consciousness. The method was continued and extended in *Clarissa*, and we do not have to lose our enjoyment of Fielding's burlesque to enjoy also the present-tense drama of Richardson's tragedy. Here, for instance, Clarissa writes a letter to her friend Anna Howe as she waits in her 'Ivy summerhouse' for a surreptitious meeting with Lovelace.

> But why do I trouble you (and myself, at such a crisis) with these impertinencies? – yet I would forget if I could the nearest evil, the interview; because, my apprehensions increasing as the hour is at hand, I should, were my attention to be engrossed by them, be unfit to see him if he does come. . . .
>
> I dare say we shall be all to pieces. But I don't care for that. It would be hard if I, who have held out so sturdily to my father and uncles, should not – But he is at the garden-door –
>
> . . . .
>
> I was mistaken! – How may noises *un*-like, be made *like* what one fears! – Why flutters the fool so!

'The fool' of Clarissa's exclamation is her heart. The letters out of which Richardson makes her story record its flutters.

Richardson coined the phrase 'writing to the moment', but it stands for much of what characterizes 'the rise of the novel'. Daniel Defoe's novels, of course, were all in the form of autobiographies, supposedly written by their protagonists. His narrators look back, in penitence, on lives of crime and adventure – of fear and opportunity. Though they tell us of events supposedly long past, they keep breaking into the present tense as they reflect on past folly or sinfulness. Truly, the drama of these texts, just as much as Richardson's epistolary tales, is 'to the moment'. It is the drama of a character who is attempting to discern the patterns of his life – and attempting to turn his life into a pattern. To be an individual – which, in the novels of both Defoe and Richardson, frequently means being on one's own – is to be committed to making oneself an example. The pretext of Defoe's narrators is that they are warnings to their readers. The present drama of narration is the narrator's attempt to look steadily at his or her past error. So Robinson Crusoe, Moll Flanders and the rest make themselves as they tell their stories, sometimes flinching from what they must say, or failing to be able to express what they once felt. Even their inadequacies of vocabulary are appropriate to the drama of an individual attempting to explain him- or herself.

For Defoe's and Richardson's protagonists, this self-explanation is also a religious exercise. The self is not yet distinct from the soul. For the eighteenth-century novelist (albeit also a clergyman) who takes most literally the lessons of empiricism, Laurence Sterne, the present tense of telling accidents and chance associations gives a shape to the self without any recourse to a Protestant creed of introspection. Sterne's *Tristram Shandy* (1759–1767) gives us its narrator's 'Life and Opinions', and conjures that 'Life' as it races across the page in a hectic yet connected progress of dashes and digressions. Tristram calls himself 'sport of small accidents'. If there were to be a novel of the Enlightenment, this should be it. Its very first page reaches for Locke's *Essay Concerning Human Understanding* to explain the odd associations that govern understanding, given shape by experiences without necessary connection. A good deal of the novel is taken up by the narrator's story of the mischances by which he came to be called 'Tristram' (Tristram being the name that his name-obsessed father most abhorred), for this is the oddest association of all. The merest accident makes the narrator what he is. Inherently, a name may be nothing, yet, once given, it *is* that person. And all the ruminations on the accidents that form an individual are happening, as we read, in the moment-by-moment inventions and self-interruptions and flights of wry fantasy of Tristram's narration.

What Sterne also discovered was that his particular 'writing to the moment' was as well adapted to mischief as to sentiment. *Tristram Shandy* uses the halts and hesitations of narration in sometimes crudely suggestive ways, and attracted the censure of many contemporary moralists. What the critics wanted were the scenes of pathos, where the narrative was stopped by feelings that the sensitive reader could relish. One of these highlights was the death of 'Le Fever'.

130

The blood and spirits of *Le Fever*, which were waxing cold and slow within him, and were retreating to their last citadel, the heart, – rallied back, – the film forsook his eyes for a moment, – he looked up wishfully in my uncle *Toby*'s face, – then cast a look upon his boy, – and that *ligament*, fine as it was, – was never broken. –

Nature instantly ebb'd again, – the film returned to its place, – the pulse flutter'd – stopp'd – went on – throb'd – stopp'd again – moved – stopp'd – Shall I go on? – No.

As in *Clarissa*, the pulse flutters. And, as with Richardson's fiction, enthusiasts wrote as if the reader's pulse also fluttered. The editor of *The Beauties of Sterne* said that he had had to keep the 'Le Fever' episode at some distance, in his anthology, from other famously affecting passages. If arranged alphabetically, as he had originally planned, these 'would be too closely connected for the *feeling reader*, and would wound the bosom of *sensibility* too deeply'. In a culture in which sensibility was valued, the experience of reading was likely to be especially affecting, even especially wounding. In a culture in which the art of being an individual involved learning to have feelings, the best kinds of fiction made for the best tuition.

Part III

ROMANTICISM

9

ROMANTIC TRAVEL

Roger Cardinal

Whereas the eighteenth century had proposed a reassuring, 'enlightened' model of the psyche, stabilized by reasoned definition and exhibiting all the cohesion of a well-tuned, visible mechanism, the nineteenth century found itself wrestling with alternative perspectives which granted space to mystery and imbalance. The hallmarks of Romantic thought were its accentuation of unconstrained impulse and its de-emphasizing of rationality as the shaping principle of art. Romantic writers, painters and musicians placed ever greater store by the individual imagination, cherishing those peak experiences wherein the creative spirit sheds the fetters of humdrum circumstance. This chapter will sketch a silhouette of the Romantic sensibility by identifying just one of its manifold manifestations – the literary and artistic documentation of the experience of travel – as representative of the whole. If one accepts that the artistic output of Romanticism was governed by an urge to transcend the familiar and the commonplace, then its practice of journeying into unknown territories may be said to have functioned as a fundamental trope for aesthetic and psychic exploration.

Romantic travel literature had first to define itself against what had gone before. In eighteenth-century Europe, travel writing had tended to fall into two broad categories. First, there were the journals of navigators who tabulated their strenuous excursions to remote parts of the world, many of them unexplored. The momentum of texts such as Louis-Antoine de Bougainville's *Voyage autour du monde* and Captain James Cook's various *Journals* is broadly fuelled by scientific curiosity, the desire to know more about the world and its peoples; only incidentally does objective documentation give way to autobiographical or self-contemplative material. Likewise, Volney's *Voyage en Syrie et en Égypte* (1787) is a strictly impersonal narrative, full of geographical and social observation and strictly unmarked by intimate authorial comment. In due course there arose a second category, the *conte philosophique*, in which the format of a narrative of travel (whether to a real or an entirely invented location) was frequently adapted for philosophical and moral debate. The didactic character of such writing is exemplified in Voltaire's *Candide* and Swift's *Gulliver's Travels*, which exploit foreign otherness as a device to scrutinize social ills back home.

Neither of these two approaches encouraged self-scrutiny on the part of the narrating subject, whose personal preferences, anxieties or yearnings remained largely unspoken. Hence, broadly speaking, the characteristic voice of the Enlightenment travel writer was disinterested, sober, analytical and philosophical. Conversely, as we shall see, that of his nineteenth-century Romantic successor would be committed, impassioned, evocative and lyrical. In effect, the adventurous ethos of the young Romantics of the new century led them to reject the values of their fathers, to privilege creative vision over good sense, and to celebrate the agitations of personal perception as being ultimately a more meaningful guide to experience than sober, objective observation. If it is true that 'travel broadens the mind', then what now becomes interesting is less the accumulation of factual travel experiences within that broadened consciousness than its curious flexibility as a recording mechanism equipped with a subjective lens. For once the Romantic traveller had thrown off any lingering scruple about objectivity, he could assume the role of director and even script-writer of the travel scenario. The Fichtean trope of the dynamic relation between the Self (*das Ich*) and the Non-Self (*das Nicht-Ich*) which it at once confronts and in a sense projects, may be taken as an image of the free Romantic consciousness as it crosses landscapes and transcribes impressions both literal and imaginary.

It is the purpose of this chapter to argue that, insofar as the prominent topoi which circulate in a given epoch mark out visible grooves of cultural reflex, so Romantic travel – by which is meant the sum of the actual journeys made by Romantics as well as their repercussions in literature, painting and the other arts – can be read as a collective discourse and a revealing cross-section of the early modern European psyche. One last adjustment of this chapter's scope needs to be completed. Undoubtedly, encounters with foreign peoples and explorations of distant cities are integral to Romantic experience, yet, in what follows, I have chosen to concentrate my remarks upon the relation of the Romantic traveller to the natural world, and more specifically upon those modes, tempi and loca-tions of travel which correspond to characteristically Romantic ways of thinking and imagining. And having started by contrasting Romantic travel with its eighteenth-century antecedents, I shall close by contrasting it (and thereby dating its decline to the late 1840s) with that post-Romantic mode of journeying known as modern tourism.

In Europe, the golden age of Romantic travel began in 1815, with the lifting of the restrictions on easy movement which had obtained through-out the Napoleonic wars. Of course, Romantic travellers had already begun to appear before this date, as witness such figures as Goethe, whose celebrated Italian journey dates back to 1786–7, or Chateaubriand, who transposed picturesque details of his North American tour of 1791 into a lushly evocative novella entitled *Atala* (1801). Moreover, several early Romantics had been mobile during the Napoleonic period. Some participated in the French invasion of Egypt in 1798, which at a stroke established the Orient as an inescapable temptation for the Romantic imagination; while Stendhal's first trip outside France took place in 1800, when, at the age of 17, he followed the French forces into Italy and enlisted in the cavalry. (In 1812 he would participate in the Grande Armée's doomed trek to Moscow and back.)

All the same, the Allied victory at Waterloo marked a watershed in travel opportunities for the younger generation and imbued the very concept of travel with an aura of the challenging, the colourful, the exceptional. If to be a Romantic meant to take seriously one's least programmed impulses, it became *de rigueur* to draw up vague yet irresistible itineraries which would guarantee experiences at odds with the norm. From now on, the passion for differentness, and the anticipation of being immersed in 'local colour', will determine the orbits of Romantic aspiration. A fashionable craving for Ossianic wildness will send Germans such as Emilie von Berlepsch, Felix Mendelssohn and Carl Gustav Carus to the remoter parts of Scotland. The French Romantics Hugo and Nerval will visit the Rhineland. Théophile Gautier will head for Spain, Algeria and Turkey; Prosper Mérimée for Sicily and Corsica; and Lamartine, Flaubert and Maxime du Camp for Egypt, the Lebanon and Asia Minor. A whole generation of Northern writers and artists will nominate the sunny climes of Italy and the Mediterranean as their spiritual home, thereby annexing the landscapes of Classical antiquity to their own Romantic geography, as witness Lamartine's poem 'Ischia', which converts a rocky islet off the Italian coast into a Romantic utopia, complete with its halo of other-worldliness:

> Sous ce ciel où la vie, où le bonheur abonde,
> Sur ces rives que l'oeil se plaît à parcourir,
> Nous avons respiré cet air d'un autre monde,
> Élise! . . . Et cependant on dit qu'il faut mourir!

(Beneath this sky where life and happiness abound, / On these shores which the eye so pleasurably scans, / We have breathed that air of another world, / Elise! . . . And still they say we are but mortal!)

Given that the obvious route down to Italy lies across the Alps, an intriguing set of associations begins to justify the Romantics' impulsive colouring of the European map: to swap the dark North for the bright South is tantamount to switching from prose to poetry, while the physical effort of toiling over steep passes on foot becomes an index of ethical commitment.

When, in Book VI of *The Prelude*, William Wordsworth relates how he walked over the Alps at the age of 20, he seems to imply that extreme muscular exertion in the mountains is a prerequisite of visionary experience. Moreover, we sense a certain elitism filtering into the discussion. Wordsworth's feat is nothing less than a rite of passage, qualifying him as an authentic Romantic, at once physically fit and metaphysically alert, receptive both to the material features of the environment and to 'the types and symbols of Eternity' which those features represent.

As another Romantic impelled to travel South in search of visions, Shelley likewise seizes the opportunity to foreground his personal engagement with the mountain setting, embarking on a lofty dialogue with nature which would be unthinkable in the lowland. The assumption which underpins his visionary poem 'Mont Blanc' is that the poet must climb up to such giddy spots as the thunderous Arve ravine if he wishes to achieve the quintessentially Romantic reconciliation of external nature and subjective mind:

> Thou art the path of that unresting sound,
> Dizzy Ravine! and when I gaze on thee
> I seem as in a trance sublime and strange
> To muse on my own separate fantasy,
> My own, my human mind, which passively
> Now renders and receives fast influencings,
> Holding an unremitting interchange
> With the clear Universe of Things around.

This interchange or reciprocity between a powerful nature and the powerful faculty of the imagination was so to affect contemporary painters as to promote the mountainscape to the Romantic genre *par excellence*. The more or less factual accounts of Swiss mountains painted by Caspar Wolf in the 1770s, and the queerly aseptic watercolours of the Aveyron Glacier made by Francis Towne in 1781, were in due course superseded by the more emphatic celebrations of the Alpine Sublime made by John Robert Cozens in the 1780s, and by the long series of dazzling mountainscapes executed by James Mallord William Turner, which began when, during a lull in the Napoleonic wars in 1802, he first spent two months in the Alps, feverishly cramming his sketchbooks with waterfalls, glaciers, lakes and snow-capped peaks. Though it is true that a sense of awe can sometimes be induced through artifice (as was the case with the Austrian Joseph Anton Koch, who constructed his grandiose views of the Tyrol mountains within the comfort of an Italian studio; or again of Caspar David Friedrich, whose emblematic *The Wanderer above the Sea of Mist* (1810) offers a vision so exaggeratedly sublime as to skirt the ridiculous), it is a tenet of Romantic art that abysses and crags must be read as authentications of transcendent physical and metaphysical experience.

Given that walking remained one of the most common means of travel throughout the first half of the early nineteenth century, especially for the young and impecunious, it is worth considering its relevance to the Romantic project. Perhaps it is the case that long-distance foot-travellers generally tend to be solitary and taciturn, and thereby to conform to one stereotype of the Romantic temperament. The typical Romantic is essentially a dawdler: whereas it is true that Wordsworth prided himself on reaching Italy after only fourteen weeks ('a march it was of military speed'), and that his friend Samuel Taylor Coleridge was a fell-walker of notable athleticism (in 1803, he averaged over thirty miles a day on an eight-day jaunt across Scotland), the Romantic prefers not to sprint through his elective spaces, but to linger, to gaze, to daydream. Physical meandering is the accompaniment of mental meandering. The young German painter Carl Philipp Fohr played the part of the wayfaring artist to perfection when he spent two summers in his teens drifting with a sketchbook along the Neckar Valley and through the Black Forest; in 1816 he hiked south to Italy, taking several weeks to reach Rome, where, in a tragic accident, he was shortly to drown in the Tiber. He prefigures the hero of Eichendorff's novella *Aus dem Leben eines Taugenichts* ('Memoirs of a Good-for-Nothing') (1826), who drifts aimlessly across an indeterminate Bohemian landscape, until circumstances tumble magically into a pattern and his destiny is revealed. In the German tradition, artist-novels such as Goethe's *Wilhelm Meisters Wanderjahre*, Ludwig Tieck's *Franz Sternbalds Wanderungen* and Eduard Mörike's *Maler Nolten* are built on the assumption that independent, unprogrammed travelling will, by definition, lead to creative insight and artistic maturity. When Karl Philipp Moritz explored England in 1782, he did so entirely on foot, and in his *Reisen eines Deutschen in England* (1783) expresses himself somewhat surprised by the local reliance on horse-drawn transport. A century later, Robert Louis Stevenson would spend a strenuous fortnight trekking through the steep hillsides of southern France: the first-person narrative of *Travels with a Donkey in the Cévennes* (1879) equates solitariness and physical exposure with states of spiritual intensity, and may be counted a late appendix to the canon of Romantic travel literature. (Equally, Stevenson's text is consistent with the thematics of 'travel-as-travail' which survives in the best-selling paperback narratives of our own century. Today's solo mountaineers and round-the-world yachtsmen almost unfailingly invoke the cliché of spiritual illumination through arduous effort.)

Of course, there are other forms of locomotion in the Romantic period which facilitated kindred states of being. The brilliant literary and philosophical output of the poet Novalis, dating from about 1796 until his death in 1801, ran parallel with a hectic professional career as a geologist and surveyor in the employ of the office of mines of the state of Saxony. Novalis once remarked that 'I have not entirely found my sphere; but one must perhaps sit in all kinds of saddle in order to find the one that is truly comfortable'. It happened that his surveying duties necessitated repeated trips across the region on horseback, so that long hours spent musing in the saddle in the open air provided the nourishment for such quintessential Romantic texts as the novel *Heinrich von Ofterdingen* (1802), with its themes of yearning and spiritual revelation. More pragmatic inspirations from horseback travel shape William Cobbett's *Rural Rides* (1830), where evocations of the English countryside are offset by sharp comments on the living conditions of the rural poor.

The back of a camel might be said to have offered a distinctive option for Europeans venturing into the uncharted deserts of the Middle East. Charles Monk, a Victorian traveller of the 1840s and author of *The Golden Horn* (1851), strikes the perfect Romantic note in observing that 'the slow and rocking movement of the dromedary tends to produce that state of reverie, when the memory recalls events long past by, and conjures up to the imagination faces and things that once were familiar'. It seems characteristic of such a lulling mode of locomotion that it should privilege inner over outer experience, and conjure up images steeped in a pleasurable nostalgia. Admittedly there were those less inclined to romanticize the desert. When, in 1849, Gustave Flaubert and his friend Maxime du Camp made a long journey through Egypt and the Holy Land, one of the high points of their itinerary was a crossing from the Nile to the Red Sea when they all but expired of thirst. In his *Souvenirs littéraires*, Du Camp records how Flaubert nearly drove him mad with his delirious ravings about lemon sorbet; and the fact that Flaubert was generally bad-tempered during the journey may account for that notorious quip in his *Dictionary of Received Ideas* which derides the orientalist as 'a man who has done a lot of travelling'. However this may be, Flaubert's flamboyant fiction *Salammbô* (1862) is uninhibited in its adherence to the Romantic myth of the Orient as the ultimate site of *couleur locale* and of sensual and metaphysical intensity. As Edward Said's classic study *Orientalism* (1978) has shown, the journey to the East played the part of a decisive mirage for the Romantics, drawing a paradoxical authority from its very lack of substance.

During the first half of the nineteenth century, travel by water remained a significant alternative to travel overland. A good many intercontinental journeys could be listed here, from Chateaubriand's transatlantic voyage of 1791 to Adalbert von Chamisso's world tour of 1815 to 1818 on the Russian brig *Rurik*. The latter journey was a scientific and exploratory mission, on which Chamisso carried out the functions of a botanist, geologist and geographer as well as of a diarist and travel writer. Prized for its novel descriptions of the Pacific Islands, his *Reise um die Welt* ('Journey around the World', 1821) is the sole instance of a Romantic circumnavigation; unless one counts Charles Darwin, whose scientific voyages of 1831 to 1836 gave rise to *The Voyage of the Beagle* (1839), a text whose scientificity is interestingly qualified by impulsive passages of a Romantic cast.

Passing mention may also be made of the great geographer and naturalist Alexander von Humboldt, who travelled in Mesoamerica and South America during the period 1799 to 1804, and in Central Asia and Siberia in 1829: his *Ansichten der Natur* ('Aspects of Nature') (1808) includes descriptions of exotic regions which were to influence such theorists of Romantic landscape art as Carl Gustav Carus and John Ruskin.

One of the most celebrated sites of the age was Fingal's Cave, a basalt formation on the remote Hebridean island of Staffa. Felix Mendelssohn's boat trip there during his Scottish travels of 1829 inspired his *Hebrides Overture*, and the trip was emulated by painters like Turner in 1831 and Carl Gustav Carus in 1844, confirming that the scientific novelty had become an accepted artistic topos. Turbulent waters are a favourite trope for the Romantic sensibility, as witness Turner's portrayals of storms in the English Channel and the North Sea; though it is surely Victor Hugo who deserves the title of *homme-océan* for having, through his two decades of exile on the Channel Islands, elaborated a grand myth of the solitary genius confronting a watery vastness which successively symbolizes night, the cosmos, death, chaos, the unconscious, the imagination and the universal abyss of dreams. Hugo's boat trips and daily swims provided the physical context for one of the most elaborate exercises in visionary Romanticism, the sequence 'Au bord de l'infini' ('On the Brink of the Infinite'), which forms the sixth book of *Les Contemplations* (1856). The poem 'Ce que dit la bouche d'ombre' ('Sayings of the shadow-voice') introduces a spectral figure who, meeting the poet by the cliff-top dolmen at Rozel, proceeds to preach in metaphors of gigantism which transfigure the Universe into a monstrous hydra with a body 'scaly with stars'.

> Là tout flotte et s'en va dans un naufrage obscur;
> Dans ce gouffre sans bord, sans soupirail, sans mur,
> De tout ce qui vécut pleut sans cesse la cendre;
> Et l'on voit tout au fond, quand l'ocil ose y descendre,
> Au delà de la vie, et du souffle et du bruit,
> Un affreux soleil noir d'où rayonne la nuit!

(There, everything floats and drifts away in a dark shipwreck; / In that abyss without margin, without skylight, without wall, / Rain down the ashes of all things that have lived; / And when one's eye dares to go down into the very depths, / It makes out, beyond all life, all breath, all sound, / An horrific black sun whence night gleams forth!)

In this same context, it is worth noting the high incidence of aquatic allusions in the poems of Shelley, as in 'Alastor: or the Spirit of Solitude', which traces a poet's career in terms of an allegorical journey through space and time. A lengthy central section details a dreamlike voyage in a tiny boat, which is swept across tempestuous seas and up a swirling Caucasian river, where the poet finally relinquishes 'the hovering powers of life'. Shelley it was, of course, who confirmed the mythic fusion of an actual and a literary journeying-to-the-limits when he drowned in a storm off Leghorn while out sailing his yacht.

For his part, the German artist Caspar David Friedrich was often inspired by an image of the sea as something cold and deathlike. Based on empirical sketches of the Baltic, which admittedly can often be uncannily still, Friedrich's seascapes typically include silhouetted human figures who stare out from the shore as if mesmerized by the horizon. Though inspired by a historical event, the heavily allegorical *Eismeer* ('Arctic Shipwreck') (1824) is a fictional image; it seems designed to delete all trace of the human, with only a few remnants of a sailing vessel to be seen amid piles of mighty ice-floes.

The Romantic generation seems to have been particularly attracted to exploring the Mediterranean by sea, that is to say, aboard a sailing-ship. Coleridge had been one of the first Romantics to seek out the Eastern Mediterranean, journeying in 1804 to 1805 to Malta, Sicily (where he climbed Mount Etna) and Naples, where he met Humboldt and Ludwig Tieck. Chateaubriand made a melancholy pilgrimage to Jerusalem in 1805 to 1806, recorded in a lengthy and typically self-absorbed memoir. Prosper Mérimée was to explore Sardinia and Sicily, appreciative both of their Classical sites and their contemporary folklore. The greatest pioneer of Romantic travel was, of course, Lord Byron, whose wanderings between 1809 and 1811 encompassed Malta, Albania, the Greek islands, Athens and Constantinople. Byron's autobiographical travel poem *Childe Harold's Pilgrimage* (1812) helped to fix his public image as the epitome of the exiled, ever restless creative spirit, an image which coloured much Romantic poetry of travel and even encouraged orchestral homages such as Franz Liszt's *Années de pèlerinage* or Hector Berlioz's *Harold en Italie* (1834). When Berlioz travelled to Italy to receive the Prix de Rome in March 1831, the Alpine passes were still closed, and his sea-crossing from Marseille to Leghorn constituted an alternative rite of passage in the form of a terrific storm.

Within the Italian sphere, ancient sites like Naples and Rome, with their Classical ruins and natural beauty, emerged as locales entirely amenable to Romantic treatment. Venice, that aquatic city *par excellence*, inspired Turner's most Romantic images, in which the painter's brush transmutes architectural shapes into wonderfully vaporous mirages. During 1834 and 1835, the Heidelberg artist Karl Rottmann visited Sicily and Greece and painted vast sunlit panoramas with archaic ruins and tiny isolated figures. Eugène Delacroix's stay in Morocco between 1831 and 1832 confirmed the Romanticization of his perceptions and his palette; while artists like Prosper Marilhat and Eugène Fromentin annexed Egypt and Algeria to the Romantic map, establishing an unmistakable repertoire of motifs expressing Arabian 'local colour', including palm trees, minarets and anonymous robed figures. The same exotic locales were favoured by early photographers such as Francis Frith, Gustave Le Gray and Maxime du Camp, who sailed to Egypt, the Lebanon and the Holy Land.

Throughout the nineteenth century, it was common practice to integrate passages of river-boat travel into any land journey of some length. Caspar David Friedrich never once made the trip to Italy which had become *de rigueur* for his contemporaries, yet he regularly left his Southern German home to spend summers on the Baltic island of Ruegen, close to his birthplace at Greifswald: the itinerary involved cross-country coach travel, but its first and longest leg was by boat from Dresden down the Elbe, a river portrayed in many of his works. Entranced portrayals of river towns were to become one of Turner's trademarks, and his sketch-books document a lifelong passion for travel along the waterways of Europe: the Rhine, the Neckar, the Rhône, the Loire, the Thames, the Severn. In the pre-Romantic poetry of Friedrich Hölderlin, the great rivers of the Danube, the Rhine and the Rhône – all rising in the Alps – provide a topographical pretext for grandiose meditations on Europe and its spiritual destiny. One early scene in Josef Freiherr von Eichendorff's enig-matic novel *Ahnung und Gegenwart* (1815) characteristically dramatizes river travel as the site of deep unconscious impulse. Having left home in search of his fate, the young Count Friedrich is descending the Danube past a dark whirlpool when he spies a beautiful girl on another boat: her eyes meet his and provoke the most intense erotic sensations, as well as inexplicable memory flashes. This primal aquatic scene is the key to all subsequent happenings and revelations in the novel. The Germanic folk-song may also be cited here, with its motifs of drifting boats, water sprites and rings dropped into the flood: Achim von Arnim and Franz Brentano collected such material in their folksong album *Des Knaben Wunderhorn* (1805), while Heinrich Heine penned his own version of a traditional tale from the Rhine Valley about an alluring siren named Lorelei. (Even French visitors like Nerval and Hugo were seduced into writing about her, while the 'Rhénanes' poems composed by Guillaume Apollinaire between 1901 and 1902, with their nostalgic reprise of the same riverine motifs, mark the persistence of these Romantic associations into our own century.)

No nineteenth-century traveller in Egypt could forgo the pleasure of going up the Nile by boat. The English photographer Francis Frith was in Egypt during 1856 and 1859 and ascended to the almost mythical region of Nubia, bringing back shots of the Sphinx and the temple at Luxor, and of at least one crocodile. Maxime du Camp likewise travelled on the Nile and took sumptuous photographs of ruins, publishing 125 original prints in the volume *Égypte, Nubie, Palestine et Syrie* (1852). It is said that as a child Du Camp had daydreams of floating to China on a wooden boat, and the anecdote lends support to the comparison of aquatic reverie in Romanticism with those naive fantasies to which Baudelaire alludes in the opening lines of 'Le Voyage', whereby the lack of actual travel experience in the child sets no limits to its greedy imaginings:

> Pour l'enfant, amoureux de cartes et d'estampes,
> L'univers est égal à son vaste appétit.

(For the child, engrossed in maps and prints, / The universe is equal to his vast appetite.)

The sensation of drifting in a boat seems especially conducive to fantasies of omnipresence and omnipotence. That liminal text of Romanticism, Rousseau's *Les Rêveries du promeneur solitaire* ('Reveries of the Solitary Walker') (1782), devotes a whole chapter to the pleasures of daydreaming while stretched out in a row-boat upon a tranquil lake. This innocuous situation secretes a dense drama of affinities, insofar as Rousseau's solitary consciousness emerges as the locus of a series of concentric circles – self, lakeside, countryside and encircling mountains being, as it were, locked within a system of interrelated magnetic energies. Here, as in many other representations in Romantic art and poetry, we discern a characteristic situation of 'centredness', whereby the focal consciousness exerts imaginative sway over its surroundings, the individual subjectivity merging into, or, more actively, absorbing, the external environment.

One might speculate about another contemporary mode of locomotion, the hot air balloon, which arguably corresponds perfectly to the Romantic ideal, given its complicity with invisible natural forces, its ecstatic buoyancy, its freedom and fickleness, in short its congruence with the myth of Icarus, wherein, as Maurice Shroder has suggested, many aspirations of the Romantic artist are figured. Serious experiments in manned flight date back to those of the Montgolfier brothers in the late eighteenth century, and despite being plagued by the innate unpredictability of air currents, ballooning continued to flourish throughout the following century. The photographer Félix Nadar, friend of writers like Nerval and Baudelaire, is known to have taken aerial snapshots of Paris from his balloon *Le Conquérant*. However, as a literary topos, ballooning remained strangely under-exploited. Among the few instances of its treatment are Jean-Paul's proto-Romantic fantasia *Des Luftschiffers Giannozzo Seebuch* ('The Balloonist Giannozzo's Logbook') (1801), Edgar Allan Poe's tongue-in-cheek tale 'The Unparalleled Adventures of one Hans Pfaall' (1835) and Jules Verne's *Cinq Semaines en ballon* ('Five Weeks in a Balloon') (1863), the first novel in his long cycle of *Extraordinary Journeys in Known and Unknown Worlds*.

Verne's narrative relates a harrowing air crossing of the African continent, and represents an intriguing mixture of genuine scientific data and the most fanciful speculation.

Perhaps the decisive mode of transport for the Romantic traveller was the horse-drawn coach or carriage. During his youth, Thomas de Quincey travelled considerable distances by mail-coach, and late in life, composed a rhapsody in its honour, *The English Mail-Coach* (1849). Both a factual essay and an exercise in poetic divagation, it includes a demonstration of those runaway images which characterize the mental fugues occasioned by the writer's addiction to opium. The four-part work opens with 'The Glory of Motion', which describes the mail-system and the giddy sensations of journeying at speed in the cheap seats on top of the coach, in the open air high above the road. De Quincey contrasts such sensations with those available on the railway train, where 'iron tubes and boilers' disconnect 'the heart of man and its electric thrillings' from the tactile immediacies of wheel, hoof and bumpy road, thereby cheating him of a proper consciousness of velocity. The 'grandeur and power' of the old mail-coach is synonymous with an acuteness of physical response which, for De Quincey, is equally a source of creative intensity.

> We heard our speed, we saw it, we felt it as thrilling; and this speed was not the product of blind insensate agencies, that had no sympathy to give, but was incarnated in the fiery eyeballs of the noblest among brutes, in his dilated nostril, spasmodic muscles, and thunder-beating hoofs.

'Going Down with Victory' evokes the glorious years between Trafalgar and Waterloo, when news of British victories was relayed by the mails; De Quincey describes a glorious nocturnal journey out of London, when the coach bore news of the victory of Talavera. 'The Vision of Sudden Death' is the nightmarish narrative of a real life incident of 1816 or 1817, when De Quincey travelled up one night from Manchester to the Lake District: perched next to a comatose coachman on the box, his senses heightened by a prior intake of laudanum, he is the paralysed witness to a hair's-breadth escape from a horrifying collision with another vehicle. The final section of *The English Mail-Coach* is 'The Dream-Fugue', a dreamlike improvisation whose headlong sequence of ecstatic images of high-speed locomotion is implicitly driven by the rhythms of the horse-drawn coach. Clearly, the attribution of a delirious dimension to coach travel also implies its kinship to the drug 'trip'; and, as Alethea Hayter has demonstrated, parallels between travelling, creative inspiration and drug-taking are standard associations in the work of several other drug-takers in the Romantic or post-Romantic orbit, such as Coleridge, Alphonse Rabbe, Baudelaire and Rimbaud.

Alfred de Vigny's poem 'La Maison du berger' ('The Shepherd's

Caravan') (1844) reveals a similar attachment, albeit with a stress on the propensity of horse-drawn vehicles to convey the traveller at slower tempi conducive to gentler reveries. The poem begins with a classic exposition of Romantic topography, contrasting the city as the site of constriction and harassment with the countryside as the realm of liberation and relaxation. Addressed to a mythic Éva, the poet's lengthy verses present the shepherd's caravan, with its soundless wheels and enclosed interior, as the perfect locus of escapist fantasy. The caravan becomes a crucible of both erotic and poetic yearning, sexual desire generating visions of passionate ubiquity:

> Je verrai, si tu veux, les pays de la neige,
> Ceux où l'astre amoureux dévore et resplendit,
> Ceux que heurtent les vents, ceux que la mer assiège,
> Ceux où le pôle obscur sous sa glace est maudit.
> Nous suivrons du hasard la course vagabonde.
> Que m'importe le jour, que m'importe le monde?
> Je dirai qu'ils sont beaux quand tes yeux l'auront dit.

(If you consent, I shall see the lands where snow reigns supreme, / Those where the ardent star devours and shines, / Those beaten by winds, those besieged by the sea, / Those where the dark pole is accursed beneath its ice. / We shall follow the vagabond trail of chance. / What care I for daylight, for the world? / I shall only declare them beautiful once your eyes have said so.)

Vigny now introduces circumstantial material into the poem with a diatribe against the modern railway system in France. This technological innovation has, so the poet contends, entirely disrupted man's natural relation to the environment. Not that Vigny is an early exponent of eco-logical awareness. Rather, he has anxieties about the impact of trains upon the human sensibility: they go too fast, they are commercial, they are dangerous. Drawing on images of bestial cruelty, he alludes to a catastrophic derailment on the Versailles line in 1842, which killed fifty-seven passengers. Above all, he insists, railways are soulless and unnatural. On trains, people sit rigidly in their assigned seats, trapped within 'a cold and calculating silence'. Vigny's argument is that railways represent a futile victory over time and space, a graceless conquest which depletes our authentic experience of the earth we inhabit.

Having so roundly dismissed rail travel, Vigny now turns to the Romantic alternative, extolling the virtues of the horse-drawn coach. The selfsame preference was voiced by John Ruskin in a nostalgic passage of *Praeterita* (1885–1889) which insists that coach-travellers were typically never in a hurry, since they could start at any hour they chose, given that the horses would always wait. Gérard de Nerval adopts a similarly carefree attitude:

I always like to rely a little upon chance. The numerical precision of railway stations, the exactitude of steamboats which arrive at a fixed hour or day, can scarcely delight a poet or a painter, or a simple archeologist or collector like myself.

As for Vigny's coach, it turns out to be a variation on the shepherd's caravan, in so far as each facilitates an imaginative focus upon external reality, which is appreciated as a sequence of vitalizing impressions and not as a numbed abstraction. 'La Maison du berger' closes with the brief portrayal of a mythic figure called *la Rêverie amoureuse* ('amorous Reverie'): her function is to allegoricize Vigny's conception of the Romantic imagination and to show that being responsive to the environment is tantamount to scrutinizing Nature's 'divine secrets'. Unfortunately, this glimpsed reconciliation of spirit and matter, of consciousness and nature, seems to be no more than conjectural, for, Vigny implies, the old modes of travel are already obsolete.

> On n'entendra jamais piaffer sur une route
> Le pied vif du cheval sur les pavés en feu:
> Adieu, voyages lents, bruits lointains qu'on écoute,
> Le rire du passant, les retards de l'essieu,
> Les détours imprévus des pentes variées,
> Un ami rencontré, les heures oubliées,
> L'espoir d'arriver tard dans un sauvage lieu.

(No longer shall we hear the horse's lively hoof / Scrape upon the highway's fiery cobbles: / Farewell to desultory journeys, to distant sounds one cranes to hear, / To the laughter of a passer-by, to delays caused by a broken axle, / The unforeseen detours of shifting slopes, / An encounter with a friend, the sensation of losing track of time, / The hope of turning up late in some wild place.)

Here lie encoded several fundamentals of the Romantic project – the fertility of unprogrammed, nonchalant itineraries; the suggestive magic of distance and wildness; the excitement of tactile engagement; the equation of strangeness with authenticity. It is true that not all Vigny's contemporaries would assent to these priorities: for many, the prospect of arriving late in some wild place would seem the height of inconvenience. Yet in taking the gamble on uncertainty and risk, Vigny distinguishes himself as a true Romantic traveller. To stumble upon otherness without foreknowledge is the experiential equivalent of launching one's creative imagination into the visionary mode, unhampered by reason. Whether we equate that 'wild place' with the natural wilderness, or whether we take a step further and equate it with the unconscious (thereby hastening a comparison with the surrealists and their capricious journeys into inner space on the imaginary vehicle of psychic automatism), the fact remains

147

that Vigny is emphatically recommending a tempo of poetic thought and a sphere of action which are not tied to routine. The appraisal of contrasted modes of travel in this poem amounts to a celebration of the authentic impulses which structure the Romantic self. Alas, the definition of Romantic travel to which Vigny gives his vote is all the more Romantic for being already doomed to extinction.

Historically speaking, the days of the horse-drawn coach were indeed numbered. As historians like Wolfgang Schivelbusch have shown, from the mid-century onwards steam-propelled forms of locomotion began to epitomize speed and efficiency, enforcing a very different tempo, while also making travel more affordable and thus more democratic. A regular cross-channel steamship link had been established as early as 1816, just months after Waterloo. Steamboats were active on the Rhine by 1828, and shortly thereafter on the Rhône and the Danube. Steamships were soon plying in the Mediterranean, where a regular link between Marseille and Alexandria opened in 1835. In England, the first railway line to carry passengers as well as freight opened between Stockton and Darlington in 1823; it ran on a traction engine. It was followed by the Liverpool to Manchester link of 1830, which exploited George Stephenson's famous 'Rocket', the first efficient locomotive. These successes were soon followed by other links, such as London to Birmingham in 1838, and London to Bristol in 1841. A rail network existed in Switzerland from 1844, and by 1846 the image of the melancholy dreamer arriving by gondola at that most Romantic of foreign cities, Venice, was superseded by the spectacle of tourist crowds pouring off the train at the terminus. A year later, despite Wordsworth's opposition, a new railway spur pierced the heart of the Lake District at Windermere. One is tempted to see such assaults on the Romantic idyll as pivotal, marking the end of pure Romantic travel and the onset of modern tourism.

As James Buzard has argued, the growth of popular tourism during the nineteenth century compelled the Romantics hastily to reassess their ideology. Hitherto, the authenticity of a Romantic sensation had always been premised on its being not only intense but also unique, always 'for the first time'. The consciousness registering such a sensation had consequently felt obliged to represent itself as distinct from mass consciousness. Now, in the space of a few years, the elective sites of an intellectual elite were being devalued, de-sacralized, recycled as so many perfunctory stopovers on a pre-established circuit; and even though early tourists may have felt genuine awe when visiting sites made famous by luminaries of the stature of a Goethe or a Byron, the repeatability of the literary pilgrimage would soon make such sensations appear secondhand and lacklustre. From mid-century on, Thomas Cook's formulaic tours, with their guides, fixed schedules and itemized options, represented in effect the bourgeois alternative to improvised, poetic travel. For although early tourism undoubtedly fed off the poetic and exotic associations of Romanticism, and although it fostered the illusion of a democratized experience of the sublime, it equally required down-to-earth travel information, including details of distances, timetables, fares and the like. Such prosaic data were supplied by John Murray's pocket-sized *Guides* and, above all, the international handbooks published by Karl Baedeker of Leipzig from 1842 onwards. With their starred recommendations, their meticulously engraved fold-out maps, their details of hotel rates and tipping conventions and their edicts as to what underwear to pack and whether or not to drink the local water, the Baedeker guides to such regions as the Alps and the Rhineland distance themselves explicitly from true Romanticism. Anonymous in their tone and normalizing in their ideology, they invite the would-be traveller to tiptoe into situations of novelty but rarely of risk; in gesturing towards sublimity, they never compromise security. By contrast, Wordsworth's account of crossing the Alps had been idiosyncratic and exceptional, and of very little use to someone actually attempting to find their way through central Switzerland. Curiously, the same Wordsworth who preferred to wander 'lonely as a cloud' would, from 1810 on, publish successive editions of his own *Guide to the Lakes*, presumably not appreciating that to invite others to share in the solitude and silence of his Romantic retreat was precisely to endanger it.

The inference is that an uncompromisingly Romantic approach to travel is in fact so extreme and so unworldly as to be impossible to realize; and that the insuperable difficulty in sustaining a Romantic experience of wild or poetic places lies in the tendency of sites to forfeit their freshness in the very occasion of being discovered. Certainly the Romantic ideal of a fertile and unsullied natural world seems to have enjoyed rather a short life, being overtaken quite soon by more realistic images of an environment fast being overtaken by an industrial age.

In his early years, John Ruskin travelled extensively in the Alps, transcribing his sensations in both diary entries and drawings. The fourth volume of *Modern Painters* (1856) is crammed with extravagant yet accurate descriptions of rock formations, grasses, waterfalls, precipices, peaks and clouds. Yet by 1869 Ruskin has begun to speak of the defilement of the Alps: their luminosity has faded, the air has become smoky, the glaciers have ebbed, and the rushing torrents are murky and foul. Whereas he had previously relied on the transparency of the lakes, Ruskin now notes that 'this morning, on the Lake of Geneva, at half a mile from the beach, I could scarcely see my oar-blade a fathom deep'. Oddly, Ruskin seems not to blame humanity for this pollution. By the early 1870s, his paranoia has reached the stage of attributing a moral failing to nature herself: faith in the uplifting character of mountain scenery reels before the evidence of her self-mocking barbarism and clumsiness. 'The deadliest of all things to me is my loss of faith in nature', he wistfully records. 'No spring – no summer. Fog always, and the snow faded from the Alps.'

It is however quite possible that the very premises of the Romantic project contained the formula for its collapse. Novalis' celebrated equation of Romantic vision with a 'qualitative involution' engineered by the sheer authority of the percipient subjectivity, secretes an implicit disavowal:

> The world must be romanticized. . . . When I confer a higher meaning upon the commonplace, a mysterious aspect upon the ordinary, the dignity of the unknown upon what is known, or an appearance of infinity upon what is finite, I romanticize it.

In drawing attention to the magisterial power of the creative subject to confer special qualities upon what lies outside itself, Novalis tacitly concedes that the world is *not* intrinsically Romantic, and must receive poetic treatment before it can fulfil itself. It follows that, if the Romantic self should ever lose its potency, the non-self in isolation will fall short of the mark. The half-admission of a potential for disappointment is echoed in a passage from Rousseau's *Rêveries* in which the author relates how the sublime feelings he had marshalled after climbing a narrow Alpine path amid pines and solitary peaks were rudely deflated when he stumbled upon a stocking factory, built beside a precipice. Rousseau's anecdote encapsulates the antithesis of the sublime and the lowly, the exceptional and the everyday, and directs our attention to the phenomenon of Romantic irony, that sardonic alternative by which later Romantics would defend an idealistic position against rampant bourgeois materialism.

Yet my point would be that, almost from the outset, Romanticism was forced to incorporate into its idealism a tacit recognition of its incompatibility with real life. Whereas one might posit a primary Romanticism in which the ideal remains forever intact, it is surely the case that a secondary, more worldly Romanticism emerges with the post-Napoleonic generation. The explicit ironies of a Heinrich Heine or a Jules Laforgue are evidence that late versions of Romanticism thrived at the very interface between blithe aspiration and cruel actuality. I suggest that in fact few Romantics were so naively entranced as to have ignored the discrepancy; indeed the lament for a lost ideal was itself a Romantic commonplace from early on.

Others took the view that, if the real world was so inadequate, it might be better not to engage with it in the first place. Writing of his desert journeys with Flaubert, Maxime du Camp records his companion's curious indifference to actual encounters.

> He was utterly opposed to movement and action. Had it been possible for him, he would have preferred to travel stretched out motionless on a divan, watching the landscapes, ruins and cities pass by before him like the canvas of a mechanically unfolding panorama.

Du Camp's reference to an illusion of travel created by artifice crystallizes a post-Romantic or decadent conception of 'armchair travel' which has its own special taint of indulgence or perversity. An attitude of splendid renunciation is characteristic of the decadent hero Des Esseintes, portrayed in Joris-Karl Huysmans' novel *À Rebours* ('Against Nature') (1884) a man who prefers to relax in the phoney English pub on the Champs Elysées rather than put himself to the trouble of crossing the Channel to set foot on English soil; or again of the eponymous hero of the play *Axël* (1890) by Villiers de l'Isle-Adam, who persuades his beloved Sara to join him in relinquishing their dreams of departure to Palmyra, Bagdad or Jerusalem in favour of joint suicide.

> The calibre of our hope no longer permits us even to consider the earth. What could we ever expect from this miserable star but pallid reflections of such moments? The Earth, you say? What has it ever made real, this drop of icy muck afloat upon the heavens? Don't you see, it is the Earth which has become the Illusion!

I would suggest that this decadent cult of apathy, this aristocratic renunciation which privileges the mirage over the tactile, corresponds to a proclivity simultaneous with the original impulse of Romantic wanderlust. Midway through his 1843 tour of the Near East which was to furnish the raw material for *Le Voyage en Orient* (1851), Nerval sent a letter home to his friend Gautier in Paris which contains a passage of ultimate insight. Despite all his exertions, Nerval has found a fundamental flaw in the Romantic travel project. Actually to undertake a journey is to compromise the perfection of the dream which motivates that very departure:

> O my dear friend, how perfectly we have enacted the fable of the two men, of whom one scurries to the ends of the earth in search of his good fortune, while the other quietly awaits it in his own domestic bed! . . . Only once, out of imprudence, you did damage to your ideal of Spain by going to see it. . . . But already I have lost, kingdom by kingdom, province by province, the most beautiful half of the universe, and soon I shall no longer know where to seek a refuge for my dreams.

If it is true that, at the extreme, the exhilaration of Romantic travel must inevitably modulate into disillusion and disavowal, it remains just possible that the frustrated wanderer might journey home and salvage something of his hopes through a cultivation of the special sensations of home-coming. Romantics in retreat from a remote and alien environment may want to find solace in a familiar, supportive one. Home-coming thus finds its place in Romantic ideology as a touching, restorative experience which offsets travail and trauma.

Friedrich Hölderlin, whose creative vision so often addresses itself to the task of projecting sublimity on to sites of purely imagined travel, such as the Mediterranean island of Patmos or the rivers of Europe and Central Asia, was also capable of writing very simple, even naive poems about the Swabian homeland he knew so well. One fragment entitled 'Heimat' ('Homeland') contains a succinct catalogue of local phenomena: rose thorns, fragrant lime trees, a cornfield at noon, a ringing bell, a stirring bird. These little signs of rural tranquillity constitute an unequivocal message of reassurance: the anxious traveller knows he has come home and that the risks he has taken are justified by the perfect concordance of his sensibility with a site of origin.

Such naive harmony might justify many minor Romantic poems on the theme of home-coming, yet is elsewhere undercut by keener intimations of uncertainty. A more typical poem of Hölderlin, also entitled 'Die Heimat', speculates that the return to a familiar environment is not necessarily guaranteed to dispel the pains of desire:

> Ihr teuern Ufer, die mich erzogen einst,
>   Stillt ihr der Liebe Leiden, versprecht ihr mir,
>   Ihr Wälder meiner Jugend, wenn ich
>   Komme, die Ruhe noch einmal wieder?
>   . . . aber ich weiss, ich weiss,
>   Der Liebe Leid, dies heilet so bald mir nicht,
>   Dies singt kein Wiegensang, den tröstend
>   Sterbliche singen, mir aus dem Busen.

(You dear banks who once nurtured me, / Can you still the pangs of love, can you promise me, / You forests of my youth, on my return, / To restore peace in me once more? / . . . But I know, I know, / The pangs of love cannot be healed so readily, / No consoling cradle-song, sung by mortals, / Can rid my heart of this.)

Although the painter Caspar David Friedrich returned, time and again and with obvious enthusiasm, to his native region on the Baltic's southern rim, it is never joyousness or a sense of plenitude that find expression in the images which these home-comings inspired. Rather, it is a kind of numbed grief which is exuded by canvases such as *Moonrise over the Sea* (1820–1826), where three figures (one of them likely to be a self-representation) huddle upon a damp rock in mute contemplation of a dark, cold seascape. Other kindred scenes contain overt Christian symbols such as the cross, yet these scarcely offset the overall bleakness of the setting. The apotheosis of anxiety is reached in *The Monk by the Sea* (1809), where the Baltic locale is dramatized in the confrontation of a single figure and the desolate immensity of sea and sky. Far from a soothing return to a site of origin, the picture seems to embody alienation, to invoke a place robbed of all trace of reassurance. Home-coming here becomes a tragic encounter with an indifferent emptiness.

Similar themes of anticipation and disillusionment recur in Gérard de Nerval's late autobiographical tale *Sylvie* (1854); it was composed not long after the writer's depressed return to France from the Orient. On the surface, the text is a flimsy travelogue about a trip the Parisian narrator makes to the Valois region north of the city; at a deeper level, the journey represents a personal emotional pilgrimage, saturated in Romantic yearning. One evening in Paris, the narrator chances upon an item in the newspaper about an archery contest at Loisy, the village where he had been brought up. A flood of powerful memories prevents him from sleeping and, in the middle of the night, he resolves to take a cab out of the city. As the vehicle speeds through the sleeping countryside, he tries to structure his recollections of the past, finding old amorous obsessions re-awakening. Arriving in Loisy at dawn, he stumbles off in a half-trance, recognizing familiar paths, forests, streams, meadows and buildings, yet experiencing them as, in effect, a series of spectres. There is a haunting glimpse of the convent where a girl named Adrienne had been a nun: we learn how the narrator had worshipped her from afar as a child. The lesson of disillusionment which Nerval had learned overseas is painfully confirmed in the homelier context of a stroll in the local fields: memories seem as evanescent as mist, nothing really *touches* him any more. The Parisian can draw little consolation from the fact that friends and relatives greet him with affection; the banal discovery that his former sweetheart, Sylvie, is now happily married with two children cuts short all Romantic aspiration, or rather sidetracks it into bourgeois sentimentality. On another occasion, the narrator confides, he had tricked an actress friend into riding out with him one afternoon across those same emotionally charged landscapes; but she quickly sensed his manipulation, accusing him of trying to get her to act out the part of Adrienne. Touching lightly on each of three modes of Romantic travel – on foot, on horseback, by coach – *Sylvie* repeatedly measures the same poignant distance between actuality and desire. The tale's wistful message is endemic to Romanticism: there is no constancy between thought and its external objects, and all desires are chimerical. As the author ruefully concedes, 'illusions drop away one after the other, like the skin off a fruit, and that fruit we call experience'.

A phenomenon so widespread and complex as the Romantic movement could hardly be sketched as briefly as this. A truer picture would necessarily account for a dozen aspects over and above contemporary travel practices: moreover, the circumstances of political, social and cultural interaction in the nineteenth century exerted a myriad points of influence upon a movement which, in any event, lingered on sufficiently long and in sufficiently different national and geographical contexts to rule out any definitive mapping of all sites of interference or intertextual affinity. Nevertheless, I hope to have shown something of the characteristic postures of the Romantic creator in relation to those modes, tempi and locations of travel which were empirically available to the Romantic generation and which provided a basic stock of shared topoi.

It must be stressed that any such common patterns of behaviour are only really telling insofar as they stand in contrast to what came before and after. It would, of course, be foolish to argue that Enlightenment ideas faltered because of changes in people's travelling habits: the Romantic rebellion against reason and the *ancien régime* must be explained in wider terms – philosophical, political, psychological and so forth. Indeed, travel options as such do not automatically define the Romantic posture, since we have seen that a Romantic might successfully cultivate his 'trance sublime and strange' in a variety of situations, from reclining lazily in a boat to dashing up a mountain. What *is* significant is that the kinds of ecstatic experiences I have evoked begin to lapse (or, more precisely, begin to take on a vulnerable or doomed appearance) at the same time as innovatory and apparently anti-poetic modes of transport start to assert themselves, and as the domains of private delight are, 'province by province', overrun by universal consumption. A certain aristocracy of the imagination may be said to have recoiled instinctively from the platitudes of cut-price tourism. Vigny's solitary, meandering coach remains an emblem of Romantic creativity insofar as it is *not a crowded train running on a regulated track*; while, as both Mark Twain and Alphonse Daudet observed, the uplifting spectacle of sunrise in the Alps becomes an immediate cliché once the hotel crowds, conditioned by Baedeker, assemble to admire it by rote. Romanticism rekindled is no more than kitsch, as was brought home to me in 1994 when I visited Fingal's Cave on a vessel packed with tourists. Arriving at the mouth of the cavern, the captain cut the motor and then let us float for several minutes with the tinny music of Mendelssohn's *Overture* emanating from the ship's tannoy.

Generally speaking, it is what *falters* which catches the Romantic's fancy – the horse-drawn coach, the folksong, the watercolour sketch – often by virtue of its naivety, its intimacy, its utter lack of programming. If a Romantic project were still conceivable at the end of the twentieth century, might it not, paradoxically, want to privilege the railway as representing the archaic, wayward, quasi-tactile option, in contradistinction to the cool, abstracted efficiency of jet travel? Perhaps the same order of contrast would obtain at the level of social instinct, with individual impulse differentiated from mass conformity. Even today, travel companies wrestle with the basic script of Romanticism in their attempt to reconcile an illusion of elite connoisseurship with popular pricing.

If there were some non-historical aspect to the Romantic project, it would lie in the impulse to escape from the commonplace and the predictable, in a sense to wander outside history itself. We have noted the Romantic appetite for outlandish destinations, for unmapped territories, for tumults and alien colours. Elective sites like Fingal's Cave, Luxor or Mount Etna certainly fulfilled a function in the Romantic period, and may do so even today, to the extent that they remain relatively inaccessible and imply some sort of effort. All in all, the Romantics were scarcely more ridiculous or admirable than many twentieth-century heroes – André Malraux, Ernest Hemingway, Joseph Beuys, Bruce Chatwin, Don McCullin – in responding to remote challenges and returning home disillusioned yet wiser, almost always bearing the marks of their mortality. If travel begins in heady idealism and climaxes in shipwreck and despair, it has at least the virtue of highlighting the fragility of the boundaries of a self envisaged as an organism resourced by independent desires.

What the Romantics gained was insight not so much into the limits of daydreaming as into the limits of a regulated, mechanistic view of the self. It was through coping with their own fallacies and mirages that they came to understand the difference between immature self-delusion and a mature self-possession. Some may find their claims to visionary illumination far too grand to ring true. Others will find the self-reflexive dimension of Romantic art to be redolent of selfishness and elitism. Yet for all its addiction to hyperbole and its engrossment in private fantasy, Romanticism secretes a deeper and arguably still resonant sense of collective truth, insofar as its many local fault-lines are symptomatic of a sensitivity to wider cultural tremors.

10

'...AS A RULE, I DOES NOT MEAN I'

Personal identity and the Victorian woman poet

Kate Flint

'I look everywhere for grandmothers, and see none.' Elizabeth Barrett Browning's comment of 1845 traditionally has been taken as a lament for the lack of a female creative genealogy, an unfulfillable desire to experience the anxiety of influence. But rather, these words should be seen not so much as a succinct summary of literary history as a performative act. They are an assertion of individuality, of pioneering identity (and possibly, of limited or selective reading when it comes to women's writing), for their accuracy is debatable. Around Barrett Browning, other women poets, rather than explicitly sharing her difficulty, were aligning themselves in relation to their literary ancestry. Above all, they were claiming the model, and, most importantly, appropriating the voice, of Sappho. In turn, this adoption of a form of classical authority was symptomatic of the way in which nineteenth-century women poets characteristically established identity not so much in terms of confessional, emotive, autobiographically personalized subjectivity as through forms of imaginative projection.

Sappho is a figure turned to by Letitia Landon (LEL) in 1824, in her popular long poem, *The Improvisatrice*. She is invoked by a fictional Renaissance Florentine woman poet – LEL presents a lineage of women's writing here – as providing a link to 'Forgotten music, still some chance/Vibrate the chord whereon it sleeps'. LEL also resurrected, in imaginative terms, the voice of the young Greek woman poet Erinna, taking her inspiration from the brief sepulchral epigram by Anipater on the young poet. 'My aim,' writes LEL, tying herself firmly to tradition, 'has been to draw the portrait and trace the changes of a highly poetical mind, too sensitive perhaps of the chill and bitterness belonging even to success. The feelings which constitute poetry are the same in all ages, they are acted upon by similar causes.' The same year, 1824, Catherine Garnett – best known as a contributor to the fashionable poetry annuals of the years which bridged Romanticism and Victorianism – published a verse drama,

Sappho. The legacy continued, although, during the early decades of the century, Sappho's poetry can often be found taking second place to her heterosexual and not particularly emulable guise as an abandoned woman, as when Caroline Norton asks, in 'The Picture of Sappho':

> Didst thou indeed sit there
> In languid lone despair –
> Thy harp neglected by thee idly lying –
> Thy soft and earnest gaze
> Watching the lingering rays
> In the far west, where summer-day was dying –

Such a sentimentalized and idealized figure is treated in terms very different from the prose and fictional polemics designed to change the laws concerning infant custody, marriage and divorce for which Norton was to become best known: polemic arising from her own resistance to resting in defeated languor in her disastrous marriage. Yet the classical figure herself comes, as the century progresses, to bear a more spirited and culturally resistant role, rather than representing a distant, lost ideal. Catherine Dawson's *Sappho* of 1889 consists of 210 pages of dramatic monologue spoken by the Greek woman, tacitly making parallels between her own life history and contemporary debates concerning women's education and social position, arguing against the popular assumption that women have an instinctive love of mastery, and showing Sappho, right up to and including her final leap, as someone who acted on rational, rather than emotional grounds. In the same year 'Michael Field', in *Long Ago*, took Sappho's fragments (using Dr Wharton's *Sappho*, a popular Victorian edition, as their source) and used them as the basis for a series of expanded lyrics, dedicated to the Greek, 'the one woman who has dared to speak unfalteringly of the fearful mastery of love'. Particularly in the context of that last phrase, 'Michael Field' raises a quite separate set of issues concerned with poetic identity, being not one person but two, Katherine Bradley and Edith Cooper, yoked by love and creativity: 'My Love and I took hands and swore / Against the world, to be / Poets and lovers evermore.' It is only in their hands that Sappho's lesbianism is reasserted: other nineteenth-century women poets (Swinburne provides the most notorious male counter-example) restricted themselves to dealing, explicitly or otherwise, with the transgressions involved in her public utterance.

Even without this deliberate fusion and confusion of authorial personality in the work of 'Michael Field', Sappho's own fragments in many ways present a paradigm for the fragmented, or rather the dispersed identities of nineteenth-century women poets. I want to argue that a major distinguishing feature in their writing is a readiness to inhabit the voices, the subject positions of others. They do not readily take on the role of seer speaking with their own, personal authority of experience; of celebrants of their own creative imaginations. Catherine Belsey, in her much lauded book *Critical Practice*, generalizes:

> It is readily apparent that Romantic and post-Romantic poetry . . . takes subjectivity as its central theme. The developing self of the poet, his consciousness of himself as poet, his struggle against the constraints of an outer reality, constitute the preoccupations of *The Prelude, In Memoriam* or 'Meditations in Time of Civil War'.

There is little space for the Romantic and post-Romantic woman poet in Belsey's delineation of the poetic figure. Nor does the Victorian woman poet fit neatly into the more subtle model, and more wide-reaching paradigm of selfhood advanced by Charles Taylor in *Sources of the Self: The Making of the Modern Identity* (1989), who suggests that the Victorian period, and indeed our own, is characterized by the appearance of the idea of a 'free, self-determining subject'. This, according to Taylor, constructs itself through a continuing battle between Enlightenment and Romanticism – between disengaged, instrumental reason (or, today, technology) and expressivism (which he more tendentiously updates into ecological orientation).

Yet in the poetic forms that I discuss here, we encounter a far less stable idea of selfhood than is presumed by this conflictual, yet relatively securely located model: a model rooted, throughout Taylor's entire study, in the belief that our sense of identity is formed through a narrative, a quest, a desire to orientate ourselves towards the good. However, Taylor's thoughtful consideration of what it means to speak of the 'self' in the first place also leads him to acknowledge the importance of language in the construction of selfhood: language is always going to be 'part of, internal to, or constitutive of the "object" studied. To study persons is to study beings who only exist in, or are partly constituted by, a certain language'. And, he continues, since a language only exists and is maintained within a language community, so 'One is a self only among other selves. A self can never be described without reference to those who surround it.' Thus, rather than focusing inwards, seeing the nineteenth-century woman poet presenting herself as 'a kind of super-subject, experiencing life at a higher level of intensity than normal people', to quote Belsey again, these remarks of Taylor's lead one back to consider how she frequently tended to use language as a vehicle to present the imagined, projected thoughts and feelings of others. The 'acts, gestures, enactments' which constitute such poems, to draw on Judith Butler's influential terminology, are performative, in the sense that they 'suggest, but never reveal, the organizing principle of identity as a cause . . . the essence or the identity that they . . . purport to express are *fabrications*'. They are bound to be such since, as I go on to demonstrate, the Victorian woman poet is, for the most part, not primarily concerned to draw on some stable sense of self out of which to write, but uses her verse as a means of exploring the fact that identity may be something imaginatively, generously, experimentally dispersed and diffuse, reachable through writing and reading which can stretch both writer and reader well beyond the bounds of personal experience. Although the dramatic monologue was far from being an exclusively woman's genre, and the remarks about selfhood and its relation to poetry apply to a large number of male writers of the mid-Victorian period in particular, it was a form which allowed the woman, as we shall see, particular freedoms.

Romantic and Victorian women's poetry is packed with interventionist dramatic monologues. These range from ballads to *Aurora Leigh*, Elizabeth Barrett Browning's 'novel-poem', as she called it, which confronts contemporary social issues head-on (exploited seamstresses, a woman sold into a brothel where she is drugged and raped, fetid housing conditions): a work which Barrett Browning characterized as an exuberant, transgressively energetic female presence, 'running into the midst of our conventions, and rushing into drawing-rooms and the like'. Partly, these many assumptions of masks may be seen as a reluctance to engage in public, self-revelatory display. There is plenty of poetic evidence which would suggest the difficulty of voicing 'one's own tongue', from Elizabeth Barrett Browning's 'With stammering lips and insufficient sound / I strive and struggle to deliver right / That music of my nature' ('The Soul's Expression', 1844) to the anxieties suggested in George Eliot's 'Armgart', a verse drama in which the woman operatic singer appears to be punished for her public stage career by being struck down by a mysterious disease which permanently damages her voice.

But there are other factors at stake, which may be illuminated by both recent and Victorian commentators. In general terms, such poetic practices correspond with Judith Kegan Gardiner's claim that 'Throughout women's lives, the self is defined through social relationships; issues of fusion and merger of the self with others are significant, and ego and body boundaries remain flexible'. They may be linked, too, to a couple of factors succinctly expressed by Patricia Waugh: 'the phenomenological perception that "I" am never at one with myself because always and ever already constituted by others according to whom, and yet outside of what, I take myself to be', and the fact that for a woman writer, there is a further implication that 'if the "I" is spoken or positioned in a discourse where subjectivity, the norm of human-ness, is male, the "I" is doubly displaced, "I" can never in any material or metaphysical sense be at one with myself.' And, using a frame of reference more historically specific to the nineteenth century – at least to the 1830s onwards – one could relate this ventriloquization of identity to the assumption, backed up with medical evidence, that women 'identified with' the feelings of others far more readily than did men. Because they were, it was presumed, biologically programmed to respond to the

emotional demands of their offspring, it could be argued that the deployment of a range of voices exhibits an internalization of the assumptions
summed up by William Roscoe in the *National Review* in 1858, that woman's
'gracious prerogative and happiest attribute [is] the power to live in
others'.

Yet the use of dramatic monologue also represents something more
radical, and something which is much less downbeat and defeatist
when it comes to considering a woman writer's engagement with the idea
of identity. First, it can allow for the woman poet to express her sense of
being objectified, letting her speak out from a position traditionally
associated with silence. Christina Rossetti commented rather sardonically
on how her brother Gabriel's proliferation of paintings and drawings
featuring his new model Lizzie Siddal reflected his own image of her: 'One
face looks out from all his canvases, / One selfsame figure sits or walks or
leans. . . . He feeds upon her face by day and night, / And she with true
kind eyes looks back on him, / . . . Not as she is, but was when hope shone
bright; /Not as she is, but as she fills his dream' ('In an Artist's Studio',
1856). Her own experience of being observed while her inner life is utterly
hidden is dramatized in the chilling sonnet where she envisages a corpse
watching a former male friend visit her on her bier, death providing an
imaginary position of knowledge and power unattainable in life:

> The curtains were half drawn, the floor was swept
>   And strewn with rushes, rosemary and may
>   Lay thick upon the bed on which I lay,
> Where thro' the lattice ivy-shadows crept.
> He leaned above me, thinking that I slept
>   And could not hear him; but I heard him say:
>   'Poor child, poor child:' and as he turned away
> Came a deep silence, and I knew he wept.
> He did not take the shroud, or raise the fold
>   That hid my face, or take my hand in his,
>   Or ruffle the smooth pillows for my head:
>   He did not love me living; but once dead
>   He pitied me; and very sweet it is
> To know he still is warm tho' I am cold.
>
> ('After Death')

Much later in the century, Dollie Radford's poem of 1895, 'A Model', gives
the thoughts of a professional model: 'Year after year I sit for them, / The
boys and girls who come and go'; and of how she was kept passive by the
imagined settings of splendour in which she was placed. The poem may be
read as an allegory of the folly of believing in a vision of womanhood which
is imposed upon one, rather than one in which one goes out and creates
for oneself:

The flowers painted round my face,
  The magic seas and skies above,
And many a far enchanted place
  Full of the summer time and love.

They set me in a fairy-land,
  So much more real than they knew,
And I was slow to understand
  The pictures could not all come true.

But one by one, they died somehow,
  The waking dreams which kept me glad,
And I sat, they told me now,
  None would believe a maid so sad.

Silence, in all these cases, is not the property of a permanently mute condition, but is transformed into a position of strength. As the Catholic poet, journalist and suffrage campaigner Alice Meynell points out in her late nineteenth-century poem, 'To Silence', the quality is to be associated not with the appropriate gendered behaviour of meek domesticity, but with the circumstances necessary to produce the most powerful art:

Thy secret is the strong that is to be.
Music had never stature but for thee,
Sculptor! strong as the sculptor Space whose hand
Urged the Discobolus and bade him stand.

Man, on his way to Silence, stops to hear and see.

The re-appropriation of silence looks forward to the reminder of the contemporary American poet, Adrienne Rich, in 'Cartographies of Silence', that it

can be a plan
rigorously executed.

Do not confuse it
with any kind of absence.

The capacity to inhabit another person's imaginative space frequently becomes a form of exploration on the part of the poet, whether the exploration is a time, or a class, or even a gender different from their own. This exploration may be very explicitly tied in to questions of identity: Christina Rossetti's 'A Royal Princess' sets herself up as a prisoner of rank and self:

All my walls are lost in mirrors, whereupon I trace
Self to right hand, self to left hand, self in every place,
  Self-same solitary figure, self-same seeking face

but she breaks out of this self-regarding solipsism to give away her gold and jewels – her father's gifts – to an angry, starving mob outside her castle. These mirrors make many reappearances in Victorian women's poetry. As Angela Leighton notes in her Introduction to the very valuable anthology she has recently edited with Margaret Reynolds, *Victorian Women Poets*, their presence is particularly felt in the latter half of the century. Citing, among other examples, Augusta Webster's 'By the Looking-Glass', Mary Coleridge's 'The Other Side of a Mirror' and Caroline Lindsay's 'To My Own Face', she comments that woman observing herself seems to supplant the more popular early motif of man looking at woman, and 'the mirror functions to bring the divided subject and object together . . . [the poems] focus on the difference between self and face, as each woman searches for some inner explanation of her socially determined identity'. Faced – quite literally – with self-division, it is easy to see how the dramatic monologue offers the temptation of an apparently stable identity which lies outside the self, which may confidently be created and projected, with any discrepancy between public and private being far more easy to control and negotiate than when one is writing with a troubled autobiographical utterance.

Another's voice may be adopted in order to express a variety of forms of social protest which stretch far beyond personal experience. This is strongly apparent in the anti-racist sentiments of the prolific, popular writer of the 1820s and 1830s, Felicia Hemans' 'The Indian with his Dead Child' ('When his head sank on my bosom, / When the death-sleep o'er him fell, / Was there one to say, "A friend is near?"/ There was none! – pale race, farewell!'), or in the painful stanzas of Barrett Browning's 'The Runaway Slave at Pilgrim's Point', raped by the slave-master, and being flogged to death for killing the child, the unbearably light-skinned reminder of her ordeal, that she bore. Or there is the voice of the Indian – in this case Asian, not native American – who, in Dawson's 'Rukhmabai', tells of the wrongs of child brides and of widows in her country, with a widow being prohibited from taking her first husband's money into a second marriage, and pleading:

> Let England rise her old strength and strike
> As Mother of Free Nations at the laws
> Which lay our millions in the jewelled dust
> Of crumbled empires and dead usages.

Notably, the voices heard here are set away from England, an unmissable demonstration of the way in which poetry could be used to break open topographical border lines, paying no attention to the alleged limitations of domesticity. And the imagination could stretch back in chronological terms, too – often, in fact, to air issues which were highly pertinent to the writer's own time, as we saw in the case of Dawson's *Sappho*, or as we find in the Jewish poet and novelist, Amy Levy's *Xanthippe* (1884). The Greek woman voices her barely repressed anger at the way she was crushed by her husband, Socrates; belittled in the company of philosophers, where only one type of clear, hard, rational mental activity seemed to count:

> . . . the high philosopher
> Pregnant with noble theories and great thoughts,
> Deigned not to stoop to touch so slight a thing
> As the fine fabric of a woman's brain —
> So subtle as a passionate woman's soul.

Finally, in the context of those who used their writing to make social points, women poets frequently ventriloquized the feelings of those less fortunate than themselves, particularly the 'fallen woman'. Levy, again, inhabits the despairing spirit of a woman dying, deserted, in a refuge: 'Nothing is known or understood / Save only Pain. I have no faith / In God or Devil, Life or Death' ('Magdalen', 1884). Pain, Angela Leighton has noted, 'is one of the keynotes of Levy's work, expressing her vision of a world which is unredeemed by faith, love or social change'. Augusta Webster's representative prostitute offers a pragmatic explanation for her position: 'The Castaway':

> . . . where's the work? More sempstresses than shirts;
> and defter hands at white work than are mine
> drop starved at last.

Her employment is driven by economic necessity, and in this she, as one who has been able to turn her beauty into a valuable commodity, refuses to draw a class distinction between her position and that of any woman who has similarly been led to sell her body:

> I say let no one be above her trade;
> I own my kindredship with any drab
> who sells herself as I, although she crouch
> in fetid garrets and I have a home
> all velvet and marqueterie and pastilles,
> although she hide her skeleton in rags
> and I set fashions and wear cobweb lace:
> the difference lies but in my choicer ware,
> that I sell beauty and she ugliness;
> our traffic's one — I'm no sweet slaver-tongue
> to gloze upon it and explain myself
> a sort of fractious angel misconceived —
> our traffic's one: I own it.

Augusta Webster is a notable poet. While some of her work, like her posthumously published *Mother and Daughter* sonnet sequence, might at first glance seem to take a conventional subject for women's poetry, she approaches the relationship in a direct and largely unsentimental manner. She more than matches Robert Browning in experimentalism, using a free verse form to indicate thoughts in progress, sometimes running on with little punctuation, sometimes faltering into broken rhythms, spattered with self-interruptions and colloquialisms. She was in no way afraid to adopt and adapt already authoritative voices: she published translations of *Prometheus Bound* and *Medea*, and in her volumes *Dramatic Studies* and *Portraits*, she speaks through mythologically and historically powerful women – Circe and Joan of Arc – as well as more deliberately sociologically typical figures.

Throughout the period, it is interesting how the adoption of a male voice often signifies a challenging of assumptions of patriarchal power. This may take the form of directing our attention – as with the Hemans poem quoted above – to male victims. Elsewhere, men are undermined by unwittingly revealing the limits of their ideological strait-jackets, as in Webster's 'Tired', where a world-weary middle-class man laments, in condescending tones that betray no self-knowledge, that his wife hasn't stayed the fresh-faced 'simple peasant girl', 'come from her cottage home / knowing no world beyond her village streets' that he married. The woman herself is allowed but a line and a half in the whole poem (though even this is more of a contribution than is necessarily conventional with the dramatic monologue form), and it is impossible to judge how much deliberate scorn is present on her part, or how much practical simplicity, deaf to the deeper meanings her lines carry to the reader, she does, after all, retain:

> Ready, love, at last?
> Why, what a rosy June! A flush of bloom
> sparkling with crystal dews – Ah silly one,
> you love those muslin roses better far
> than those that wear the natural dew of heaven.
> I thought you prettier when, the other day,
> the children crowned you with the meadow-sweets:
> I like to hear you teach them wild flowers' names
> and make them love them; but yourself –
>
> What's that?
> 'The wild flowers in a room's hot stifling glare
> would die in half a minute.' True enough:
> your muslin roses are the wiser wear.

In her prose writings, published under the misleadingly domestic title *A Housewife's Opinions*, Webster elaborates on the issue of writing dramatic monologues. The essay 'Poets and Personal Pronouns' draws a clear distinction between the practice of creating characters in fiction and in

164

verse. Novelists should make us feel as though the people they create are alive, 'the presentment of some special person known in the flesh': by contrast, the poet's task is to represent feelings and thoughts 'in a way which shall affect us as the manifest expression of what our very selves must have felt and thought and done if we had been those he puts before us and in their cases'. The self that is at stake, in other words, is not just that of the poet, but of the reader. In the light of this, she recoils from the common assumption that the poet is 'believed to be his own lay figure. He is taken as offering his readers the presentment of himself, his hopes, his loves, his sorrows, his guilts and remorses, his history and psychology generally' (she is careful to point out, a few sentences later, that these generalizations apply equally to women as to men). As proof against this unquestioning belief that what a poet does is to pour out a troubled or a joyous soul, she advances the number of multifarious beings whom one encounters in modern verse, and suggests that the very fact that writers are capable of the materialistic tasks of correcting their proofs and seeing their volumes through the press is proof positive of the fact that 'as a rule, I does not mean I . . . few poets are even ostensibly autobiographical; and it is hard on them to investigate them as if they were putting themselves through a process of vivisection for the public to see how they were getting on inside'.

Traditionally, the kudos for establishing the importance of the dramatic monologue in the nineteenth century has gone to *Robert* Browning: poems like 'Andrea del Sarto' and 'The Bishop Orders His Tomb' have been read alongside his essay on Shelley, with its praise of 'objective' writing, in which the personal biography of the poet is hidden, and 'The work speaks for itself, as we say.' But LEL was there first, writing in 1824: 'Poetry needs no preface, if it do not speak for itself, no comment can render it explicit.' The multiplicity of poetic voices assumed by women during the nineteenth century acts as a challenge to the identification of women with the purely subjective, the personal, the sensual, the incapacity to grasp the wider vision: an identification blindly practised by many contemporary reviewers in their attempt to devalue so-called 'effeminate' poetry – poetry which, ironically enough, was actually being written by *men* like Dante Gabriel Rossetti and Swinburne.

For *women* poets of the period, crossing the borders of the self becomes a way to explore the possibilities of identification with others, to establish selfhood not as a form of isolation, but as something grounded in a perpetual dialogue between similarity and difference. Hence, such boundary crossings work against any attempt to over-generalize about the 'nature' of the woman writer's self, either generically (as bearer of a range of characteristics conventionally, casually associated with 'the woman poet') or as a representative of her gender. Indeed, they call into question the stability of the markers of identity: writing the dramatic monologue is a form of literary transvestism, allowing slippage between gender positions, between classes, between races. They – to borrow Judith Butler's phrase – refuse to allow 'the idealization of the heterosexual bond': not just in the subject matter of their writing, but in their refusal to take up any stance of complementarity towards male poets, however much critics, on occasion, might try to pigeon-hole them. The work of these women provides a continual exemplification of George Eliot's firm reminder, in *Daniel Deronda* (1876), that 'Our consciences are not all of the same pattern, an inner deliverance of fixed laws: they are the voice of sensibilities as various as our memories'. More than this, the continual production of new identities in which they engage – repetition (the act of writing poetry) with difference – may be read as anticipating some current theoretical postulations about the nature of gendered identity. Such identity, they (just as much as Butler) suggest, is not something which is innate, nor something which follows a developmental model, but is produced – through utterance, through writing, through performance. The ease with which their own lives may, in many cases, be readily severed from the voices through which they speak offers eloquent testimony to this, while at the same time giving the writers a range of observational stances on their society: stances from which they may do the gazing, and judging, and relish in the hidden power which another's voice can give them.

11

MAPPING THE SELF

Gender, space and modernity in mid-Victorian London

Lynda Nead

This chapter looks at the role played by space in the formation of social relations and gendered identities in the mid-Victorian period. It does not come up with any cut and dried account of the experience of modernity for men and women at this time; what it does suggest is that within the sites of the modern metropolis, identity was diverse, unfixed and open to constant negotiation. Subjectivity was not already in place when men and women occupied the streets of Victorian London, but was formed through the encounters, interactions and experiences of that occupation. Social space, in this context, is not a passive backdrop to the formation of identity, but is part of an active ordering and organizing of the social and cultural relations of the city.

These configurations of space and identity should be grasped in terms of precise historical and cultural contexts. Conventional histories of Victorian society have accounted for bourgeois femininity through the figure of the 'angel in the house'. Social historians have traced the gradual separation of the public and private spheres within bourgeois class formation. Whereas in the eighteenth century, it is claimed, the home tended to be above the workplace in the city and women might be involved in both the commercial and the domestic realms, by the beginning of the nineteenth century the bourgeois home tended to be geographically separated from the work-place, with the paterfamilias travelling between the home and work in the city and the woman carrying out her roles of wife/mother/home-maker in the domestic sphere. The ideology of respectable domesticity is thus iden-tified as a central component within the formation of bourgeois identity. The implications for the gendering of identity would also seem clear. Whereas men could move between the public and private spheres, female respect-ability was exclusively defined in terms of its identification with the private domestic sphere. This account produces a somewhat sensational image of the Victorian city: one peopled by men and unrespectable women. Unaccompanied women in the city are classified as street-walkers, in the sense that they are prostitutes. According to the ideology of separate spheres, women lose their respectability when they leave the private sphere and enter the public and commercial spaces of the city. In the spaces of commercial exchange, they themselves become commodities and go on sale.

Although it is reasonably clear that the notion of separate spheres did function as an ideological construct in the period – that is, that it was circulated through a number of discourses and described a type of ideal of gendered difference – it is far less convincing that it can be seen as an explanation for women's *actual* occupation and experience of the public domain. Respectable women quite obviously did move alone through the city streets and these experiences could be accommodated within either an individual or a shared notion of respectability.

Take a coloured lithograph from around the middle of the 1860s (Plate 11.1). It shows a woman in a street being approached by an evangelical clergyman who, believing her to be a prostitute, tries to reclaim her. She rejects his attempts and assures him: 'I am not a social evil, I am only waiting for a bus.' The print demonstrates the disjuncture between a religious fantasy of femininity and everyday practice. The cleric is the embodiment of the ideology of separate spheres, of female respectability being tied to the domestic realm: the woman whom he approaches is testimony to a different populating of the city streets. A respectable woman, on her own, waiting for public transport. The confusion which follows is an instance of the negotiation of uncertain identities and relations in the social spaces of the modern city.

Consider another example from the period. In a postscript to a letter, dated 4 January 1856, one young woman writes to her friend:

> When I got to the station on Tuesday the train had gone so I walked to town I hadn't gone far when a gentleman in a 4 wheel chaise offered me a ride but I was like you bashful and said no. If you had been [there] I should [have] said yes.

This correspondence between two respectable, lower-middle-class women also presents a range of possibilities: of female, unaccompanied travel through the city and of the city as a site of sexual flirtation and risk for women as well as for men.

The premise of both the print and the letter is that women's presence in the city is part of everyday experience and that metropolitan encounters necessitate a constant appraisal of one's own and of others' identity. In order to explore these ideas in more detail, we can look at the commercial, social and cultural relations produced through one particular London street, at a very precise historical moment in the nineteenth century. It is a study of how the modern city creates a modern visual culture and how a public for that culture is constituted. It is a study of Holywell Street, formerly in the parish of St Clement Danes, Westminster (Plate 11.2).

Plate 11.1 (C. J. Culliford), *Scene in Regent Street. Philanthropic Divine:*
'May I beg you to accept this good little book. Take it home and read it attentively.
I am sure it will benefit you.'
Lady: 'Bless me, Sir, you're mistaken. I am not a social evil,
I am only waiting for a bus.'
Coloured lithograph, *c.* 1865 (private collection)

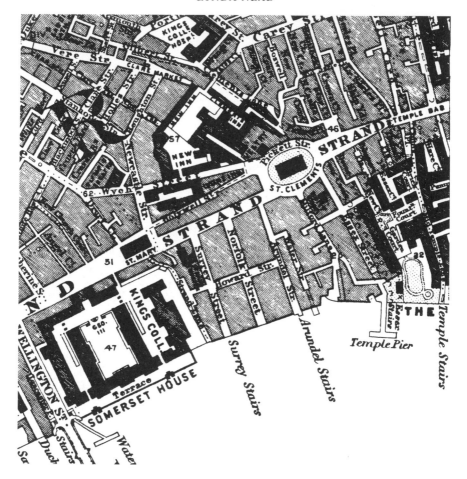

Plate 11.2 'The Strand and Holywell Street',
Stanford's Library Map of London and its Suburbs (detail), 1862

Holywell Street was always 'coming down'. From the first years of Queen Victoria's reign through to the end of the century, plans were submitted for the demolition and replanning of the ancient courts and alleys north of the Strand which included Holywell Street. There was even a story about a young man from the country who found himself in this part of London one winter's night, intending to make a short journey of a few yards to the main thoroughfare of the Strand. He soon became lost in the labyrinthine alleyways and it was said that his ghost haunted mid-Victorian London, wandering round and about, constantly returning to the original starting point of the journey. He never escaped from the narrow, dark, irregular alleys and never reached the Strand.

170

Holywell Street always seemed on the brink of extinction, of crumbling into history; a precarious monument to Elizabethan London and a deserving sacrifice to the modernizing Victorian metropolis. On New Year's Day in 1853, nature intervened; the *Illustrated London News* carried a report of a hurricane which had blown off the roof of a house in Holywell Street. In 1861, the *Builder* responded to a parliamentary bill to clear the area, by publishing an illustrated article on 'Elizabethan London' (Plate 11.3). The article expressed the view:

> Much as we may admire the picturesque and value old structures – landmarks in our history – we can express no sorrow in this case. We have thought it desirable, however, to preserve a memorial of their appearance. . . 'One of the views, it adds, shows Holywell Street, of evil notoriety.

Leaving aside, for the moment, the question of what constituted the 'evil notoriety' of Holywell Street, it is helpful to look at the visual image of the street. The view includes a number of elements, such as deep bays, over-hanging eaves, high gables, crescent moon shop sign and a number of print shops which recur in most visual representations of this site throughout the century. There is a significant number of pictures of Holywell Street. Prints and watercolours were commissioned by collectors in the nineteenth century who wanted a visual record of this historic area. Within this imagery there are variations; sometimes the width of the street varies, or the shops and houses become more cliff-like with the cobbled street gorged out below (Plate 11.4), but otherwise it is a remarkably consistent iconography. It is as though a particular range of architectural elements is routinely included which constitutes an aesthetic of the metropolitan picturesque.

What is far more changeable is the representation of the public which moves through this urban space. There is a real ambiguity about the class of the people who pass through Holywell Street and its environs. Holywell Street therefore poses important questions about the ways in which social and moral identities are constructed and perceived in the heterogeneous public spaces of mid-Victorian London.

By 1870, the antiquarian value of Holywell Street had become more pronounced. As successive plans to rebuild the area failed to be carried out, the picturesque qualities of the housing and streets were increasingly romanticized, perhaps precisely because their eventual destruction was so inevitable. The *Illustrated London News* of 1870, imagined the building of 'a new street – a wide and straight one – . . . through the labyrinth of fetid alleys . . . a thoroughfare not precisely straight, but nearly so'. Seizing the opportunity of a quick dig at the aesthetics of Baron Haussmann's Paris, with its miles of new, straight boulevards, the article imagines the creation of a new kind of urban space, allowing a different form of social circula-tion. In contrast to the unregulated and purposeless movement embodied in the meandering lane of Holywell Street and symbolized in the story of

Holywell Street, looking towards the East.

Plate 11.3 'Elizabethan London', *Builder,* 6 April 1861

Plate 11.4 W. Richardson, *Holywell Street*, Watercolour, *c.* 1870
(The Museum of London)

the ghost of the lost country visitor, a straight thoroughfare enables circulation with purpose and movement without contact.

It is in this opposition of labyrinthine alleys and wide, straight thoroughfares that one sees two contrasting nineteenth-century urban aesthetics at work: the first, picturesque, picaresque, romantic, retrospective; the second, modernizing, cleansing, for which locations like Holywell Street are a sign of physical, moral and political contagion. The self in the nineteenth-century metropolis is thus placed within a number of different mappings of the city: economic, social, moral and aesthetic. It is entirely appropriate, therefore, that one Edwardian commentator observed that Holywell Street was 'A joy to the artist . . . a sorrow to the sanitarian', for this relationship between subjectivity, hygiene, morality and aesthetics was replayed through the century in discourses on the city.

On the eve of its demolition in 1898, the *Architectural Review* illustrated Holywell Street in its series on 'Disappearing London' (Plate 11.5). Curiously, the subtitle given in this instance is 'Coming Down London'. Holywell Street could not just disappear, its timbers, chimney pots, gables and windows had to 'come down'; but then, it was always coming down.

I have become interested in Holywell Street because it presents an extraordinary micro-history for a broader re-examination of the construction of the self in the modern city and of the gendering of public space in Victorian London. Recent art history has tended to address the issue of modernity through the work of Charles Baudelaire and Walter Benjamin, adopting their focus on the central figure of the city – the flâneur, the man on the street. Within Baudelaire's formulation and its surrealist reworking, woman is excluded from everyday urban experience. Apart from being positioned as prostitute, or street-walker, women are spectral absences from this theorization of the city. They may be part of the furnishing of the street, objects of erotic fantasy or longing; the locus of sexual and moral transaction and contamination: but they have no active agency. They do not construct urban space in the ways their male counterparts are imagined to do; they do not move through the spaces of the nineteenth-century city with the same diversity as men.

An historical analysis of Holywell Street turns up a different picture. It proposes a concept of space where individuals explore and negotiate multiple urban identities. Within this study, space actively constitutes the self and subjectivities inflect the symbolic meanings of space.

The micro-study also develops recent feminist revisions of the idea of 'separate spheres' as an organizing concept for the history of middle-class, or, more broadly, respectable women, in the nineteenth century. This essay takes respectable women away from their conceptual incarceration within the private, domestic sphere and replaces them within the discourses of the city: shopping, walking, looking in windows, brushing up

Coming-Down
London:
No. 2.

"THE ARCHITECTURAL
REVIEW": SEPTEMBER, 1898

Holywell Street:
From St. Clement Danes Church.
Strand: Drawn by
F. C. Emanuel.

Plate 11.5 'Coming-Down London: No. 2',
Architectural Review, September 1898

against obscenity *and* respectability and forcing constant renegotiation of modern identity in the urban context.

The focus of this story of Holywell Street is the debates leading up to the passing of the first Obscene Publications Act in 1857. The 1857 Act did not redefine what should count as obscene, but it introduced substantial new powers of policing in the city. The 1857 Act authorized police to seize obscene materials and to destroy them if their 'publishers' could not prove the non-obscenity of the work. The bill was introduced in the House of Lords by Lord Campbell, the Lord Chief Justice. On 9 May 1857, Campbell had presided over the trials of two men charged with the sale of obscene publications. The cases clearly had an enormous impact on him. The first case, that against William Dugdale of Holywell Street, was a dramatic affair. The defendant entered the court in an excited state, by turns protesting against the conduct of his arrest, proclaiming his innocence, pleading mercy for the sake of his children, and finally threatening the court with a knife.

The second case, against William Strange, was brought for the publication of two obscene libels, *Paul Pry* (Plate 11.6) and *The Women of London* (Plate 11.7). Witnesses were called to vouch for Strange's good character, including a certain George Vickers, who kept a bookshop next door to Dugdale's in Holywell Street. Both defendants were found guilty and given prison sentences. Summing up the case, Lord Campbell expressed his horror that obscene papers, such as those seen in these cases, were sold publicly in the streets of London for as little as one penny. Hitherto, there had been some check to such publications, arising from the high price which was charged for them, but now these obscenities were cheap and easily obtainable; they were a source of national disgrace and more pernicious to society than any form of chemical poison. What is striking to a modern viewer of the prosecuted materials is the mildness of their sexual content. It seems that the law was not concerned with the prosecution of the most sexually explicit materials but with regulating the boundaries of the obscene; that is, with policing those representations which came closest to the limits of respectable culture.

Campbell pursued the metaphor of obscenity as cultural poison when he announced his intention to the House of Lords to introduce a bill to regulate the exhibition and sale of obscene publications. Using the opportunity of a debate on legislation to regulate the sale of chemical poisons, he reported to the House:

> that there was now carried on a sale of poison far more fatal than prussic acid or strychnine, he meant indecent publications. . . . He thought it was the duty of the Government to take the necessary measures for immediately putting a stop to those publications.

The following day, press responses to Campbell's announcement were generally favourable. The *Daily Telegraph* supported legislation because:

PAUL PRY.

The Inquisitive, Quizzical, Satirical, and Whimsical Epitome of Life as It Is.

No 1.　　　PUBLISHED WEEKLY,　　　Price One Penny

CASINO-TAP, HOLBORN.

Plate 11.6 'The Casino-Tap, Holborn', *Paul Pry*, No. 1, 1856

A NIGHT-HOUSE IN THE HAYMARKET.

on a wreath, which gave her the appearance of a ballet-girl.

"What is that for?" asked Agnes.

"Oh! Jimmy will have it. He says it has a good effect. Now I'm ready; are you? I want to get down again. Jimmy is in a bad temper to-day. You see how I'll bully him and tease him. You need not take off your bonnet; you can sit by my side, or near me, and if you feel hot at all you can take it off downstairs. I shall tell Jimmy that you have come to help me, as his custom and business is increasing so largely, and has been getting larger ever since I became one of the ornaments and attractions of the establishment. When I add that you don't want any pay, he wont raise a single objection."

"Wont he?"

"Not he. I know the old sweep; he is as fond of money as a miser is of guineas, or a Jew of old gold. Would you like it, do you think? You need not stop longer than you like. If you're tired you can have my key and go home."

"Your key?" said Agnes.

"Yes, mine; you are going to stay a day or two with me. Don't say no; because it would be telling an unnecessary story. I must have my way for once. We have not seen one another for a very long time, and I am not going to part with you so very easily. Now, say you agree."

"I agree, then," said Agnes, carried away by her friend's impetuosity, and the torrent of words she rained down upon her.

"That's a good girl. Now, come on. Are you all right? I'll go first. Mind you don't fall down these beastly stairs."

"No fear," replied Agnes, treading carefully.

The door in the wall soon revolved a second time, and the girls were again in the café.

Charlotte walked up to a small bar in one corner of the room, and going behind it, took her place on a high chair, which, but for the canopy, resembled a throne. She had changed her dress upstairs, and now wore a gorgeous bro-

No. 12.

Plate 11.7 'A Night-House in the Haymarket', *The Women of London* (London: George Vickers, *c.* 1860)

178

If this is done with the requisite energy, we are quite sure that Holywell-street will soon be purged of its many abominations, and one source of pollution, which is vitally injurious to the morals – more particularly of the female part of the community – will at once be extinguished.

This axis of obscene publications, Holywell Street and women as the consumers of these goods recurs consistently throughout the months of debate which followed Campbell's announcement to the Lords.

Following the Bill's third reading, Campbell expressed his hope that it would soon pass into law:

and that the time would soon come when Holywell Street would become the abode of honest, industrious handicraftsmen, and a thoroughfare through which any modest woman might pass.

Here there is a significant shift in the terms of the debate: from women as consumers of obscene materials, to women as pedestrians in Holywell Street. As we shall see, the two conditions are, in fact, dependent upon each other. Women are consumers of obscenity because they move through the space of the street. As an independent subject within the modern city, woman takes on the mantle of cultural consumer. Obscene publications are rogue commodities; promiscuous in their address, the outcome of dissident producers and transgressive consumers. The legislation seeks to correct the morality of this commercial and social system and women become a key element in the attempted transformation.

The significance of obscene publications legislation within the context of urbanization is that it focuses on the problem of 'seeing'. It responds to a specific form of viewing/looking, made possible by mass cultural production and the spaces of the modern city, where the *display* of visual commodities enables their *consumption* merely by movement through the space of the street. What becomes clear here is the centrality of space in the formation of modern subjectivity, in which *who* you are is determined by *where* you are and *what* you see. The law seeks to enforce a regime of visibility and to control the casual and indiscriminate possibilities of metropolitan sight.

So, as well as seeking to regulate the *sale* of obscene publications, Campbell's Act also sought to control the *visibility* of these objects through prohibiting their public display. Visibility, in this context, enacts the ultimate promiscuity: to pass by may be to see, which, according to a certain realist aesthetic (still dominant in current debates on pornography), may mean to be affected by. If honest women are passing through Holywell Street, they become subject to this chain of possibilities. Just prior to the Bill's discussion in the House of Commons, a leading article in *The Times* suggested:

We would only ask any member of the House of Commons who may feel any doubt as to the propriety of applying some remedy to this evil, to step aside for five minutes in his walk from the West-end to the City, and to mark the age and dress of those who may be seen hanging about the windows of [Holywell Street] . . . and then, if he be a father, to ask himself how he would like to know that his own children were exposed to similar temptations.

The public debate was thus organized around two main issues: visibility and audience.

What also emerges emphatically from these debates is that in the nineteenth century, Holywell Street and obscenity were synonymous. Although the proposed bill was national in its scope, almost all the public debate and subsequent arrests were focused on one area, Holywell Street. It is clear, then, that the street's reputation was already in place by 1857 and that the evocation of space, in this context, is metaphorical and symbolic rather than simply topographical.

Holywell Street was a narrow lane extending parallel with the Strand, from the church of St Clement Danes to St Mary-le-Strand (Plate 11.2). Donald Olsen has described the paradox of Victorian London, that whereas the quiet residential streets were broad and straight, the busy commercial streets and major thoroughfares were likely to be narrow, irregular and crooked. Such was Holywell Street. The Strand was a major London thoroughfare, with an additional symbolic importance of connecting the City of London (financial district) with the West End (commercial and residential area) and Whitehall (official/parliamentary). But frequent bottlenecks limited the Strand's value as a major through highway. The site between St Clement Danes and St Mary-le-Strand, the location of Holywell Street, was one particularly bad traffic bottleneck. At this point, the Strand narrowed so that traffic had to be channelled through the nearby narrow old lanes to the north. On 23 July 1857 *The Times* leader lamented:

It is a fact that in certain parts of London, and notably in Holywell-street, which is a feeder of the most important thoroughfare of the metropolis, prints, song-books, and other publications of the most disgusting character are exposed to public view.

It seemed that as a consequence of a deliberate lack of urban planning, people were being systematically guided through a crumbling, quaint old lane which was synonymous with the dirty book and print industry.

The street's name referred to a holy well which stood on the spot, at which pilgrims bound for Canterbury may have stopped to take a drink from what were believed to be curative waters. As a site of commerce, Holywell Street was first occupied by mercers, and the carved sign of the 'Half Moon', allegedly the oldest shop sign in London, was a remnant of this original occupation (Plate 11.8). As the mercery trade declined, the trade in costume

Plate 11.8 J. W. Archer, *Old Entrance to Lyon's Inn, Holywell Street, Strand. April 1847*. Watercolour, 1847
(Trustees of the British Museum)

dress (masquerade) and second-hand clothes took its place. By the middle of the eighteenth century, old booksellers began to replace the costume hire and dress shops; and by the nineteenth century, the street was largely given over to the book trade. But this book trade was of a very particular kind. The street was occupied by radical pressmen, free-thinkers who published tracts on politics, religion and sexuality and who, in the decades following the French Revolution, were spied on by police informers and prosecuted for sedition, blasphemy and obscenity. William Dugdale's publishing activities in this period included the production of a number of key free-thinking texts on birth control and its implications for human sexuality.

Holywell Street bore the traces of this political radicalism through the nineteenth century, as its activities shifted from free-thinking to pornography. Its identity as the main source of indecent and immoral literature was installed around the beginning of Victoria's reign. In *Radical Underworld*, a study of the early nineteenth-century radical press, Iain McCalman vividly describes the transitional moment during the 1830s when radical pressmen such as William Dugdale turned their attention in a wholesale way to the production of pornography.

But over and above Holywell Street's radical history, or its particular significance as a traffic bottleneck at a point where the City is linked to the West End, or as a medieval site which undergoes certain economic and commercial transformations, Holywell Street had accumulated an incredible degree of symbolic meaning.

In 1857, two years after the formation of London's first municipal government, the Metropolitan Board of Works, Holywell Street stood as a symbol of old London against the modernizing, cleansing thrust of the new city. It was disordered, crumbling, labyrinthine, rather than straight, singular and purposeful. Built on the site of an old well, it was the physical and moral antithesis of the drive to re-map London through a complex of drains and sewers. It was stagnant and corrupting, but also quaint. A picturesque survival of old London, it would have to come down before the march of modern improvements.

This was the site in and through which modern identities were re-defined in 1857. The Obscene Publications Act was passed in September 1857. On 23 September, police served a number of search warrants on shops in Holywell Street. The occupants, it was claimed, were completely taken by surprise. The police blocked the approaches to the street and to individual houses to prevent any property being removed. Books, prints and stereotypes were seized and summonses brought against a number of shopkeepers. Reviewing the success of the Act in December 1857, Lord Campbell told the House of Lords:

> This siege of Holywell Street might be compared to the siege of Delhi. The place was not taken in a day, but repeated assaults were necessary, and at last . . . it was now in the quiet possession of the law.

It is certainly true that reports of the assault on Holywell Street occupied exactly the same pages of the daily newspapers as reports of the fighting in the Indian colony and both endeavours can be seen as aspects of Britain's imperial project. Delhi and Holywell Street constitute two manifestations of the 'other' for imperial Britain – one outside the nation, the other poisonous, within the capital.

How, then, are women positioned within this history? Speculating on the new mass audience for the publications of William Dugdale, Iain McCalman suggests that it:

> cut across middle- and working-class boundaries. It included . . . artisans, clerks, army and navy officers, students, journalists, professionals, businessmen, government officials and tourists.

The implication here is that the audience is male, and that the audience reads rather than views. *Viewing* radically changes the constituency of audience and the relationship between self and space. Viewing is mapped on to and by the city, so that a passage through Holywell Street is a passage across complex definitions of gender and the subject's relation to desire, pleasure and power in looking.

Women were present in Holywell Street, both as consumers and as producers of obscene publications. Among the first summonses brought through Campbell's Act against shopkeepers in Holywell Street was a certain Mary Elliott, aged 49 years, of 14 Holywell Street, at whose premises indecent books and prints had been seized by the police. She pleaded guilty, but her defence pointed out that since the charge had been brought, Elliott had closed her shop and had promised never to resume trading in obscene publications again. Elliott was found guilty; the prosecution showed that, immediately following the first seizure, a second search had been made of the premises which revealed a fresh stock of obscene material. The prosecution claimed that the shop was open and trading at the very moment of the trial. In summing up, the recorder described Elliott as a defiant and determined pornographer and sentenced her to twelve months' imprisonment with hard labour.

As far as the identities of the audiences for this material is concerned, the issue is more complex. Holywell Street seems to have presented a peculiar illegibility as far as the specific identities of its public was concerned. A leading article published in the *Daily Telegraph* on 17 June 1857 describes the coexistence of respectable and non-respectable booksellers in Holywell Street. This blending produces an analogous condition in the public who move through the street. Lawyers from the nearby Inns of Court; professors from King's College on the Strand; medical students seeking second-hand copies of anatomical texts; bibliophiles and antiquarians come to Holywell Street for what the newspaper assumes to be legitimate purposes. But within the public space of the street, they come up against the dissolute and the immoral who are brought to Holywell Street by its trade in dirty books. According to *The Telegraph*, the situation is complicated even further by a deliberate misreading of identities among this audience. As the professors and lawyers browse through respectable-material 'they are elbowed . . . by the dissolute and the brutal, who intentionally misconstrue the purpose of their visit'. The respectable public can only visit Holywell Street 'at the risk of having one's pocket picked, or of being assailed by a volley of ribald jokes'. What we are presented with here is a series of negotiations around social identity – transactions, transgressions, appropriations – which suggest the partial and incomplete nature of urban masculinity during this period. The article continues:

> It is positively lamentable, passing down these streets, to see the young of either sex – often, we blush to say, of the weaker – and in many cases evidently appertaining to the respectable classes of society, furtively peeping in at these sin-crammed shop-windows, timorously gloating over suggestive title-pages, nervously conning insidious placards, guiltily bending over engravings as vile in execution as they are in subject.

Here we have it, then: evidence of a most fearful situation. Respectable middle-class women looking at and consuming the obscenities of Holywell Street. But in its fiercest denial, the newspaper articulates an even more dreadful possibility. What if these women are not timorous, nervous or guilty, but bold, daring and desiring?

Some general observations concerning the Victorian construction of self may be drawn from this history of Holywell Street. First, it becomes clear that the constituency of the public on the streets of London forced a constant reappraisal of gender and social identity. The intermingling and proximity presented by public spaces such as Holywell Street demanded a continual process of redefinition and negotiation of self. Neither masculinity nor femininity were fixed; gendered identities could be adopted or assumed for a time and then relinquished. In July 1857, Amelia Roper, the young woman who declined that offer of a lift on her way to town wrote about a visit, with friends, to the Olympic Theatre in Wych Street (a few yards from Holywell Street):

> [We] all went to the Olympic Theatre last Monday fortnight, and it was most lovely I can't describe it to you. I wished you could have been with us, they were all quite amused by my 'greenness'. I couldn't keep from saying Oh my! now and then, it was most affecting in some of the parts. We went full dress I had a *low body* on. We felt quite *screamers* I can assure you.

In her letters, the writer shows herself to be aware of the social possibilities of metropolitan life and of the different kinds of feminine identities open to her. But this is not simply a question of the city offering unprecedented potential for women; neither is it an issue of the city as a site of sexual danger. Rather, the city should be understood as offering a set of spaces for the everyday negotiation of self and identity.

Second, there are significant implications for our historical under-standing of the nature of cultural consumption. The modern city enabled new forms of mass consumption, where audiences could be constituted by movement through the city streets and by viewing goods on display, rather than through traditional structures of social and cultural distinction. Within this context, the category of the obscene could be seen as the paradigmatic modern commodity. Cheap and mass-produced, it could be read as a cipher for the loss of social differentiation threatened by the city generally.

And finally, the moment of regulation embodied in the Obscene Publications Act in 1857 enables us to look in a more historically grounded way at the monolithic category of 'Victorian morality'. Indictments and other legal records present detailed evidence of prosecuted materials which testify to the energy with which obscenity, in all its forms, was contested in the period. But it needs to be recognized that the issue here was not one of controlling the sexually explicit, but of guarding culture. Official regulation of obscenity was a battle against cheapness and availability and was part of a larger debate concerning the relationship of subjectivity and cultural consumption in the modern period.

In December 1857, Lord Campbell reported to the House of Lords that Holywell Street had been successfully cleaned up, that goods had been destroyed and shops had ceased trading. In February 1858, *The Times* announced that 'The Royal Academy of Filth in Holywell Street has been shorn of its dirty honours and dirty profits' and in an attempt to signify a clear change in the street's reputation, the Metropolitan Board of Works proposed to alter the name to 'Bookseller's Row'; but the new name would not stick. It is difficult to assess with absolute certainty the extent of the transformation of Holywell Street; many of the shopkeepers continued to trade under the same names, and the street's notoriety remained. What is more certain is that as a micro-history of mid-Victorian London, Holywell Street suggests that the city and its public were heterogeneous and resisted clear categorization, the need for which was so clearly and consistently articulated elsewhere in Victorian cultural ideology.

Holywell Street did finally come down at the very end of Victoria's reign to make way for the Aldwych and Kingsway, but it survived through the nineteenth century as a testimony to the compexity of Victorian urban history and to the economic, social and moral transactions which were at stake in the Victorian mapping of self.

12

STORIES OF THE EYE

Daniel Pick

Critics and historians have often described the late nineteenth century as an unmistakable cultural turning albeit of a shadowy nature. This chapter is concerned with changes in the language of observation as well as in the perception of perception itself in that period. It asks whether a more complex understanding of the processes which enable us to make sense of visual phenomena coalesced with an increasingly intricate understanding of the construction of the mind. The aim is also to sketch some of the key reference points we need in order to analyse this putative transformation in the story of the eye.

The 1890s, according to E.H. Gombrich in *Art and Illusion* (1960), witnessed the beginnings of a discussion in which 'the whole comfortable idea of the imitation of nature disintegrated, leaving artists and critics perplexed'. There was gathering interest in that disintegration and in the very texture of that contemporary perplexity in art and science. The blind spots of what had been dubbed by Claude Bernard 'the experimental method' (and which in his view could involve a total separation of the processes of observation and interpretation) became as interesting as what could be directly witnessed by the scientist. The enigmas of mental and visual processes raised interlocking questions about lost and remote sites of sensation, perception and memory, but also provided reciprocal metaphors. 'The obscure' became something of a tag to identity the *fin de siècle* itself along with the dark colours and shadow lines so often described in its novels. Stories united by little else often seemed at least to share an intense preoccupation with sombre shades, fading lights and dim worlds beyond immediate recall.

Blindness became a frequent motif of Victorian fiction, just as, more tragically, it had sometimes been the fate of early nineteenth-century optical investigators, who stared for too long at the sun as they recorded the impact of dazzling light on their eyes and minds. Turner's empirically impossible head-on painting of the sun, *Light and Colour (Goethe's Theory) – the Morning After the Deluge* (1843) bore scintillating witness to this unattainable desire, as Jonathan Crary has shown in his important study of vision and modernity, *Techniques of the Observer* (1990). The difficult journey towards some inaccessible – invisible – physical place or into contact with some forgotten mental state or moral condition was documented in numerous tales. The hazy borderland between madness and sanity was to become the much explored theme of Henry Maudsley's influential psychiatry. The most notable literary example of this propensity to trace visual and psychological 'borderlands' is provided by Conrad. Gloomy hues, shrouded evolutionary mysteries and impenetrable moral ambiguities became his very trade marks. In *Heart of Darkness* (1902), the primeval dark is conveyed in this celebrated passage:

> We penetrated deeper and deeper into the heart of darkness. . . . We were wanderers on a prehistoric earth. . . . We were cut off from the comprehension of our surroundings; we glided past like phantoms, wondering and secretly appalled, as sane men would be before an enthusiastic outbreak in a madhouse. We could not understand because we were too far and could not remember because we were travelling in the night of the first ages, of those ages that are gone, leaving hardly a sign – and no memories.

In the 1880s and 1890s popular fiction as well as esoteric human sciences focused upon the relations of blindness and insight, visibility and invisibility in a variety of ways. Blurring and masking recurred strikingly in the fiction and essays of Oscar Wilde and, in the present context, one might want to consider how far hidden faces and attic-confined portraits were indicative of wider *fin de siècle* concerns with the mentally obscure and the morally unseen. In still more explicitly symbolist terms, notice the insistent eye motif in the art of Odilon Redon: here the organ of sight itself provided an image of the fragile membrane separating and connecting the inner and outer world. One might add to these varied turn-of-the-century examples of cultural attention to light and dark, sight and sightlessness the sun-dead future of Wells' *Time Machine* (1895) or, very differently, the devastating personal crisis of blindness recounted in Du Maurier's *The Martian* (1896), which is followed by a quite different kind of internal mental vision, achieved via some remarkable interplanetary telepathy. Mind and cosmos were thus figuratively interrelated in and beyond the genre of 'science fiction'. In short, it was not only major writers such as Conrad and James who made unprecedented 'uses of obscurity' (to borrow Allon White's phrase) in their narrative technique, and furthermore the novel was only one instance of a much wider set of contemporary transfigurations in cultural and political thought which questioned the sharper epistemological and ethical definitions offered by some earlier writers. Materialism was given new theorizations in political and scientific thought, yet also came under fresh challenge, not only in terms of an already long-running conflict between Victorian secular and religious ideologies (sometimes caricatured as the battle of science versus faith) but also among advocates of progressive ideas and experimentalism.

Yet whilst nineteenth century's last decades demonstrated a notable cross-disciplinary preoccupation with how we see and what we see, it would be simplistic to imagine some absolute epistemological or artistic break. Indeed, it has been compellingly argued that the real shift in the cultural meaning of vision can be seen emerging by the beginning of the nineteenth century. As Crary has put it, 'in the aftermath of Kant's work there is an irreversible clouding over of the transparency of the subject-as-observer.' The science of vision was increasingly understood to involve human physiology and psychology rather than (as in the hitherto domi-nant model of the *camera obscura*) questions about the mechanics of light and optical transmission. In brief, the body now obtruded rudely into the hitherto rather detached language of vision. A whole range of new inventions emerged in the first half of the century, demonstrating the fact that our experience of sight was no simple registration of the truth of the outside world. Moreover, retinal after-images, although known since classical times, acquired a new significance. The after-image undoubtedly bore witness to something; but what? If it was a verifiable experience, it was not simply the record of a present stimulus. It brought into focus the temporal aspect of 'observation' and the ambiguous relationship of external and internal processes.

Other developments, in part technical, in part conceptual – from dioramas to stereoscopes – were also altering the learned and popular culture of observation. The causes and effects of these changes are complex and cannot be encompassed here, but, as Crary intriguingly demonstrates, even ahead of the invention of photography, codes of seeing were undergoing some of the profound revisions which we usually attribute to photography. A vogue for gadgetry such as the thaumatrope, or 'wonder-turner' (demonstrating the effect of after-images) can be linked with more erudite philosophical and aesthetic speculations about perception. Instead of earlier models of unified vision, modernity frequently seemed to involve recognition of sensory fragmentation and dispersed psychological experience. As Schelling wrote: 'We do not live in vision; our knowledge is piecework, that is, it must be produced piece by piece in a fragmentary way, with divisions and gradations.' Other writers were exploring at around this time the complex relationship of perception to memory. Words such as *mélange* or *fusion* become commonplace in the critique of classical optics and its model of pure isolated sensation. Herbert, Kant's successor at Königsberg, wrote about how we fend off as well as take in an unmanageable stream of sensory inputs. The mind extracts as well as obscures other images in order to perceive.

Thus, late nineteenth-century doubts about vision's grip on 'objective reality' emerged out of longer-standing debates in science, art and fiction.

The relationship between vision, consciousness and memory had already been understood to raise interconnecting problems, although the answers ventured had diverged across periods as well as within them. There was a number of earlier literary and philosophical 'foils' used by modern writers to mark the distance they had travelled and the novelty of the current conjuncture. In his *Philosophy of the Unconscious* (translated in 1884), Hartmann attacked Locke's simplistic view that consciousness or 'having ideas' was coterminous with mental life. Moreover, Descartes and Locke inhabited a quite different tradition of thought on the nature of vision from that of, say, Goethe, Müller or Helmholtz; in different ways all three had come to stress the irreducibly subjective and corporeal dimension of seeing. Vision could not be abstracted from the bodily processes of the viewer: this became the repeated, but none the less startling, finding of a broad span of nineteenth-century investigators.

Whatever the judgement we may now make as to the degree of rupture and continuity which marked these themes, commentators around 1900 often viewed the Victorian twilight years as a time of radical intellectual, emotional and moral transition, not least in their intensified or even unprecedented recognition of the invisible and the unconscious. In a footnote added in 1914 to *The Interpretation of Dreams*, Freud drew our attention to another late nineteenth-century author, C. Du Prel (*Die Philosophie der Mystik* 1885), who, he felt, had also offered some significant points of departure on just these matters:

> The problem of the nature of the mind evidently calls for a preliminary investigation as to whether consciousness and mind are identical. This preliminary question is answered in the negative by dreams, which show that the concept of the mind is a wider one than that of consciousness in the same kind of way in which the gravitational force of a heavenly body extends beyond its range of luminosity.

In the same text, Freud, like Marx and Bergson, also expressed his scepticism about the old *camera obscura* model of truth. The night-time world which lay beyond the 'range of luminosity' was being opened up in strikingly original, indeed revolutionary, ways by Freud and others, but it would be a mistake to imagine, teleologically, that all earlier thinkers on dreams and other mental underworlds were but faint precursors of the dynamic unconscious or that they were entirely in the dark about the kinds of blindness psychoanalysis went on to explore. In any case the perception of a changing intellectual climate was an important stimulus to new thought in its own right. The declaration of difference may be a quasi-'performative' utterance, helping to produce the change by virtue of the claim itself, rather than simply commentating upon an intellectual metamorphosis which has already taken place. A sense of change was marked out in self-consciously modern colours and symbols as well as in avowedly path-breaking arguments; explicit philosophical critique as well as a new tone and style drew attention to the partiality of the truths constructed by the classic age of the Enlightenment.

The story so far: in the late Victorian period it was perceived that a set of earlier beliefs in a sharply defined and securely describable visual field was giving way to a more ambiguous inner space, the confidence in 'clear seeing' dissolving in the face of a renewed preoccupation with how we see objects and how we have 'insight'. It was well noted by a number of commentators that we would surely view the world and our own minds differently if we could only escape conventional codes. Theorists explored what has since become an unexceptional truth: that expectation and precedent weigh upon our minds, informing and indeed making possible our grasp of the visual world. The question of how far observation could be said to be at the same time hidebound interpretation of sensory experience had already become the stuff of intricate exploration in the first half of the century. This was consolidated in the 1850s and 1860s, for instance, in John Ruskin's influential views on the art of drawing or Friedrich Lange's work on materialism which will provide my concluding illustrations.

Today, some of these provocative nineteenth-century debates seem culturally obvious, hardly worth stating. To 'observe' a photograph, for example, is also to read it and clearly we have to learn how to read. What a photograph would mean, how the image would look to the uninitiated is a moot point, the subject of anthropological experiment. Different kinds of naivety are obviously possible: from ignorance of the frame of reference and meaning of photography to the kind of unexamined familiarity which takes for granted a perfect congruity between the image and the world 'snapped'. In the period, various photographers experimented with composite pictures or with retouching; the possibility, and the recognition of the possibility, of 'doctoring' pictures could not be avoided. Significantly many of the early photographers had had prior careers as illusionists. 'Trick photography' led to growing concern among cultural commentators. Hence the appearance of articles with titles such as 'The Lies of Photography' in magazines and a more general scepticism about the truthfulness of representation which had initially been promised for the age of the camera, as Martin Jay has shown in *Downcast Eyes* (1993). But how far do history and experience bear upon vision itself, not just the interpretation of art and photography? It had long been contended that the blind person to whom eyesight was later restored would not immediately and by dint merely of the physical change 'see normally'. Certainly these far from new broad questions did lead to significant cultural explorations in the second half of the nineteenth century. The suspicion of over-familiar 'sight' prompted the desire for something else, such as a liberating moment of blindness followed by the return of some infantile uncoded vision. It is said that Monet wished he had been born blind and only later had his sight restored (at a stroke), thereby to free himself from stultifying habit. The longing for such freshness of perception often went together with a desire (expressed by many nineteenth-century painters) to see 'as a child'. Infancy was equated with visual innocence and both sides of the equation were used to articulate the artistic yearning to break free. If one could only catch the play of light upon the eye at its very inception; thus John Singer Sargent's comment on Monet:

> [he] was not content with using his eyes to see what things were or what they looked like as everybody had done before him, [he] turned his attention to noting what took place on his *retina* (as an oculist would test his own vision).

In the novel and in painting (most notably in the development of impressionism) as well as in other cultural forms of the period, we can see the starkest evidence of this complex (and long emerging) problematic of vision and modern representation. 'Form' became the subject of renewed speculation and debate. To paraphrase the familiar contention about the novel, 'classic realism' (with its belief in writing as a potential mirror reflecting the world) gave way to something more hazy, a semi-visible pattern of lights and shadows. But realism *and* modernism arguably both inhabited a new and disturbing world of vision, which had lost its classical optical bearings. None the less, while formulations setting Victorian realism against modernism easily risk travestying the discursive complexity of the former, it is clear that the process of representation came to be problematized in significantly different ways. Realism, as J.P. Stern put it, designated 'a creative attention to the visible rather than the invisible', although this should not be taken to mean that the finest nineteenth-century realist novelists merely confirmed such an attention. On the contrary, what very often emerged was a powerful tension between the conceptual commitment to such codes and quite other resonances, intimations of processes which were neither visible within, nor containable by, the conventional terms of such narratives. Life, declared Virginia Woolf later in a famous essay on modern fiction (which aimed to repudiate commonplace late Victorian and Edwardian tropes), is not a series of gig-lamps symmetrically arranged, but a semi-luminous envelope with which art, she felt, must engage. It is one of the curiosities of this history that the cultural developments in attitudes to light and dark, vision and blindness which are described in Woolf's essay occurred in a period notable, in a material sense, for its widening luminosity. Perhaps more even than a curiosity, it might be argued that there was a link between these apparently counterbalancing processes. Electric light increasingly flooded the cityscape, leading in one sense, as Wolfgang Schivellbusch argues in his memorable book (1988) to the 'disenchantment' of the night. Yet even as the lights went on, numerous commentators, as I have been suggesting, pointed in the other direction, to all these 'dark regions' where science and technology, reason and realism were unable to penetrate.

The reducibility of the mind to organic terms of explanation was a further assumption undergoing intellectual re-examination. The field of the unconscious, the primitive and the regressive, as well as the ghostly and the telepathic, all these wonders and horrors of heaven and earth undreamt of in the more confident materialism and naturalism of previous years, returned to the fore. Such pursuits often had a liminal quality; the investigator poised between scepticism towards and enthusiasm for the fleeting and the fantastic. It was the age of Henry James' *The Turn of the Screw* (1898). In the mid-1890s, Henry's elder brother William, much engaged by such epistemological departures, for instance, the experiments and questions posed by the Society for Psychical Research, declared 'the exploration of the subliminal region' the task of tasks. In the 1880s and 1890s, many investigators committed themselves to 'psychical research'; new understandings of 'the unconscious' were emerging, often poised between a kind of 'ape-in-man' post-Darwinian excitement and disturbing intuitions of psychic meanings and sexual investments which had little to do with mere 'selection' and 'reproduction' or so-called racial memory. Popular novels such as Robert Louis Stevenson's *Strange Case of Dr Jekyll and Mr Hyde* (1886), Emile Zola's *Dr Pascal* (1893) or Bram Stoker's *Dracula* (1897), although caught up in the nomenclature of apish spite, hereditary decline and criminal brains, were also upon the cusp of a new language of dreams and desires.

Late nineteenth-century writers so often charted the dark and the night-time, often seeking to prise open *another* domain of meaning, intimating shapes and truths which eluded vision or which could just be glimpsed out of the corner of the eye. In *The Interpretation of Dreams*, Freud drew on images of telescopes and ideas about virtual reality, but also kept showing how visual images might just as well stand in for something else in the unconscious; what was seen was not necessarily what was really meant. The image was as much disguise as revelation. The visual impression of the dream provided the beginning rather than the end of the story of signification. At one point, in a later textual addition to the dream book, he cited Hans Sachs' remark that 'we ought not be surprised to find that the monster which we saw under the magnifying glass of analysis turns out to be a tiny infusorian'. In literature, as well as in the origins of psychoanalysis, the position of the self-confident observer was very much in question. This sense of observational displacement or even visual opacity could either be seen as a gain or as a worrying symptom. In some accounts, weak sight or blindness were taken as symptoms of a wider crisis of modern degeneration and decline. *The Time Machine* suggested a future in which a grotesque underclass suffer exactly such a fate: 'You can scarce imagine how nauseatingly inhuman they looked – those pale, chinless faces and great, lidless. pinkish-grey eyes! – as they stared in their blindness and bewilderment.' Whether as exciting experimental possibility or doom-laden prophecy, the 'out of sight' was certainly not 'out of mind'.

Even Darwin's one-time kindred spirit Alfred Russel Wallace would turn back increasingly from the hypotheses of materialism and evolution to the realms of the spirit, and eventually the eternal and the cosmic. Wallace's intellectual journey was by no means unique; even that most strident of European materialists, Cesare Lombroso, ended up by the 1900s in the company of a medium, communing with the dead in darkened hotel rooms. This was a *camera obscura* of a very different kind from that so confidently inhabited by earlier draftsmen and optical theorists. Many members of the Victorian intelligentsia had trooped since the mid-century for purposes of conversion or refutation, through the curtained rooms of the table turners and spirit-communicants. Wallace also looked at the sky and the stars with renewed wonder. The affinity between the two theorists of natural selection had only ever been partial. In any event Darwin could but express the forlorn hope that his fellow scientist had not 'murdered too completely your own and my child' in the process of qualifying his earlier views. Mind, Wallace now argued, just could not be explained away in Darwinian terms. Despite Darwin's admonitions, the younger man continued his new lines of enquiry into evolution and much besides. The title of one of Wallace's later books, *Man's Place in the Universe: A Study of the Results of Scientific Research In Relation to the Unity or Plurality of Worlds* (1903) was entirely characteristic of this kind of odyssey, a far cry from *Man's Place in Nature*, the work of Darwin's 'bulldog, Thomas Huxley, forty years earlier. Some psychologists sought to build upon or surpass earlier Romantic intuitions, mesmeric ideas or spiritualist claims, moving towards new models of 'automatism', multiplex personality' and all sorts of uncanny mental phenomena beyond the reach of consciousness, not least in the sphere of the hypnotic state. While in one sense the later nineteenth century witnesses the consolidation of psychiatric materialism as epitomized by the work of Griesinger, Magnan, Meynert (Freud's teacher) or Maudsley, there was also a renewal of interest in the psychological causation of mental disturbance in the two final decades of the century. The term 'psychotherapy', Gauld remarks in his *History of Hypnotism* (1992), entered into circulation in the 1880s.

This *fin de siècle* 'crossroads' in attitudes to the visible and invisible can also be located in the shift from the confident observer Jean-Martin Charcot to Freud. The Parisian neurologist had asserted that 'all I am is a photographer, I describe what I see'. In his appreciative but also critical obituary, Freud had written that Charcot: 'was not a reflective man, not a thinker: he had the nature of an artist – he was, as he himself said, a *"visuel"*, a man who sees.' For Freud, however, there was a notable 'blindness of the seeing eye'. His move from hypnotism to the 'talking cure' removed the need or even the desirability of being (and seeing) 'eye-to-eye'. It has been widely remarked that the visually restricted arrangement of the consulting room marked out an important element in the specificity of the psychoanalytic enterprise. There is another sense, or course, in which Freud's work came to constitute a new suspicion of sight, and an attention to all it may conceal, namely, the sense in which he took the eye itself as standing in symbolically for something else, notably the penis; this is as true of Oedipus' self-blinding, Freud remarks, as of E. T. A. Hoffmann's extraordinary story *The Sandman* (1816). As Freud puts it in *The Uncanny* (1919): 'A study of dreams, phantasies and myths has taught us that anxiety about one's eyes, the fear of going blind, is often enough a substitute for the dread of being castrated.' Freud's judgement here raises a question which might be worth reconsidering. Whatever the castration fears that Hoffmann's story may or may not articulate, *The Sandman* was perhaps the most remarkable of all the nineteenth century's fictions about madness and the anxiety about losing the means of sight. Can vision really be redirected so quickly to other still more basic anxieties?

In Hoffmann's tale, Nathanael never gets over an early warning he is given when a child about the terrifying figure of the Sandman. It is a rich and complex story which I cannot recount here, but let me just quote the passage in which the child has just asked who is this dreaded character of the title. His mother's answer does not satisfy him, so Nathanael enquires of his youngest sister's old nurse: 'Why, Natty', replied the old woman, 'don't you know that yet? He's a wicked man who comes to children when they don't want to go to bed and throws handfuls of sand in to their eyes; that makes their eyes fill with blood and jump out of their heads, and he throws the eyes into his bag and takes them into the crescent moon to feed his own children, who are sitting in the nest there; the Sandman's children have crooked beaks, like owls, with which to peck the eyes of naughty human children.' Freud was not blind to the privileged place accorded to sight in Charcot's psychiatric performances, Sophocles' drama or Hoffmann's tale; but he displaces the focus from the eyes themselves. In Freud's later theories of civilization, the visual sexual stimuli are anyway understood, phylogenetically, to have been superimposed upon earlier olfactory gratifications at an evolutionary stage when we were still on all fours. He had scented the possibility that sight has not always been more important than smell. Certainly Freud devotes considerable attention to the visual domain in other respects, and to deal adequately with this theme would take far more scrutiny than I can offer. If Freud's interpretation of Hoffmann's *The Sandman* seems not to do justice to the richness of either of them, surely Freud was right to find the tale exemplary and important. Nathanael's madness follows from the loss of his eyes and his sense of self; madness and the 'eye thief' descend upon him together. Freud rightly declares it an uncannily disturbing story, but the question of why it is so disturbing remains to be debated.

In recent years, we have been confronted with a plethora of studies on sight and blindness in the past. Such literature takes many forms; from analyses of the motif of vision (or its loss) in poetry and painting to histories of ophthalmology. Rather than an aesthetic choice to address the problems of seeing differently in the later nineteenth century, some commentators have argued that the key issue was altogether more organic: painters were not engaged in a theoretical departure from previous ways of looking; rather they were victims of poor eyesight, groping about in the blur or semi-dark. In a well-known book, *The World Through Blunted Sight* (1970), the doctor turned art critic Patrick Trevor-Roper seeks to offer such a medical explanation of what was going on in the history of painting. Trevor-Roper points to Monet's and Cezanne's myopia and notes how such diagnoses were prevalent in criticism at the time. Thus he cites Huysmans' comment on Cezanne: 'An artist with a diseased retina, who, exasperated by a defective vision discovered the basis of a new art' and reports the following remark from *L'Eclair* in 1906: 'An incomplete talent, in which an imperfect vision resulted in work that was always incomplete and sketchy.' Many degenerationist writers of this period, it should be added, were prone to link artistic and literary experiment with constitutional insanity or feeble powers of perception. Certainly those late nineteenth-century challenges to the conventional way of painting and describing were perplexing to contemporaries. While some commentators stressed the readability of the human face and body, the attack on physiognomical naivety was also in full swing. Much work in painting, literature and the human sciences had hitherto gone into attempting convincingly to code the face and body, to turn physiognomical folklore into scientific truth, as Mary Cowling shows in *The Artist as Anthropologist* (1989). The nineteenth century had been the golden age of such solemn inventories: the laws of character supposedly revealed in the nature of the face and eyes, charted in innumerable taxonomies of racial features, Jewish glares, criminal ears and eyebrows, social 'types'. Even Darwin tried to use photography to codify the expression of the emotions in 1872; but as he had laboured on the project amidst a torrent of images of his own children, animals and the insane, he seemed to become increasingly doubtful about the fixity of the phenomena he tabulated.

Darwin was a keen observer of nature but at the same time a sceptic about some of the wilder claims for a science of appearances. It might perhaps be recalled here that the eye was in other respects too a particular problem for Darwin. It was used as a clinching case by one of his most troubling critics, St George Jackson Mivart, the proof that natural selection was an inadequate explanation of evolution. Darwin was much exercised in trying to find an answer to the point, made by Mivart and others, that incipient structures of the eye did not produce sight. It was argued therefore that the fact that the feature persisted and 'evolved' could not be explained by virtue of its initial utility; it must have been envisaged by a designer who had an end point in mind, not simply as a function of selection, Mivart concluded in *The Genesis of Species* (1871). Earlier still, in *Natural Theology* (1802), a book which was of great significance to Darwin, William Paley had argued that the eye was a perfect demonstration of the fact that God was the creator of the human body and of everything else too for that matter. To imagine no such creator or 'artificer' was to enter into the 'absurdity' of atheism, the 'irrationality of irreligion', in the historian John Hedley Brooke's phrase. The eye constituted a particularly intricate and important case study in Paley's book. The eye is designed for vision, he proclaimed, just as a telescope is made for assisting it. Eyes are spectacularly well adapted to their varied use across the animal kingdom in birds, fishes, human beings. The eye is unmistakably 'fashioned'; to contemplate such an orb was the best cure Paley could provide for atheism. As much as any inanimate telescope or *camera obscura* (with which it has 'a complete resemblance'), the eye should be regarded as an instrument. The divine designer's aim was clear vision. Paley argued that in an animal, unlike in a telescope or an automatic statue, the process of causes and effects can only be traced so far until it disappears, as it were, into the mystery of creation. In short, the eye demonstrates the existence and the genius of the Creator: 'Can anything be more decisive of contrivance than this? The most secret laws of optics must have been known to the author of a structure endowed with such a capacity of change.' Darwin was altogether more doubtful.

The late nineteenth-century material on vision in art and science which I have outlined above should also be situated against the backdrop of at least a century of advances and institutional developments in the medical understanding of blindness. The seventeenth- and eighteenth-century philosophical fascination with what the born blind, united with their sight in adulthood, would 'see' was confronted, by the late eighteenth century, with the growing promise of medical cure. Alongside the technical advances, however, increasingly extravagant boasts were being made about the moral and psychological redemption which now lay at hand: the treatment for blindness as a panacea for much else besides. Rehabilitation and redemption, as well as improvement in the provision for the blind were the order of the day; Louis Braille suggested this in his revolutionary script in 1835, originally to aid blind musicians. The quasi-sacred role of the eye doctor and dire warnings about the knavery and humbug of fringe practitioners were the dual messages of the medical schools. In the century of rising institutional progress for the medical specialism it is not surprising that prominent eye surgeons such as MacKenzie, Middleton and Lawrence made large claims for their importance and that sight was considered without question to be the most important of the senses, essential to the enjoyment of any of the others. Almost by definition, the blind, especially the poor blind, were understood to have been reduced to 'a dreary, blank, dark, solitary and cheerless existence' (Lawrence). New textbooks, lecture series, specialist hospitals and expert journals as well as vital new medical inventions (most notably the opthalmoscope) transformed the relationship between the doctor and the blind. In short, the nineteenth century was the great age of the medicalization and institutionalization of eye treatments.

But if medical actions and treatments constitute part of our story, so too does interpretation: particularly with regard to the issue, in parts organic, psychological and philosophical, of what seeing involves. Twentieth-century studies have amply confirmed to us the fact that vision involves an active process of construction. As M.H. Pirenne shows in his important book, *Optics, Painting and Photography* (1970), in order to see, we need to do something more than just be passively receptive to light. Although the process whereby light enters into the eye from the outside world is a purely physical one, which occurs inside the living as well as in the dead eye, or in a camera, yet we are not merely receivers of sensations. Eyes are ceaselessly moving, framing different scenes. If we succeed in keeping our eyes very steady in one position, then vision loses its clarity. Activity and movement are crucial. Moreover, we do not simply 'see' our retinal image; we interpret it. As Pirenne puts it, the relationship between the physiological event in the brain and the psychological process of vision 'is part of the philosophical riddle of the relationship between body and mind, and largely remains a mystery'. Gombrich's own work (cited above) also provides an important intervention into that enduring twentieth-century debate, showing that the world as we see it involves the viewer's construction. Our eyes undergo stimulations on the retina which result in 'sensations of colour'. But it is our minds that transform sensations into perceptions. Our conscious vision of the world is grounded in experience and expectation; it is not simply a registration of some self-evident external reality. But how much of this process was known in the last century? Was it only in the 1890s or beyond that the sense of the complexity of vision – its intricate mind–body conundrum – really crystallized?

In fact many earlier discussions were moving in this direction. Turner's friend and champion, Ruskin, understood, ahead of impressionism, that our knowledge of the visible world creates the difficulties of art. We do not simply see afresh as we look through our eyes; our vision today is slave to our experience. If we could forget what we already know, we would see differently, better, he declared in *The Elements of Drawing* (1857):

The perception of solid Form is entirely a matter of experience. We *see* nothing but flat colours; and it is only by a series of experiments that we find out that stain of black or grey indicates the dark side of a solid substance, or that a feint hue indicates that the object in which it appears is far away.

He urged the novice artist to try and envisage a book or a table as a patchwork of colours. It was crucial to free oneself as far as possible from any presumption of knowledge. All great artists, Ruskin proposed, have a capacity to look anew at shapes and colours; to see the world with what he took to be a childlike innocence.

I want to end with some related observations from the closely, contemporaneous work of Friedrich Lange, a teacher and radical who turned to commerce and journalism before returning to the university late in his life, as professor in Zurich in 1870 and then at Marburg in Germany from 1872. He died in 1875, ten years after producing a massive and sympathetic critique of materialism. Lange wrote about Darwin; he corresponded with Engels (Marx, however, thought him stupid and misguided), and his book is to be found in Freud's library in London – with a pencil mark against a passage on vision – indeed on the eye and the imagination. Some critics were dismissive of his work; the Marxist Plekhanov, for example, considered much of it pure Kant, since Lange viewed the 'thing in itself' as unknowable. Plekhanov also complained that Lange had failed to address the importance of Marx and dialectical materialism, concentrating instead on Vogt, Moleschott and evolutionary naturalism. In fact his work seems to me to be less clearly located than either that attribution of Kantean or evolutionary materialist pedigree would suggest, as we can see with regard to his observations on sight. Vision, Lange shows, is inseparable from interpretation; to the man born blind who receives his sight by an operation, the objects of visual perception appear oppressively near; the child reaches out for the white crescent in the night-time sky; even to the adult the figure of the moon or the sun is hardly more distant than the figure of the hand which covers the moon with a threepenny bit. He merely *interprets* this figure differently, and this interpretation reacts of course on the immediate impressions of the object of vision. Lange speaks of the ego, the consciousness or some other imaginary being sitting within the skull and regarding the retinal picture. He links it with the splendid illusion of a diorama as well as with the laws of perspective and the technical apparatus of a camera. Lange is addressing the crucial question not just of how do we see but where is 'I' or 'the ego' in the psychological process of seeing. What is inner and what is outer? And he also wants to know in the light of these observations how materialism might go forward without returning to idealism.

In quasi-Darwinian terms, Lange asks how we select what we see from the vast variety of possible objects within our field of vision at any one time.

How does the struggle for survival of the image occur? What do we see and what do we ignore? Lange confronts the materialists with something he classes 'unconscious thinking' and is not sure whether or not it can be explained away as a phenomenon of a merely corporeal nature. Lange explores how what we know we are seeing and how we know we are ourselves are interlocking questions. Materialism and realism he suggests, have to be understood as involving codes of seeing.

> The idea of the Ego is meanwhile, as it is originally with man, quite inseparable from the idea of the body; and this body is the diorama body, the retinal picture body, fused with the body of the sensations of touch, the sensations of pain and pleasure.

The fictional aspect of the unity of the person is also stressed by Lange. Somehow our sense of seeing connects with our sense of ourselves as unities; so we are able to see, as though from one visual and psychological place; but despite the fusion of the functions of the sensoria, nevertheless the enigma – 'the metaphysical riddle' – remains: 'how out of the multiplicity of the atomic movements there arises the unity of the psychical image.' This is the central mystery. Observation is nothing less than 'a colossal paradox', even a 'philosophical fantasy'. His point of reference is Müller's *The Physiology of Sight* (1826), which explores the complex adjustment which takes place to the inverted nature of objects in the process of sight. Lange is alert to the way in which the historical realization that sight was thus mediated (literally turned upside down) was revolutionary.

It could be argued that the nineteenth-century material I have sketched in this chapter is merely a footnote to an age-old history: the classics, the Bible, pre-modern literature are all replete with examples of the sightedness of the blind and vice versa. Alongside the legendary instances of blindness, from Oedipus to Gloucester in *King Lear* (to say nothing of the Victorian period's own Rochester in *Jane Eyre*), we might also want to include for consideration the many sight and blindness myths which have been collated by historians and anthropologists from across the globe: eye goddesses, peeping Toms, innumerable evil eye beliefs. But this essay has suggested that in several nineteenth-century discursive contexts, a significantly new understanding about the nature of vision was emerging. Furthermore, it came to be acknowledged that how we come to look at or within ourselves, how indeed we turn ourselves into a unity, a first-person singular, links in complex ways with how one sees the world. I have also suggested that this more sophisticated problematic of vision was not only a characterization made in the subsequent historiography, but was topos of the *fin de siècle* itself. And it may well be that the presumption of stumbling around in unprecedented cultural darkness facilitated the new insights and visions which did emerge in those years.

Part IV

MODERN AND POSTMODERN

13

THE MODERN AUDITORY I

Steven Connor

THE SELF-SEEING I

Depending on who you believe, modernity is identified both with the making and the unmaking of the self. One story about modernity would identify it with the apprehension of the self's autonomous self-grounding, the positive precipitate of the act of expelling all inauthenticity and error from the self. Only by such an act of autogenetic faith, it appears, can the self give rise to itself in the characteristically modern, modernist and, some would say, rather more than implicitly masculinist manner. But the very condition of such a bootstrap lifting stunt is that there is, after all, nothing to *guarantee* the modern self – nothing, that is, except its abandonment, in the mode of reflection or of delirium, of all external guarantees. So, according to the other story, the absence or impotence of God, the Church, the king, tradition, makes the modern subject more liable to come apart at the seams than ever before. The very strength of the modern self is its weakness, just as its weakness is the ultimate source of its strength.

If the modern self wills itself into being, then, from Descartes onwards that willing has a particular form and reach; it is an epistemological willing, or a will to know. The stubbornly ineffaceable flicker of self-reflection in the *cogito* that Descartes could not reasonably continue to doubt was both a pure assertion of the self and, almost instantaneously, a mirroring back to the self of that assertion. The modern self is an epistemized self, its will-to-self a will-to-self-knowing, even in its most radical assertions of the need to go beyond merely rational or cognitive categories.

The epistemized self which takes itself as an object of self-knowledge also constitutes itself in terms of the epistemological regime of the eye which has become increasingly dominant in the West since the Renaissance. The rise of scientific and technological rationality, as Heidegger and others have shown, was accomplished by a separation of the active, transforming self from a nature progressively conceived as passive, constraining and un-conscious; with this separation came what Heidegger called the *Gestell*, or visual enframing of the world, as a separated object of knowledge. Visualism

203

signifies distance, differentiation and domination; the control which modernity exercises over nature depends upon that experience of the world as separate from myself, and my self-definition in the act of separation, which vision seems to promote. Where knowing is associated so over-whelmingly with seeing, then the will-to-self-knowing of the epistemized self has unavoidably taken a scopic form.

Martin Jay has argued that the twentieth century has seen, alongside the consolidation of the visualist paradigm, the maturing of a philosophical tradition, especially in French thought, in which the powers of vision are subject to hostile investigation. The idea of the self as a seeing and self-seeing entity similarly comes under sustained assault throughout the twentieth century. This produces a philosophical interest in those relations between the self and its environments which cannot be reduced to sight. However, in the many examples of antiocularcentrism arrayed by Martin Jay, the suspicion of sight often takes the more abstract form of an inten-sified scrutiny of vision, a scrutiny which amounts to a kind of vision raised to a higher power. This would then offer no simple alternative to vision, but a turning of visual modes against themselves, though always in the mode of vision. The work of Lacan and Foucault provide signal examples of this phenomenon.

This chapter aims to suggest some of the defining importance in modernity and beyond of the sense of hearing, and the other non-visual senses with which it is associated. I document examples of the growing identification of the self and the ear in some areas of characteristically modern experience, as well as in some important literary, philosophical and psychoanalytic texts of modernity and postmodernity, and read this alongside the emerging acoustic technologies – of the telephone, phono-graph, radio – which dominated the period between 1875 and 1920. I finish by offering some suggestions regarding the audiovisual constitution of self in postmodernity.

SOUND TECHNOLOGY

It is too often assumed that technology and visualism are in a necessary and invariant relation; that the instrumentalization of the world by technology is necessarily a reduction of it to an object for sight, the 'conquest of the world as picture' condemned by Heidegger. Such an assumption imper-fectly recognizes the importance of the other senses, and especially the sense of hearing, in technological development. The period between the invention of the telephone and the gathering of the great powers for the Second World War marks that second great wave of technological innova-tion, defined by Lewis Mumford as the era of 'neotechnics', which was characterized not so much by the development of industrial machinery or means of physical transport – technology aimed at a general augmentation of physical speed and power – as by the enhancement of the senses. Much of the technology of the twentieth century had already been invented during the nineteenth, but we think of the twentieth century as the era of modernity primarily because of this shift from industrial to communicational technologies; from technologies that are an elongation of the arm (or the penis) to technologies that are, as Marshall McLuhan has it, an extension of the central nervous system. The steam-engine, rifle and cannon give way to the computerized missile system; in the Gulf War, we remember, the missiles with video cameras in their nose-cones themselves had eyes – *were* eyes.

It is a striking fact that, from the mid-1870s to the mid-1920s, the impetus of innovation was not only in visual technologies – with the development of the cinema in the early years of the century and, more humbly, though with more far-reaching effects, the invention of the electric light bulb – but also in auditory ones, from the near-simultaneous invention of the telephone and the phonograph in 1876, through the rapid development of the microphone and other devices for amplification, of radio and of recording technologies.

Such auditory technologies produced responses which cannot easily be accommodated to the otherwise all-encompassing model of visualism, stimulating subjective experiences formed round the auditory rather than the visual, or at least formed in a certain contest between the two. The awareness of such a contest may be glimpsed at the exhilarated beginnings of the telephone age in an article in *The Times* on 19 November 1877, which speaks of the 'invidious superiority' enjoyed by the eye over 'the weakest and most treacherous of our faculties'; the eye,

> not to speak of its celestial achievements over other worlds, or of kingdoms of the earth it could see in a moment of time, [had] encroached successfully on the dominance of the ear, by beacons and telegraphs, and all kinds of signals.

The advent of the telephone seemed to promise a regime of the auditory, in which distances and separations were collapsed in an uncannily intimate proximity. Early commentators on the telephone were fascinated, not so much by its capacity to convey messages and information as by its faithful preservation of the individuating tones and accidents of speech and even the non-verbal sounds of the body. *The Times* characterized the revolutionary potential of the telephone as follows:

> There is no reason why a man should not hold conversation with a son at the Antipodes, distinguish his voice, and, if the instrument be applied as a stethoscope, hear his heart's throb. Next to seeing – nay, rather than seeing – what would parents give to hear the very voice, the familiar laugh, the favourite song, of the child long separated by a solid mass 8,000 miles in diameter?

The shocked delight at hearing the intimate sound of the heartbeat is matched in a contemporary telephonic fantasy by Kate Field, an American journalist and early convert to the telephone. As well as organizing a 'telephonic soirée' for Queen Victoria, Field also put together a celebratory history of the invention from Alexander Graham Bell's collection of cuttings in 1877 (she never returned them, much to Bell's chagrin). Under the persona of 'Puss', writing to her friend about the pleasures of the telephone, she describes her flirtation with an invisible interlocutor:

> Didn't I laugh when my unknown acquaintance sang, 'Thou art so near and yet so far!'
> 'Why did you laugh?' asked the Invisible, at the conclusion of his song.
> 'Did you hear me? My mouth was some distance from the Telephone.'
> 'I heard you perfectly. Now hear me breathe.'
> When that breath came to my ear I was startled, Ella. Then we whispered to each other, and finally the Invisible exclaimed, 'Just one more experiment,' and he kissed me! I heard him. I can't honestly say that this final experiment was as satisfactory in its results as the ordinary way of performing the operation. It is not likely to supersede old-fashioned osculation, but *faute de mieux*, it will serve.

The capacity of the telephone to convey bodily sounds as well as verbal messages recommended the device to the medical profession; the first discussions of the telephone in the *Lancet* were in fact concerned with its capacity for electronic diagnosis at a distance. If such diagnosis is in one sense a recruitment of the auditory to the service of a scopic epistemology – the telephone as telestethoscope – the startling experiences imagined and reported by *The Times* and Kate Field suggest a different, more fluid interchange of separated spaces, in which the interior of one body is transmitted, almost without mediation, to the inner ear of the listener. The telephone offers a quasi-controlled collapse of boundaries, in which the listening self can be pervaded by the vocal body of another while yet remaining at a distance from it. The development of telephonic sex around a century later in the context of anxieties about actual physical interchange consequent upon AIDS, as represented, for example, in Nicholson Baker's novel *Vox*, testifies to a similar libidinization of the aural.

These small examples point to what is perhaps the most important distinguishing feature of auditory experience, namely its capacity to disintegrate and reconfigure space. With the development of radio in the early twentieth century, this effect was intensified. The rationalized 'Cartesian grid' of the visualist imagination, which positioned the perceiving self as a single point of view, from which the exterior world radiated in regular lines, gave way to a more fluid, mobile and voluminous conception of space, in which the observer–observed duality and distinctions between separated points and planes dissolve. Most importantly, the singular space of the visual is transformed by the experience of sound to a plural space; one can hear many sounds simultaneously, where it is impossible to see different visual objects at the same time without disposing them in a unified field of vision. Where auditory experience is dominant, we may say, singular, perspectival gives way to plural, permeated space. The self defined in terms of hearing rather than sight is a self imaged not as a point, but as a membrane; not as a picture, but as a channel through which voices, noises and musics travel.

The transmission of radio waves in particular could be seen both as a sublation and a literalization of the Romantic idealization of sound, which stressed the capacity of sound both to pervade and to integrate objects and entities which the eye kept separate. Sound is omnipresent, non-directional and mobile, where vision is intermittent, separative and fixating. The dependence of sound upon the principles of resonance, transmission and induction implies the mutability and transparency of objects and bodies in space. Douglas Kahn, in his introduction to one of the few books in recent years to take seriously the auditory experience of the modern, describes the effects of the idea of sympathetic vibration which was often attached to sound:

> wherever sound occurred, it was always manifested elsewhere, or other things were manifested through it; a sound had no autonomy but was always relational, being somewhere or something else, a constant deflection that ultimately stretched out to spiritually organize everything from essence to cosmos, always ringing with the voice and music.

Since traversal and transference are in the nature of sound, it also becomes the privileged figure of sensory interchange. The aural technologies developed in the late nineteenth and early twentieth centuries were based upon the principles of electrodynamic convertibility and reversibility – the well-established fact that fluctuations in electrical current produce magnetic variations, which can then be translated into movement, and vice versa. Thus the telephone used the vibrations of a tympanum to induce a variable current which was then converted back into sound, just as the phonograph turned the vibrations transmitted to a stylus into electrical signals and thus into sound. The electrodynamic principles of the telephone, phonograph and microphone were the scientific equivalents of the principle of synaesthesia, or the correspondence of the different senses, which held such fascination for late nineteenth-century and early twentieth-century artistic culture. Sound is thus oddly positioned with regard to synaesthesia, for it is both one sense among many, and therefore itself subject to conversion into colour, tactility, electric impulse and so on, and also the privileged figure for the process of synaesthetic and electrodynamic exchange itself.

The synaesthetic power of sound is a central feature of the synthetic magical system of Esoteric Buddhism developed by H. P. Blavatsky, as well as the synaesthetic systems developed by Arthur Rimbaud, Aleksandr Scriabin and the Russian futurists Alexei Kruchenykh and Velimir Khlebnikov. Many of the visual artists interested in synaesthesia were particularly drawn to the relations between sound and colour, an example being Wassily Kandinsky, who in 1909 scripted an opera entitled *The Yellow Sound*. One might suggest that the promotion of colour over line by artists such as Seurat, Monet, Kandinsky and Cézanne represents an attempt, not merely to decentre the perspectivalist system of vision inherited from the past, as Martin Jay argues, but also to approximate to auditory effects within the visual. With the development of radio, sound's power to transform and to be transformed seemed to be intensified. The telephone, the phonograph and the microphone had suggested the interconvertibility of sound and matter – the *Manchester Guardian* proclaimed that Alexander Graham Bell had 'literally succeeded in making iron talk' – but the technology of the 'wireless' apparently did away even with this material mediation, as sound became the enacted form of electromagnetic fluctuation itself. In 1913, F. T. Marinetti had praised the 'wireless imagination' and associated it with the liberated language of futurism. Twenty years later, Marinetti coined the term 'La Radia' to signify an art that would burst free from every containment or constraint. La Radia signified an art modelled on the conditions of radio, and would be characterized by

> The immensification of space. No longer visible and framable the stage becomes universal and cosmic. . . . The reception, amplification and transfiguration of vibrations emitted by living beings or dead spirits [and of] vibrations emitted by matter.

Marinetti's claims for the radiomorphic sensibility of La Radia anticipate some of the claims made more recently for the cybernetic sensibility of postmodernism. La Radia, he declared, would go beyond time and space, since

> the possibility of receiving broadcast stations situated in various time zones and the lack of light will destroy the hours of the day and night. The reception and amplification of the light and the voices of the past with thermoionic values will destroy time.

The new art of Marinetti is also formed on the model of a new kind of human subjectivity, which is continuously being traversed, dissolved and remade. The new instability of the modern self, its understanding of itself in terms of its interception of, and by, experiences, events and phenomena, rather than its reception or perception of them, is frequently embodied in terms of sound, and in particular electronically broadcast sound, rather than of sight. We might date the inauguration of this self-understanding in Walter Pater's Conclusion to his *The Renaissance*, first published in 1868. The Conclusion scarcely mentions sound, but evokes 'the passage and dissolution of impressions, images, sensations . . . that continual vanishing away, that strange perpetual weaving and unweaving of ourselves' characteristic of modern subjectivity in ways that suggest the auditory rather than the visual, or, so to speak, show the visual being 'auditized' or passing across into the auditory (and as we have seen, the very action of passing across may in itself suggest the auditory).

THE NOISE OF THE MODERN

Cultural historians have no doubt been right to point to the importance of visual technologies in the emergence of modern life. Jean-Luc Comolli speaks for many in referring to the 'frenzy of the visible' brought about by the social multiplication of images and visual technologies from the second half of the nineteenth century onwards. But this exclusive focus may have caused a neglect of some of the more intensely auditory experiences of modernity. Undoubtedly, the world has got vastly noisier since the onset of industrialization. (In most countries, there was no legislation to control noise before the twentieth century.) Perhaps the most significant fact about this noise is not its increased level but its endogenous nature; modern man is surrounded by man-made noise. The indeterminacy of sound – about which I will have more to say later on – is heightened by the fact that it can be attributed definitively neither to the realm of culture nor of nature. The vulnerability to the alterity of sound – or to sound as the sign of alterity – is a vulnerability to the doubled self of the man-made; man-made sound emanates from 'us', but assails and pervades us from an enigmatically indefinite 'out there'.

It is this man-made noise which predominates in the workplace, the street and the battlefield. The booming, chattering onomatopoeic sound-poetry of F. T. Marinetti's *parole in libertà* (words in freedom) which was so important an influence in Dadaism and Surrealism, was first developed as a report on the battle of Adrianopolis in the Balkan War, entitled 'Bombardment'. Martin Jay suggests more generally that the loss of stable perspective that was so common an experience of the chaotic, crowded and cacophonous conditions of the First World War, did much to reorganize its participants' psychological lives in terms of sound rather than sight.

It might similarly be suggested that the teeming, protean life of the city also seemed to require the positing of a mode of mental life which was auditory rather than visual. The figure of the flâneur, the strolling, detached observer, is in this sense to be understood less as an expression of the experience of the city than as a heroic, counterfactual compensation for the molestations of vision brought about by urban experience; the figure of the flâneur reasserts visual distance against perceptual and affective conditions that assail the immunity of the eye. The unsteadiness of the ways of looking and seeing characteristic of city life – the glance or the glimpse rather than the sustained gaze – goes along with a sense of shifting and saturated space of which the plural, permeable ear can evidently make more sense than the eye. The urban consciousness of Joyce's *Ulysses* (1922), for example, is predominantly a vocal-auditory consciousness; the city of Dublin is very imperfectly and intermittently seen in *Ulysses*, being experienced rather as an agitated polyphony of travelling sounds and voices, in which the seemingly private 'interior monologues' of Leopold Bloom, Stephen Dedalus and others are subject to every kind of auditory interference, including songs, jingles, sayings and non-human sounds. This reaches its comic-nightmarish apogee in the ventriloquial bacchanal of the 'Circe' episode in the brothel, in which the entire novel, and the city with which it is isomorphous, is rewritten as a kind of radio play.

Virginia Woolf's *Mrs Dalloway* (1925), which may itself be seen as a response to *Ulysses*, balances a sense of the compressive but dissevering eye and the diffusive but assimilatory ear. In the opening sequence of the novel, the multiple perspectives on an aeroplane flying above London are condensed and sublimated into

> a bright spark; an aspiration; a concentration; a symbol (so it seemed to Mr. Bentley, vigorously rolling his strip of turf at Greenwich) of man's soul; of his determination, thought Mr. Bentley, sweeping round the cedar tree, to get outside his body, beyond his house, by means of thought, Einstein, speculation, mathematics, the Mendelian theory.

But there is also the sound of Big Ben, unrolling its sonorous hours through the novel in 'leaden circles [which] dissolved in the air', as well as the sound of St Margaret's chime which 'glides into the recesses of the heart and buries itself in ring after ring of sound, like something alive which wants to confide itself, to disperse itself, to be, with a tremor of delight, at rest'.

In the twentieth century, the experiences of war and of urban life have been horrifyingly conjoined in the experience of the air-raid. The terror of the air-raid consists in its grotesquely widened bifurcation of visuality and hearing. On the one hand, there is the dominative distance of the bomber's aerial perspective, or the even greater and more decorporealized ballistic visuality of the guided missile; on the other, there is the absolute deprivation of sight for the victims of the air-raid on the ground, compelled as they are to rely on hearing to give them information about the incoming bombs. The inhabitants of cities subjected to aerial bombardment during the Second World War and after have had to learn new skills of orientating themselves in this deadly new auditory field without clear coordinates or dimensions, but in which the tiniest variations in pitch and timbre can mean obliteration. The terror of the air-raid is therefore at once the reduction of sound to sight, since those deprived of vision are reduced to the condition of targets and nothing more, and the epitomization of the disturbing self-sufficiency of sound in some kinds of modern experience.

The city solicited representation in the new medium of cinema, of course; but the title of one of the most striking and celebrated cinematic renderings of the city, Walter Ruttmann's *Berlin: Symphonie einer Großstadt* ('Berlin: Symphony of a City') (1927), expresses the sense of visuality passing across into auditory form. Ruttmann himself literalized this passage in a short work of the following year, *Wochenende* ('Weekend') (1928), which employed the technology of the cinematic sound-track to produce an entirely acoustic rendering of an individual urban story. Ruttmann's use of the film sound-track, which enabled him to cut and mix complex sounds in a way that would not be generally feasible until the spread of magnetic tape technology after the Second World War, is inventive and improvisatory. It also makes a kind of philosophical sense, for it invites us to consider the product, not as a *Hörspiel*, or radio play, but as a sound-film requiring a kind of listening eye, a gaze mutated into the conditions of hearing. Once again, the essential condition of the auditory is to be grasped in the synaesthetic transitions it enables; the coalescence of the visual and the auditory is itself a kind of auditory effect.

Ruttmann's sound-film anticipates a more recent technological conjoining of the auditory and the urban. The Walkman has the reputation of bringing about a solipsistic and antisocial withdrawal of its user from his or her environment. But it is better understood as a way of translating the experience of the city into auditory terms. Unlike fixed hi-fi headphones, the Walkman does not remove its user from his or her environment; rather, its portability deepens the experience of the body as it moves through an urban scene transformed by the cadences and colorations of the inner sound-track. The Walkman offers the pleasures of a mastery exercised over an otherwise potentially over-mastering saturation by auditory stimulus in the city, but it does so not by switching the attention of its user from an outer to an inner experience, but by making available a different (auditory) kind of attention to the non-auditory aspects of the city. Like Ruttmann's sound-film, the Walkman auditizes the urban.

One might also associate the auditory with a more abstract condition of modern life, which we may call the switchboard experience. The development of the telephone again offers us a way of understanding this. Early telephone systems necessitated direct and dedicated cable links between each subscriber. But once it became clear that the telephone was to have

211

general social uses, as well as more limited military and industrial applications, it also became clear that exchanges and complex switching networks would be necessary to allow the large numbers of private subscribers to communicate with each other. The earliest testimonies to the telephone reflect the excitement of unmediated, confidential, person-to-person conversation; but, within a decade or so, subscribers had become accustomed to the idea of the switchboard, actualized in the voice (almost from the beginning, by conscious design, a female voice) of the operator. The immediacy of telephonic speech was achieved therefore only after one had surrendered oneself to the impersonal distributional networks of the telephone system.

The telephone system was only one of a number of such networks that were being constructed from the later nineteenth century onwards. If the experience of the city was that of an unpredictable, complex collage of experiences and perspectives, this was accompanied in the early twentieth century by the awareness that the packed, pullulating overground of the city was overlaid and underpinned by a 'networked city', with its vital aerial and subterranean systems of drainage, communication, power and transport. Surely no better example can be imagined of the dominion of abstract rational seeing than the reconfiguring of the city as a networked diagram in this way? Well, yes: but we should remember that networking systems, especially the auditory networks of the telephone and the radio, do not spontaneously present themselves as visual phenomena. Often, they must themselves be subjected to visualization, and, as the example of the London Underground map shows, this did not happen quickly or easily. Until the act of visualizing which seems to constitute the network is itself made an object of vision, until one is brought to see the network's act of seeing, the network may be experienced as pervasive, dispersive and disorientating. The subscriber placing the call through the operator had to learn to construct and inhabit an imaginary – as we might now say, virtual – switchboard space, which was in essence unassisted by the eye, and may be said to be modelled on the auditory.

THE RAPTURE AND CAPTURE OF SOUND

All of these effects are interpreted and amplified by that steadily deepening suspicion of the eye in philosophy and social theory in the twentieth century which Martin Jay has described as 'antiocularcentrism'. This runs from the attacks on spatial thinking to be found in the work of Bergson, through to the assaults upon the idea of the unitary optical self in the psychoanalysis of Jacques Lacan, and the analysis of the scopic regimes of power in the work of Michel Foucault, as well as the reduction of the Hellenic privileging of sight and 'Hebraic' preference for the ear to be found variously in the work of Emmanuel Levinas, Luce Irigaray and

Jean-François Lyotard. Thomas Docherty perhaps provides a convenient generalization of this current of thinking when he defines postmodernism as a 'prioritisation of the aural over the visual', and, more specifically 'a mode of hearing, of *entendre*, which will not allow for an easy slippage into "understanding"'.

My point is to suggest that we can understand the coming into being of this postmodern renewal of aurality in terms of certain important experiences of the modern world. However, the idea or ideal of a self structured around the experience of hearing, whether this be taken to be modern or postmodern, encounters a serious difficulty. For, perhaps because of the very dominance of the visual paradigm in conceptions of the self, the auditory or acoustic has often been experienced and represented, not as a principle of strength, but as a disintegrative principle. Indeed, it was precisely this aspect of the aural which may have recommended it to the arts of dissolution practised by futurism and dadaism. One of the problems of building an aesthetic around the principles of sound and hearing is the fact that they are hard to consider as autonomous. An important aspect of this insufficiency of hearing is identified by accounts of the role of sound in film. As Rick Altman has argued, sound in film is always in fact subsidiary to image; a 'pure' or unattributed sound is always marked by doubt and menace until it can be tracked to and synchronized with its source, which is usually to say, visualized. This sense of the defining insufficiency of sound, and defining asymmetry of sound and vision, is echoed in the work of other commentators on cinema sound such as Christian Metz, Pascal Bonitzer and Michel Chion. We ask of a sound 'What was that?', meaning 'Who was that?', or 'Where did that come from?' We do not naturally ask of an image 'What sound does this make?' Indeed, for both Western and Eastern aesthetic traditions, the more silent an image, the more independent of the raggedly contingent world of time and change it will appear to be. If all unlocated sounds are enigmatic, then unlocated voices are particularly so, and particularly so in the case of represented voices in film or television, where we have no other information with which to supplement the experience of the voice. Thus, in cinema, we appear to need the specific verification of seeing a speaking mouth at the very moment of its utterance in order to exorcise the magic or scandal of an unattributed voice; the confirming opposite of this being the uneasiness induced in us by inexpert dubbing, or the faulty synchronization of image and sound. Rick Altman remarks aptly that 'fundamental to the cinema experience is a process – which we might call the *sound hermeneutic* – whereby the sound asks *where?* and the image responds *here!*'

The sense of the insufficiency and insubstantiality of hearing makes the definition of the self through it a problem. How can the modern psyche be said to be organized around an otology which is so regularly defined as the deficit of ontology? Some provisional answers seem to be emerging from psychoanalysis, although it has only recently begun to attend to the auditory determinants of the self. The work that has been done in this area, by William Niederland, Guy Rosolato and Didier Anzieu, confirms the fact that sonorous experience, though it is of vital importance in early infantile life, represents a particular threat to selfhood; it is at once the ego's source and its jeopardy. The ego is formed, according to Freud and those who followed him, not from the inside out, as it were, but rather as a kind of defence mechanism; as a filter, channel or buffer against intense excitations coming from the outside. In recent years, Didier Anzieu has turned French psychoanalysis back to the question of the formation of the ego and therapies designed to repair it. Anzieu's work is a development of a throwaway remark in Freud's *The Ego and the Id* (1923) that 'the ego is ultimately derived from bodily sensations, chiefly from those springing from the surface of the body'. Central to Anzieu's work is a conception of what he has called the 'skin-ego', by which he means the ego formed as 'a containing envelope, a protective barrier and a filter of exchanges, as a result of proprioception and epidermal sensations and the internalisation of skin-identifications'. Anzieu suggests that chief among a number of imaginary containing volumes parallel to the skin-ego is the experience of a 'sonorous envelope', or bath of sounds, especially those of the mother's voice, that surrounds the infant, soothing, supporting and stabilizing it. This imaginary envelope is the auditory equivalent of Lacan's mirror-stage, in that it gives the child a unity from the outside; it can be seen, therefore, as a 'sound-mirror or . . . audio-phonic skin'. Without the satisfactory experience of this sonorous envelope, the child may fail to develop a coherent sense of self; there will be rents or flaws in the ego, leaving it vulnerable to inward collapse in depression, or invasion from outside, leading to the formation of an over-protective artificial skin in certain forms of autism.

Anzieu's analysis has been carried forward recently by Edith Lecourt, who makes more explicit the implication of Anzieu's work that the sonorous binding which a 'good-enough' experience of parental sound provides is in fact a protection against the otherwise diffusive and dis-integrating conditions of sound itself. These conditions Lecourt defines as the absence of boundaries in space – 'sound reaches us from everywhere, it surrounds us, goes through us' – and in time – 'there is no respite for sonorous perception, which is active day and night and only stops with death or total deafness' – as well as its disturbing lack of concreteness – 'sound can never be grasped; only its sonorous source can be identified'. All these conditions are summed up, says Lecourt, in its quality of '*omnipresent simultaneity*'.

Anzieu's and Lecourt's conception of the sonorous envelope carries forward the insights of some earlier psychoanalysts. In a paper of 1958 entitled 'Early Auditory Experiences, Beating Fantasies, and Primal Scene',

William Niederland narrated the case histories of patients who derived erotic satisfaction from being subjected to physical and sexual abuse accompanied by violent vocal assault. Niederland suggests that the patients must be understood as attempting to introject and control frightening and traumatic experiences of sound, the 'early fear of bodily extinction by intense, ego-overwhelming auditory sensations', or the threat of impending 'auditory extinction' which Niederland believes may in fact be a feature of all infantile experience. One of Niederland's patients was a homosexual man, who was driven to seek masochistic sexual experiences specifically at times when 'the noises of the city – experienced as crude and intensely felt primitive sounds – assail him and threaten to overwhelm his ego'. In doing so, Niederland suggests, 'he "*structures the situation*," that is, he transforms the threatening unorganized noise into organized meaningful sounds emitted at his own behest'. Niederland draws this analysis from earlier suggestions by Heinz Kohut regarding the psychological process whereby ego-assailing noise is mastered by being structured as music, as well as from a paper by Otto Isakower which builds on some of Freud's undeveloped insights regarding the relations between audition and the formation of the super-ego. Despite differences of emphasis, this psychoanalytic work therefore concurs on the question of the defining contrast between threatening and disorganized noise, which is perhaps to be identified with the conditions of sound itself, and organized sound, or music; it is suggested that it is in the passage from one to the other that the self is formed, in a process in which power and pleasure are intricately interwoven.

This analysis coheres well with Jacques Attali's explication of the larger cultural process whereby noise is captured, socially ordered and then, as music, used to order social life.

> More than colors and forms, it is sounds and their arrangements that fashion societies. With noise is born disorder and its opposite: the world. . . . Everywhere codes analyze, mark, restrain, train, repress, and channel the primitive sounds of language, of the body, of tools, of objects, of the relations to self and others. All music, any organization of sounds is then a tool for the creation or consolidation of a community, of a totality.

Attali suggests that the most important factor in the move from noise to music, which he sees in Adornian fashion as an important part of the coming of the wholly administered society, is the development of technologies for reproduction. Before the development of the phonograph, the auditory realm was wholly transient, immaterial and temporal. The opening of the self to and by the auditory was an experience both of rapturous expansion and of dangerous disintegration. In making it possible to fix and preserve the auditory experience which had previously

215

been identified with uncapturable temporal passage, the phonograph came as the culmination of a range of different attempts through the nineteenth century to formalize and control sound, from the efforts of German philologists such as Bopp and Grimm to understand the laws of phonetic change in language through the automata and speaking machines which periodically fascinated audiences in European capitals, to the systems of 'visible speech' developed, for example, by Alexander Melville Bell, the father of the inventor of the telephone, which he claimed made it possible to render every actual or conceivable sound in written symbols, and the stenographic shorthand system known as phonography from which Edison's invention derived its name.

These efforts to control sound are parallel to the desire to complete sound by giving it a visible source in the talking film, as well as to the attempts to reconstitute the threatened ego described by Niederland, Anzieu and others. But Attali's analysis of the remorseless colonization of noise by formalized music is insufficiently attentive to the intertwining of auditory rapture and acoustic capture at the levels both of psyche and society. The two alternatives are dramatized in the contrast between the telephone and the phonograph, in their respectively diffusive and reproductive capacities. The telephone and later the radio posed the threat of the 'vocalic uncanny', or the sourceless voice which is in excess of the locating eye. Suddenly, Romantic theories of the mobility of the voice with, on the one hand, its diffusive power to cross and dissolve boundaries and, on the other hand, its integrative power to conjoin separated entities, seemed to be literalized. Against this, the phonograph is a technology which renders sound (and to begin with especially the sound of the human voice, since the technology would need to develop quite a long way before it was possible to record music satisfactorily) equivalent to sight. Douglas Kahn suggests that the phonograph is sound governed by the figure of inscription rather than transmission; it may also perhaps be seen as a mechanized form of that 'audiophonic mirror' spoken of by Didier Anzieu. As Charles Grivel writes:

> A machine arrives in the nick of time to capture all this [the dissolution of the philosophical authority of the voice] and give it an appearance. It is reproduced, and one can see that it is reproduced: a box with wheels tells us so. The visualization of the process implies its irreversibility, its irremediability.

Such a contrivance appears to be sound, not as self-diffusion, but as self-completion, as what Grivel describes as 'a perfected ear trumpet [that] compensates for a deficit in the symbolic that I am: I never have enough ear, for I am never enough myself'. But, as the work of Jacques Derrida has so amply suggested, the distancing and exteriorization of the voice accomplished in all forms of acoustic and graphic technology also

216

introduces absence, spacing and exorbitance into the voice. If the voice, as what Guy Rosolato has called the infant's 'greatest power of emanation', is the enactment of the fantasy of omnipotence and omnipresence, the material embodiment of this fantasy in the phonographic voice is the self split off into simulacrum, set apart from itself.

It is for this reason that there appears to be such a close relationship between auditory technologies and death. Such technologies make the dead speak in two distinct but related senses. First of all, they make the dead world of matter the bearer of meaning; in the spectral dance of the cinema, and the other-worldly voice that crackles from the phonograph or the telephone, it is as though matter itself had snatched a fetishistic kind of life. Second, because such technologies preserve the speaking, moving evidence of animate life, the dead could indeed continue to speak through them. In 1922, in *Ulysses*, Joyce has Leopold Bloom, ever the gadgeteer, musing at a funeral in 1904 about the possibility of a necrophonic archive:

> Besides how could you remember everybody? Eyes, walk, voice. Well, the voice, yes: gramophone. Have a gramophone in every grave or keep it in the house. After dinner on a Sunday. Put on poor old great-grandfather. Kraahraark! Hellohellohello amawfullyglad kraark awfullygladaseegain hellohellohello amawf krpthsth.

I imagine that Joyce did not know that, in the famous painting by Francis Barraud of the dog Nipper, which was so famously associated throughout the century with the HMV gramophone record company, the dog staring into the horn from which his master's voice is presumably emanating, is sitting on a coffin, though it confirms the cultural associations between death and phonography.

One can see a psychocultural response to this kind of threat in the attempt to separate out the two techno–acoustic aspects represented by the telephone and the phonograph, distinguishing the active and excursive self-augmentation of the voice from the deathly passivity of its mechanical replication; these two aspects are strongly gendered as masculine and feminine respectively. They are conveniently dramatized in Villiers de L'Isle Adam's misogynistic science fiction fable of 1886, *L'Eve future* ('The Future Eve'). The central character of the novel is the already mythical 'Wizard of Menlo Park', Thomas Edison, who has secretly developed the capacities of the telephone and the phonograph far beyond what had been displayed in public. The masculine aspect of technologized sound is manifested in the seemingly limitless acoustic power which Edison exercises by means of the telephone, for example, in the scene in which he rouses a sleeping assistant 150 miles away by means of a kind of massively amplified telephone he calls an 'Aerophone'. Edison's telephonic power is associated with the power of electricity itself, which is both an

image of sound and its antagonist; for Edison's dream is to use electricity
to recapture the lost sounds of history:

> – Yes, said the great engineer, continuing his meditation, I have this
> little spark . . . which is to sound what the greyhound is to the
> tortoise. It could give the sounds a start of fifty centuries and yet
> chase them down in the gulfs of outer space, ancient refugees from
> the earth! But on what wire, along what trail, could I send it? How
> teach it to bring the sounds back, once it has tracked them down?
> How redirect them to the ear of the investigator?

The feminized aspect of sound is embodied in the female android he
creates for his friend Lord Ewald, who is to synthesize the manner and
voice of Alicia Clary, the woman he loves for her physical beauty but
despises for her meanness of soul:

> She will have the voice of Miss Alicia Clary, as she will have the rest
> of her properties. The songs and words of the Android will forever
> be those that your lovely friend will have dictated to her – unknow-
> ingly, without ever laying eyes on her. Her accent, her diction, her
> intonations, down to the last millionth of a vibration, will be
> inscribed on the discs of two golden phonographs . . . perfected
> miraculously by me to the point where now they are of a tonal
> fidelity . . . practically . . . *intellectual*! These are the lungs of Hadaly.
> An electric spark sets them in motion, as the spark of life sets ours
> in motion. I should warn you that these fabulous songs, these extra-
> ordinary dramatic scenes and unsounded words, spoken first by the
> living artiste, captured on records, and then given new *seriousness* by
> her Android phantom, are precisely what constitute the miracle,
> and also the hidden peril of which I warned you.

This opposition between the fantasy of androtelephonic as opposed to
gynophonographic sound is found in different forms throughout the late
nineteenth and twentieth centuries. It is there in the production and
staging of hysteria by Jean-Martin Charcot at the Salpêtrière hospital in
Paris, in which, as Janet Beizer has shown, the uncontrollable mobility
of the female hysterical voice was named and placed by the practice of
dermographically inscribing the diagnosis on the flesh of the patients
and recording them in photographs. It reappears in George du Maurier's
Trilby (1894), in which the wicked musical genius Svengali exercises his
mesmeric-ventriloquial power over the beautiful Trilby to induce in her a
divine singing voice and earn him celebrity and wealth. It is dramatized in
the famous case of Daniel Paul Schreber, who introjected the command-
ing god-like voice of his father by subjecting himself in female fashion to
the voices that speak to, and through him; and in the case of Christine
Beauchamp, whose multiple personalities were carefully distinguished and

orchestrated by Morton Prince. The dichotomy between male-telephonic sound and female-phonographic sound is borne out also by Kaja Silverman's analysis of the asymmetries of voice in the Hollywood sound-film; Silverman argues that there is a conspicuous contrast between the male voice which can speak outside the frame of the film, as narrator or controlling voice-over, and the female voice which is typically required to be made visible and corporeal in the synchronized speech of the female character. This structure of acoustic privilege 'locates the male voice at the point of apparent textual origin, while establishing the diegetic contain-ment of the female voice'. In running together a history of the coming of sound to the cinema with a narrative about the technical manufacture of a female voice, a film like *Singin' in the Rain* establishes the close relation between gender and technology in the production of the voice.

AUDIOVISION

All this suggests the compelling importance of the auditory in the cultural, clinical and technological constitution of the modern self. Certainly, the idea of the auditory self provides a way of positing and beginning to experience a subjectivity organized around the principles of openness, responsiveness and acknowledgement of the world rather than violent alienation from it. The auditory self discovers itself in the midst of the world and the manner of its inherence in it, not least because the act of hearing seems to take place in and through the body. The auditory self is an attentive rather than an investigatory self, which takes part in the world rather than taking aim at it. For this reason, the auditory self has been an important part of phenomenology's attempt to redescribe subjectivity in terms of its embodiedness: 'My "self",' declares Don Ihde, the most enthu-siastic of audiophile philosophers, 'is a correlate of the World, and its way of *being-in* that World is a way filled with voice and language. Moreover, this being in the midst of Word is such that it permeates the most hidden recesses of my self.'

But I have further suggested that acoustic experience is also experienced as a principle of rapturous exorbitance, as what goes beyond, or may not be encompassed in the regimes of sight and demonstrability. It might be that we could see such exorbitance as part of the 'autonomization' of the senses which Fredric Jameson suggests took place at the end of the nineteenth and beginning of the twentieth century in response to, but also in mimetic rivalry of, the alienating effects of a rationalized, commodified world:

> The very activity of sense perception has nowhere to go in a world in which science deals with ideal quantities, and comes to have little enough exchange value in a money economy dominated by considerations of calculation, measurement, profit, and the like. This

unused surplus capacity of sense perception can only reorganize itself into a new and semi-autonomous activity... [in which] an objective fragmentation of the so-called outside world is matched and accompanied by a fragmentation of the psyche which reinforces its effects.

Certainly there is evidence in the clamorous activity of the avant-gardists in early modernism, as well as in the cooler, postmodern avant-gardism of figures such as John Cage later in the century, of a foregrounding of sound and hearing as the most disruptive sense, as the privileged way to an ecstatic exceeding of, or receding from the propriocentric self. As such, the notion of the auditory self prepares the way for many of the claims for the disintegrated, libidinized, pulsive self argued for by Lyotard, Kristeva, Barthes and others. But we have seen that the auditory is also an insufficiency, in that the auditory always leads to, or requires completion by the other senses. The instability of the auditory self is such that it dissolves the very autonomy which seems to bring about the psychic unseating of the visual in the first place. To say that the auditory is the channel of alterity in the self is to say that it leads or resonates beyond itself. Apparently, the auditory can furnish a principle of psychic organization only by dint of being subject to forms of organization – the rationalization of 'pure' sound into music, of psychic threat into psychic reintegration – which subordinate and denature it.

This is not merely to argue, however, that the auditory is always merely recuperated or recaptured, to the benefit of the self-seeing, self-knowing, spatialized self. For the auditory also has the capacity to enter into other forms of sensual organization, contaminating and creatively deforming them. Fredric Jameson sees the utopian potential of the autonomized senses as related to their echoing of the fetishism of the commodity, which holds the economic object magically distinct from the world of exchange that produces it. In my view, by contrast, the utopian potential of the acoustic lies in its intensified mimicry of the process of exchange itself, now the mark not of seriality and the subordination of commodities to the single abstract equivalence of the money-form, but the anticipation in the interior and exterior reorganization of the senses of a more polymorphous transformation of value.

So it is not in a pure, autonomous faculty of audition that the greatest effect of the revival of the prestige of the acoustic has been seen. Rather, it has been in the very principle of relativity that defines the acoustic, the insufficiency that makes it impossible for the acoustic to stand alone. So, bizarrely, the most far-reaching effects of the return of the acoustic may be in the transformations it has allowed in visual concepts and ways of feeling. To give only one example: the development among geographers and social theorists of new concepts of produced or social space, especially the overlaid, multiple spaces of city experience, in opposition to the flat rationality of Cartesian cartography, seems to employ the resources of the ear to give density and dimension to its accounts of social space. Just as the space of the city resounds across definitions rather than being contained by them, the new geography attempts to achieve what is invisible to the cartographic eye. The sense of hearing is only occasionally heard of in such work, but it operates markedly upon it, not as an alternative kind of centring, but rather as the switchboard which allows for intrasensory communication and the mutual transformation of the senses.

The massive increase in reproductive technologies characteristic of our own postmodern epoch may assist the diversification of such switchboard effects. These reproductive technologies, from the simple games-console all the way through to the most sophisticated multimedia spectacles and virtual reality rigs, represent more than an extension of the powers of what Freud described as the 'auxiliary organs' of the 'prosthetic god' that modern man has made of himself. Where early modern technologies extended and amplified the powers of ear and eye, contemporary technologies offer the prospect of sensory recombination and transformation as well. The digitization and consequent universal convertibility of information may make the synaesthesias dreamt of by the late nineteenth and early twentieth centuries a common actuality, creating new aggregations of the visual, auditory, haptic and olfactory senses. Undoubtedly the dominance of vision in the constitution of the self would be put at risk in such a new sensory dispensation, since that dominance depends upon the separation of the senses one from another, and the existence of vision as an arbitrating meta-sense, capable of distinguishing, overseeing and correcting the operations of the other senses. To be sure, visual technologies will continue to be enhanced, and the remorseless drive to see, be seen and make visible will also continue unabated. But it may be that the energetic impingements and abrasions of the senses one upon the other may make the ear, with its acceptance of plural stimulus, and hearing, with its qualities of openness, complexity and interpenetration, a richer and more responsive metaphor for the self and its sensory composites and concretions than the self-detaching eye.

It has already been said that a pure and autonomous experience of hearing is not possible, such that a self formed around the experience of the ear in the same way as it may previously have been formed around the eye is inconceivable. It may help, however, to understand the importance of hearing in the newly unsettled venue of subjectivity, between the eye, ear and the other senses, to borrow a term from the theorist of film sound, Michel Chion. We might expect a modern self to understand itself as what Chion calls an *acousmêtre*, which he defines in cinematic terms as an acoustic agency whose position with respect to the screen is undecidable, in that it is present and audible and effective within the visible scene, but is not *seen to speak*. The *acousmêtre* is thus to be distinguished on the one hand from the 'natural' (though in fact synthesized) voice which is simultaneously seen and heard, and on the other from the *acousmatique* voice, which is heard but does not emanate from the action on the screen (for example, the voice-over, or narrating voice). The voice of the *acousmêtre* can emanate from a character hidden from view in the scene (Polonius behind the arras), or from a non-human mechanism, like a robot or a tape recorder; the classic example, however, is the figure of the Invisible Man in James Whale's film of 1933. The *acousmêtre* exists between sound and vision, and is to be identified with neither, but rather with a complex and fascinating process of transfer and interchange between them, in which we must see their sound and hear their physical shape, location and movement. The passage of hearing and vision into one another induced by the insufficiency of stimulus induces the compensatory involvement of other senses too, as we begin to supply by imaginary tactile means, for example, the absent volume of the audible invisible man.

To begin to experience *oneself* as an acousmêtric phenomenon could be either anguish or enlargement, or both. Such experiences are forecast in some of the works of late modernism, which begin to explore the consequences of the eye's diminished privilege. One example might be Joyce's *Finnegans Wake* (1939), whose punning, overloaded 'soundspeech' multiplies the collisions and coalescences of eye and ear and, particularly in Book III, Chapter 3, anticipates the switchboard effect of the modern auditory-technological imagination. A 'character' embodied at various times under the name of Shaun and Jaun, and here called Yawn, is asleep, but under interrogation by four chroniclers, who seem to summon up through his person, by means that may be spiritualist or radiotelephonic, other characters. 'I have something inside of me talking to myself', Yawn declares at one point. Among the voices that overtake or 'outspeak' him are those of his mother A(nna) L(ivia) P(lurabelle), Kate, the servant in the pub seemingly kept by his father, his father, H(umphrey) C(himpden) E(arwicker), and Oscar Wilde. At various points in the text, we seem to hear other voices breaking into the interrogation, like the noise of static between radio stations: 'Is the strays world moving mound or what static babel is this, tell us? – Whoishe whoishe whoishe linking in? Whoishe whoishe whoishe?' At another point the text seems to be affected by a crossed line, and we hear the voice of the switchboard operator:

- What is your numb? Bun!
- Who gave you that numb? Poo!
- Have you put in all your sparepennies? I'm listening. Sree!
- Keep clear of all propennies! Fore!

The reply of HCE, whom this interchange has interrupted, is 'Mr Televox, Mrs Taubiestimm and invisible friends!' To read *Finnegans Wake* is to experience an exacting enrichment of the auditory sense. It is not merely, as Joyce and his readers have sometimes claimed, that the book has a kind of acoustic rather than semantic intelligibility; it is that the force of sound is made so pervasive as to interfere with the processes of visualization that are otherwise to the fore in reading.

We might point also to Samuel Beckett's *The Unnamable* (1952), a text in which an unnamed character, motionless in an indeterminate and uncertain space, speaks, in a tormented, unstinting soliloquy, of itself and of its condition. As the text proceeds, we ourselves become increasingly uncertain as to whether we are to visualize a space or scene within which the act of speaking (or writing pretending to be speaking) is taking place, or whether we are to understand the scene as an emanation of the voice which talks itself into various kinds of existence in various kinds of location. Read from the perspective of the still incipient future of the displaced eye, *The Unnamable* seems like a kind of premonition of what it might be like, not only to suffer, but also to have found a means of subsistence and self-invention in the condition of ontological insufficiency consequent upon the demotion of the eye and the values associated with it. The speaker imagines itself as a grotesque aural prosthesis, as 'a head . . . grown out of his ear', and multiplies otological images in its efforts at self-understanding:

> I shall transmit the words as received, by the ear, or roared through a trumpet into the arsehole, in all their purity . . . in at one ear and incontinent out through the mouth, or the other ear, that's possible too. . . . Two holes and me in the middle, slightly choked. Or a single one, entrance and exit, where the words swarm and jostle like ants . . . I'm in the middle, I'm the partition, two surfaces and no thickness, perhaps that's what I feel, myself vibrating, I'm the tympanum, on the one hand the mind, on the other the world, I don't belong to either.

What remains unresolved is how the more abstract, ethical qualities associated with modern selfhood – the integrative qualities of will, decision and moral choice, on the one hand, and the collective qualities of empathy, understanding and responsibility on the other – will be affected by different kinds of self-apprehension and self-construction. Perhaps all that may be said with certainty is that there appears to be no necessity for such qualities either to depend wholly and solely upon visualist self-picturing or to dissolve with the coming of other modes of self-apprehension and self-devising.

14

ASSEMBLING THE MODERN SELF

Nikolas Rose

In the first volume of *The Man Without Qualities*, Robert Musil remarked upon the way in which 'experiences' seemed to have made themselves independent of individuals, to have gone on to the stage, into books, into exhibitions and the reports of scientific institutions, into communities based upon religious conviction. Once having achieved their independence, they return with a new authority. 'Who today can still say that his anger is really his own anger,' Musil wrote, 'with so many people butting in and knowing much more about it than he does?' (1979, pp. 174–5). Musil's words capture something fundamental about our contemporary experience of ourselves. Our feelings, beliefs, desires, hopes and fears are suffused with the descriptions, injunctions and evaluations of those who claim to know more about what is good for us than we do ourselves. Most of those who Musil mentions still chatter in our ears. But over the last half century, they have been overpowered by new 'experts of experience'. These experts rest their authority upon claim to truth, to science and objectivity, to facts, experiments, findings and statistics, to long hours in the consulting room and the hospital. They impress us because their advice seems to rest on evidence within reality itself, although evident only to those who know how to look. These are the specialists of psy: psychologists, psychiatrists, psychotherapists, psychiatric social workers, management consultants, market researchers, opinion-pollers, counsellors. Their murmerings into our outer and inner ears are not confined to our periods of frank madness or despair. They accompany us from the moment of our conception and birth through all the phases within which they have framed our lives: childhood, adolescence, sexual desires, relationships, mid-life crises, illnesses, old age, mourning, even death. They have shaped the vocabularies and activities of all those other authorities who now seek to manage human conduct: our judges, doctors, policemen, prison officers, managers, economists, investment consultants, politicians, pundits, talk-show hosts and soap-opera scriptwriters have come to speak in psychological dialects. These specialists of psy have enmeshed themselves inextricably with our experience of ourselves.

224

Musil writes of these authorities 'butting in'. But their intrusion can take many forms. There are, indeed, many times when it is a matter of the knock at the door, the uninvited presence, the demand for admission: the social workers descending upon those suspected of abusing their children, the industrial consultant 'enriching' the working routines of labourers in factories and offices, the psychiatrist assessing the defendant before charge, verdict or sentence or running 'therapeutic groups' in prison or reformatory; the doctor evaluating a disturbed individual with a view to compelling them to receive psychiatric treatment. But, eagerly or reluctantly, we all too often ask them in, seek out their knowledge in books and magazine articles, listen to them on radio phone-in programmes and confessional television talk shows, take ourselves to counsellors, therapists and marriage guidance. And the presence of psy in our contemporary experience is not limited to our encounters with the experts. When we speak to our friends and acquaintances about the ills that trouble us or the hopes that animate us, our conversations will be studded with psychological terms – stress, anxiety, motivation, personality, self-esteem and so on. Even when we are alone, in our most intimate experiences of ourselves, psy allows us to understand the actions of those around us, to describe our personality, passions and hopes, to understand our sorrows and calibrate our disappointments, to project and embark upon a future for ourselves. In being acted upon and acting upon ourselves in these ways, modern human beings (in different ways for women and for men, for the young and the old, for the rich and the poor) have become psychological selves.

'Modernity' in 'the West' has long been credited with the 'invention of the self'. The link between 'individualization' and 'modernization' was a recurrent theme in nineteenth-century social thought, developed in various ways in the writings of Jacob Burckhardt, Karl Marx, August Comte, Emile Durkheim and Max Weber. These stories of individualization in nineteenth-century social theory concerned the rise of the atomized and discrete subject of morality, politics, law and culture. More recent writers have stressed the rise of the psychological and ethical individual: the self. Thus the anthropologist Clifford Geertz has claimed that

> [t]he Western conception of the person as a bounded, unique, more or less integrated motivational and cognitive universe, a dynamic center of awareness, emotion, judgement and action, organized into a distinctive whole and set contrastively against other such wholes and against a social and natural background is, however incorrigible it may seem to us, a rather peculiar idea within the context of the world's cultures.
>
> (Geertz, 1979, p. 222, quoted in Sampson, 1989, p.1; cf. Mauss, 1979)

Philosophers such as Charles Taylor have argued that our modern notion of what it is to be a human agent, a person or a self, and the issues of morality with which this notion is inextricably intertwined, is 'a function of a historically limited mode of self-interpretation, one which has become dominant in the modern West and which may indeed spread thence to other parts of the globe, but which has a beginning in time and space and may have an end' (Taylor, 1989, p. 111). And Michel Foucault, in his 'archaeology' of the human sciences, concluded that 'man', as the subject and object of knowledge, 'is an invention of recent date' dependent upon a particular modern configuration of thought: if that were to crumble 'then one can certainly wager that man would be erased, like a face drawn in sand at the edge of the sea' (Foucault, 1970, p. 387).

Of course, one finds evidence of intense concern about the kinds of people that humans are in other times and other places. There is no need to repeat the sterile debate between 'universalists' – who believe that there could never have been a culture without concern for the human individual – and 'relativists' – who believe that 'traditional' societies thought of people as a kind of undifferentiated mass. My point here is a different one. I want to suggest that the *relation* to ourselves which we can have today has been profoundly shaped by the rise of the psy disciplines, their languages, types of explanation and judgement, their techniques and their expertise. The beliefs, norms and techniques which have come into existence under the sign of psy over the last century about intelligence, personality, emotions, wishes, group relations, psychiatric distress and so forth are neither illumination nor mystification: they have profoundly shaped the kinds of persons we are able to be – the ways we think of ourselves, the ways we act upon ourselves, the kinds of persons we are presumed to be in our consuming, producing, loving, praying, sickening and dying. They have become woven into the practices that fabricate and sustain the 'psy' interior that has been hollowed out within us as our truth, this psychological being which has been placed at the origin of our passions, our speech, our ills, our wants and our conduct. We need to abandon the belief that we are 'in our very nature' discrete, bounded, self-identical creatures, inhabited and animated by an inner world whose laws and processes psychology has begun to reveal to us. On the contrary, we are 'assembled' selves, in which all the 'private' effects of psychological interiority are constituted by our linkage into 'public' languages, practices, techniques and artefacts.

ENGINEERING HUMAN RELATIONS

Reflections upon the nature of human beings occur in all cultures and all historical periods. To suggest that something profound has happened in our own recent history might seem merely fashionable historicism. But something does seem to have occurred, at least in North Western Europe and North America, in the fifty-year period from about 1875 to 1925. One dimension was the birth of psychology as a 'discipline' – as a scientific specialism with its own subject matter, journals, courses, credentials, and as a profession with its own organizations, criteria and role as expertise (cf. for what follows Rose, 1985). When the first volume of the journal *Mind* appeared in January 1876, it proclaimed itself 'the first English journal devoted to Psychology and Philosophy' and set itself the aim 'to procure a decision as to the scientific standing of psychology'. Wilhelm Wundt is usually considered as having inaugurated modern scientific psychology when, in 1879 at the University of Leipzig, he set aside some space for conducting psychological experiments. Wundt's own methods would be rejected in the course of the scientization of psychology in subsequent decades, but 'the laboratory', with all its resonance of white coats, experiments and objectivity was to be a vital element of the scientization of psychology (Danziger, 1990; on the invention of objectivity, see Porter, 1995). William James established a 'rudimentary demonstration laboratory' at Harvard in 1876 – the same year when he 'urged young men with professorial ambitions to study recent trends in scientific psychology' and predicted that they would soon find vacant places calling for their peculiar capacities in departments of philosophy (O'Donnell, 1985, p. 2). Two years later James began work on his *Principles of Psychology* and Stanley Hall received Harvard's first Ph.D. in psychology. In 1883, after a visit to Wundt, Hall set up his own laboratory at Johns Hopkins. James Sully, who was the Grote Professor of Philosophy of mind and logic, established the first English laboratory for experimental psychology in October 1897 at University College, London, and a similar laboratory was founded in Cambridge in the same year. Psychology, in Britain as much as in the USA, would become a discipline, in part at least, by virtue of the ways in which it could mobilize laboratories, experiments and a whole rhetoric of scientificity in support of its truth claims. In this way it would gradually (and incompletely) distinguish itself from philosophy and ethics on the one hand and medicine and biology on the other, to form itself into a single, though inherently divided and fractured, discipline.

Psychology in the first half of the twentieth century would not only become a discipline; it would become a profession. America was the examplar. The American Psychological Association was founded by Stanley Hall in 1892, dedicated 'to the advancement of psychology as a science'; according to O'Donnell, by 1903 its original membership of thirty-one had quadrupled and it doubled again by 1913 (O'Donnell, 1985). By 1929, Edwin Boring, in his *History of Experimental Psychology*, claimed around 1000 psychologists in the United States alone, in over 300 academic institutions (Boring, 1929). Boring wrote his book in part to stake a claim for a scientific and academic psychology in the face of the proliferation of psy as a technical and practical know-how. But psy was to blossom precisely because exceptionally productive alliances were formed between the world of the academy and the requirements of practitioners (for details on the following, see Fryer and Henry, 1950). As early as 1908, Hugo Münsterberg published *On the Witness Stand*, the first book on psychology as a legal resource; he would propose a programme for an industrial psychology in 1912, in *Psychology and Industrial Efficiency*. Frank Parsons inaugurated psychology's role in vocational guidance in 1909 with *Choosing a Vocation*; by 1914 the first bureau for vocational guidance would be established in the public school system. E. L. Thorndike formalized the pedagogic calling of psychology in 1913 with the publication of *Educational Psychology*. Walter Dill Scott proselytized for the psychologization of profit in *The Psychology of Advertising* (1910) and *Influencing Men in Business* (1911): he was appointed the first university professor of 'applied psychology' in 1915 and would found the Scott Corporation, the first private business in psychology, in Philadelphia in 1919. By 1915 psychological tests were being used for selection of telephonists and telegraphists for Western Union. Since such tests were used for the selection of chauffeurs for the German army as early as 1916, it is no surprise that in 1917 the US Army created a Committee on Classification of Personnel, established a training school for military psychologists at Camp Greenleaf, Georgia and embarked upon a whole programme of psychological testing and assessment of military personnel (described in *Psychological Examining in the U. S. Army*, published in 1921). In the post-war period, dignified by its military service, psychology would flourish in public and private organizations, in academic departments and associations of applied psychology, and in private enterprises such as the Psychological Corporation, founded in 1921: from personnel departments to life insurance offices, from clinics for children to centres for the rehabilitation of the aged, psychologists would become indispensable. And while it went under the title of 'applied psychology' there was little 'application' about it – innovations did not usually flow from discoveries in the laboratory to devices in the 'real world' but in precisely the reverse direction.

Britain followed the same path, although a little further behind and on a more modest scale. The British Psychological Society was inaugurated in October 1901 and the *British Journal of Psychology* first appeared in 1904. The growth of academic psychology in Great Britain was remarkably slow: at the outbreak of the Second World War there were only six university chairs in psychology and a combined lecturing staff of about thirty. As in the United States, it was outside the academy that psychology would find its growth points in Britain. Psychologists together with doctors and philanthropists played a key role in the eugenic movement, with its concern for the identification of 'feeble-minded' schoolchildren which led to the development of the intelligence test: Charles Spearman's famous paper '"General intelligence" objectively determined and measured' was published in 1904; the Chief Medical Officer of the Board of Education recommended the use of 'psychological and educational tests' for differentiating the normal from the feeble-minded child in his report of 1911; Cyril Burt was appointed as psychologist to the London County Council in 1913 and William McDougall published his article 'Psychology in the service of eugenics' in 1914 (for details of all these examples, see Rose, 1985). Burt and other psychologists were important figures in the vociferous mental hygiene movement of the 1920s and 1930s, were involved in setting up the Tavistock Clinic in 1920, the Child Guidance Council in 1927, and the first mental health course for psychiatric social workers which started at the London School of Economics in 1929. Charles Myers urged the establishment of 'institutes of applied psychology in each of our largest cities' in his 1918 lectures on 'Present Day Application of Psychology with Special Reference to Industry, Education and Nervous Breakdown' and established the National Institute of Industrial Psychology in 1921, and Edward Glover set up the Institute for the Scientific Treatment of Delinquency in 1932.

These bare facts suffice to make one central point: despite the importance of the laboratory and the whole apparatus of scientificity – experiments, proofs, statistical tests of significance, replications and so forth – the 'disciplinization' of psychology was not a matter of the discovery, in some moment of pure thought, of the laws of mental functioning. It would be around its claims as a discipline of behaviour, a knowledge of the norms of conduct and the techniques for its management, a provider of devices for diagnosing and ameliorating pathology, that psychology would coalesce. The laboratories that were crucial for the emerging expertise of human conduct in the first half of the twentieth century were not inside the academy but outside. Psychologists could find their laboratories in any organization or institution where human beings were operating according to norms that were set for them by the apparatus itself, where human conduct could be observed, judged against these norms, evaluated as normal or deviant. This ensemble of knowledge, standards and judgement ensured that the norms which were to become psychological – of intelligence, of personality, of adjustment, of development, of attitude – were inescapably institutional and regulatory: they were the norms of the classroom, the norms of the factory, the norms of the prison, the norms of the military apparatus. Each of these apparatuses could host a hundred little experiments for forcing into visibility the minutia of human conduct, its origins in individual differences, its vulnerability to the pressures, conditions and characteristics of the environment. Each classroom, each prison, each factory, each battalion could be studied, documented, the conduct of those within it classified, compared over time, analysed statistically and significant differences identified. Once identified, these differences could form the basis of new norms for maximizing workplace efficiency, school performance or military effectiveness, and for identifying those who were potential threats or stumbling-blocks in the search for efficiency and for directing them to individual treatment. It would be these institutional and technical norms that psychologists, over the first half of the twentieth century, would attempt to regularize and ratify through theory and experiment, and then to give back to practitioners in scientific form.

Consider, for example, the psychological normalization of the intellect. The school and the army in the early decades of this century functioned as huge laboratories for the assessment, calibration and quantification of human capacities. The school had been the first site for this project, in particular the problematization of those children who were not capable of benefiting from the systems of universal education introduced in the late nineteenth century – the problem of the 'feeble-minded'. The IQ test lashed together an older endeavour to define something called 'intelligence' with a eugenic concern with the consequences of the inheritance of human abilities for the efficiency of the population. The test, in its normalized, statisticalized and standardized form, seemed to provide authorities with the ability to quantify human qualities: a practical device for differentiating human individuals in all those practices where the particular characteristics of human beings were administratively pertinent. Military life provided a further opportunity for a massive experiment in psychometrics. The US Army testing programme was under the direction of Robert Yerkes, President of the American Psychological Association at the outbreak of war and also chair of the Eugenics Research Association's Committee on Inheritance of Mental Traits. The Army Alpha group intelligence tests, specifically devised for assessment in the US Army, were administered to two million American soldiers in the First World War; the non-linguistic Army Beta tests were administered to 100,000 soldiers in 1918 alone. By 1922, following the path opened by this enormous effort at the psychologization of differences, three million school children a year in the US were being tested by group tests of intelligence (Hornstein, 1988, p. 19). For the many American eugenicist psychologists, these testing programmes confirmed their fears about the links of race and intelligence and the implications of immigration: psycho-eugenics was crucial to the malign politics of race in the first half of the twentieth century.

In his presidential address to the first meeting of the Personnel Research Foundation in 1921, established under the aegis of the US government's National Research Council, Yerkes declared that 'there is every reason to believe that human engineering will shortly take its place among the important forms of practical endeavor' (quoted in Gillespie, 1988, p. 133). Important as eugenics was, it did not define or limit psychology's practical role. On the one hand, psychology would accord a new legitimacy to teachers, managers and all the authorities of human conduct operating in the schools, the courts, the prisons, the factories and the like.

On the other hand, in demonstrating the multiple 'practical applications' of psychology, these alliances would enhance the academic significance of the discipline itself – indeed these reciprocal relations were, as Danziger and others have shown in great detail, the very conditions for psychology's disciplinization (Danziger, 1990).

The professional attention of psychologists would rapidly spread from pathology to normality. The norms and criteria established for the identification and classification of the pathological would be extended to normality itself – the normality of the normal child, the normal worker, the normal parent, the normal consumer would need to be understood, safeguarded, enhanced and acted upon in areas as diverse as child development and advertising. In countless other areas of human existence, we now learned to see and to judge ourselves and others with psychological eyes, in terms of a psychological relation between the visible, external features of conduct and its inner, invisible but none the less real psychical determinants. Take, for example, the notion of 'normal child development'. Arnold Gesell discovered normal development in his laboratory established at the Yale Psycho-Clinic, which opened in 1911 for the assessment and treatment of children having problems at school (see Rose, 1990, Chapter 12). Here, in a specially constructed dome allowing one-way vision, he would quantify children's capacity to make piles of wooden blocks, walk, run, climb small artificial sets of stairs, draw different shapes, use their own name and so forth while others filmed and took notes. Gesell had a commitment to a metaphysical idea of development, but this abstract philosophy of time and growth could now be materialized in life itself, through meticulous examination of the films, frame by frame, which enabled the identification of behaviour that was common – or 'normal' – at particular ages and its differentiation from that which was 'advanced' or 'retarded'. In this laboratory, norms were not discovered: they were forced into existence by the apparatus themselves, made visible by techniques, then written down, concretized, turned into charts and tests which could become the model for a hundred different scales of development to be utilized by childcare workers and disseminated to parents: the child was now the inevitable subject of normalizing psychological gaze and vocabulary: 'he certainly is advanced for his age'.

Relations among human beings also became psychological. The Hawthorne works of the Western Electrical Company on the outskirts of Chicago have become famous because they served as the laboratory for a series of experiments starting in 1924 and extending over fifteen years which forced these 'human relations' into the open. They appeared to reveal the effects of workplace organization upon worker productivity and job satisfaction: experimental methods in the workplace would provide a key foundation for the claim of psychology to provide a disinterested knowledge of economic life with major practical implications (these much discussed experiments are well analysed in Gillespie, 1988). The group, the complex of psychological interpersonal relations that formed whenever individuals were gathered together for whatever common purpose, was born in a whole variety of other studies carried out in the 1930s and 1940s. These ranged from Lewin's experiments on styles of leadership among boys at the Iowa Child Welfare Research Station prior to the outbreak of war, through Leighton's studies of the Japanese relocation camp at Poston Arizona after the entry of the United States into the War, to Wilfred Bion's experiments in group treatment to resolve the problems of indiscipline in the training wing of Northfield Military Hospital in 1943. From this point on, psychologists could become specialists in the design and redesign of human collectivities. They were not only able to ameliorate problems that arose in any context where individuals were gathered together, from the hospital to the workplace, from the boardroom to the classroom. They could also advise those who would manage individuals in groups as to the best ways of achieving their objectives and harmonizing the psychological contentment of the managed with efficiency of the enterprise: a combination of neutral expertise and mutual benefits. Could anyone genuinely concerned with the improvement of human relations gainsay such an endeavour?

Of course, the birth of psychology, as a discipline and as a profession, is only one aspect of the psychologization of experience in the twentieth century. Psychology, as it disciplined itself in the late nineteenth century and into the twentieth, had no monopoly on attempts to understand the 'inner person', to render the human soul amenable to rationalized knowledge and esoteric technique. There were all those controversial endeavours dating back to at least a century earlier – such as mesmerism, hypnotism, phrenology and so forth – which claimed to understand, diagnose and act upon the troubles, ills and fates of the human being through engaging with some inner realm. There were the proliferating activities of nerve doctors whose principal remit was the minor troubles of emotion and conduct of the wealthier classes and predominantly of their women. And there were the growing claims of medical psychiatrists, who controlled the space of the public and private asylums, had made forays into the institutions of the law and courts, and increasingly claimed jurisdiction over the diagnosis and treatment of the pathologies of mind. As the twentieth century progressed, and especially during and after the Second World War, there were innumerable professional disputes between and within each branch of the burgeoning empire of the psy. In particular, doctors denied the capacity of those without medical training to practise except under the direction of medics, exponents of organic psychiatry disputed the claims made by those who sought purely psychological explanations of mental disorder, many of those who advocated psychological treatments of minor mental troubles decried the psychoanalysts for their pan-sexualism and claimed that their therapeutic results were as often to worsen as to improve the condition of their patients. Further, the encroachment of psy specialists into the territory of other experts was not uncontested. Not for nothing is the carpenter Moosbrugger a recurrent figure in *The Man Without Qualities*: the question of his responsibility for his horrific murder of a prostitute – of psychological determinism or jurisprudential free will – was the subject of dispute between lawyers, newspaper reporters, politicians and psychiatrists. Across the past century of psy, lawyers have resisted the incursion of psy into the courts and into the prisons, military men have resisted its incursion into the armed forces, managers and factory owners have doubted its capacity to do much for labour relations or productivity, families or those who speak for them have resisted the incursion of psychologically trained health visitors and social workers into the 'private space of the family'.

Nevertheless, over the course of all these little struggles and resistances – over territory and authority, public and private, personal and political – there has none the less been a spectacular proliferation of psy experts throughout our present experience. Once more, the bare numbers are instructive. The British Psychological Society grew from 1164 members in 1945 to around 5500 in 1975: by 1994 the membership was over 18,000. There was a corresponding growth in a whole array of other practitioners of psy. Take the psychotherapies and counselling. Classical psychoanalysis grew at a sedate pace: the membership of the British Psycho-Analytical Society was around 100 at the end of the Second World War, reaching 378 in 1985 (at which date, according to Roudinesco, 1990, there were 6210 psychoanalysts world-wide) and under 500 in 1995 – only about a dozen new analysts qualify in the UK each year. But by 1995, just one other school of therapy, that committed to the use of hypnosis, could name over 300 practitioners in its National Register of Hypnotherapists and Psychotherapists, and the British Association for Counselling lists over 2000 individual counsellors and psychotherapists in over 250 counselling and psychotherapy organizations ranging from the Adlerian Counselling Centre, through Bottlefed, Therapy Services for Adult Children of Alcoholics, Oxford Male Survivors Sanctuary, to the York Centre for Gestalt Development.

Britain, of course, cannot compete with America. From 531 members in 1931 (when Fernberger was already remarking that the organization had the character of a big business) membership of the American Psychological Association grew to over 11,000 in 1964, with 1600 psychologists employed directly and fulltime by the Federal government alone. By 1973 the organization had 35,000 full members and its convention in Montreal attracted 19,000 attendees; and by 1993 there were over 76,000 members and 42,000 affiliates. The American Psychoanalytic Association

233

had reached a membership of over 2000 by 1985 and around 3000 in 1995, with at least thirty-five affiliated societies and twenty-seven institutes. Readers may amuse themselves by estimating the numbers of psycho-therapists and counsellors in the land of the unquiet self.

These figures are not simply indicators of the spectacular growth of the business empire of the self over the last one hundred years, they are evidence of the birth of a new type of person. For human beings are the kinds of creatures who have no universal ontology, no essence whether this be spiritual or genetic. Our ontology is historical: it is both temporal and spatial. What humans are – perhaps better, what human beings are capable of, what we can do – is variable, historical, situational – not an originary 'being' but a mobile 'becoming'. The significance of the growth of psy in the twentieth century is the evidence it provides that, in all the little practices, gestures, pleasures, desires, norms, values, judgements, conflicts and sufferings of everyday life, human beings are becoming psychological selves.

IS THE HUMAN SOUL MADE OF LANGUAGE?

Language is one of the keys to our assembly as psychological beings. It is, after all, only possible for us to delineate our passions, formulate our intentions, organize our thoughts through lexicons, grammars, syntax and semantics. Our culture enjoins each of us to follow the edict 'know thyself'. But how is such knowledge to be gained? Can this be by a pure act of intro-spection, turning our own gaze inwards to focus on the configurations of an inner experience? How are we to see this self which we are commanded to know? What are we to look for? How are we to articulate this to ourselves, let alone to others? What consequences follow from the things we discover about ourselves when we turn our eyes to our hidden self, attune our ears to the voice within, make ourselves the object of our own gaze?

No, our reflexivity – our self-inspection, self-scrutiny, self-judgement – is not, can never be naive. When Augustine urged his contemporaries in late antiquity to 'return to yourself, it is in the inner man that truth dwells', the inner man whom he sought was a very different character from the psychological self we are urged today to discover as our truth (cf. Hadot, 1995, p.65). The gaze of our inner eye is configured by words, phrases, explanations and valuations: we can experience ourselves as certain types of creatures only because we do so under a certain description. The birth and history of psychological descriptions of individuals and their conduct hollows out a certain kind of self, locates certain zones or fields 'within' that are of significance, requires us to speak of ourselves in particular vocabularies, to evaluate ourselves in relation to certain norms. Traumas, emotional deprivation, depression, repression, projection, motivation, desire, extroverts and introverts – we have a psy vocabulary – or rather a family of divergent vocabularies – to describe ourselves. And whatever the origin of these languages of the self, they are indispensable to the ways in which we can make ourselves the objects of our own reflection.

The anatomy of the psychological self was put together over this century through a cluster of organizing terms: intelligence, personality, motivation, role and so forth. Take, for example, 'attitude'. From being a visible composition of the body – one could adopt a 'defiant attitude by posture, gesture, facial expression – the word moves in the early decades of this century to designate an invisible psychological state. The significance of the psychologization of attitude was the promise of a science of action itself. As Thomas and Znanieki put it, 'every manifestation of conscious life . . . can be treated as an attitude, because every one involves a tendency to action' in relation to 'social values' (Thomas and Znanieki, 1918, p. 27). Social psychology would be 'a general science of the subjective science of culture' (ibid., p. 31). By 1928 William Thurstone had devised the principles for the quantification of this new field of subjectivity, and could declare that 'attitudes can be measured': each attitude could be rated by giving numerical values to verbally expressed opinions and beliefs – for example, about abortion, capital punishment or Italians – along a scale ranging from positive to negative (Thurstone, 1928). By 1935, Gordon Allport could define attitude as 'the cornerstone of social psychology' which could explain such phenomena as prejudice, patriotism, loyalty, crowd behaviour, control by propaganda and much more: an attitude was a 'mental and neural state of readiness, organised through experience, exerting a dynamic influence upon the individual's response to all objects and situations with which it is related' (Allport, 1935). The social psychologists engaged in a multitude of investigations to chart these newly discovered 'attitudes': attitudes could account for the different propensities of women and men to favour prohibition or the tendency of Jewish students to favour birth control more than Catholics or Protestants. Industrial discontent, racial prejudice, the morale of citizens and the like could be described in terms of variations of attitudes. Organizations such as factories or armies could be managed in the light of a knowledge of the attitudes of their workers or soldiers. 'Attitude surveys' or 'morale surveys' were required if one was to ensure that problems did not arise from 'failures of communication'. But while attitude surveys revealed that consensus did not exist on basic beliefs and opinions, they also held out the hope that consensus could be engineered by attitude change. In the US during the Second World War, psychologists employed by the governments and the military engaged in a vast endeavour for the inscription, calculation and transformation of attitudes: morale surveys could be used to chart changing support for the war effort in general and for different policies; broadcasting techniques could be evaluated in terms of their success in changing attitudes. Everyday language for describing the determinants of conduct

– one's own and that of others – was reshaped. Children and workers were troublesome because they had 'attitude problems', conflicts were to be resolved by 'changing one's attitude'; one would do badly at a particular task because one did not have the right attitude. The vocabulary of attitude thus provided a new means of linking the subjective and the political: we govern our own conduct, and are governed by others, in terms of a novel psychological language of the internal dispositions which shape our actions.

Or consider the term 'trauma'. Ian Hacking has examined the psychologization of this term while studying the recent disputes in the United States over the status of 'recovered memories' of child sexual abuse (Hacking, 1995, p. 183 ff.). Trauma, Hacking reminds us, was once a surgeon's word referring to a wound on the body, most often the result of battle. Only gradually was trauma psychologized, as a result of a chain of little shifts in the late nineteenth century: the idea that head injuries without manifest external or neurological damage could cause loss of memory and paralysis gradually became linked with existing arguments which in turn linked hysteria and amnesia to lead to the notion that psychological shock could itself produce hysterical symptoms in a patient while itself being hidden to memory. The human actors in this process of psychologization were the great men in the history of the discipline: Pierre Janet, J.-M. Charcot and Sigmund Freud. But the chain of connection was established around a tangle of more mundane concerns in the 1860s and after: about the insurance costs and consequences of railway accidents which produced disability in sufferers without any visible lesion, about the possible links between the symptoms of such victims and hysteria, about the possible moral effects of physical trauma, terror or revulsion and so forth. Trauma had already become psychological when, in the 1880s, Janet argued that horrifying experiences were alone enough to produce hysterical symptoms, and that these could be removed by hypnosis which acted upon the memory of the original trauma. When Freud argued that the core of a hysterical attack was not a specific event but a memory which, most often, has the content of a psychical trauma, trauma had become fully psychological.

Once psychologized, we can think of any number of events and experiences that are traumatic – in terms of the damage they do, not to the limbs, the head or even the brain, but to the psyche, to personality, to development, to self-esteem. In early life, it now appears, traumatic events such as bereavement may cause irreversible psychological damage. In the case of adults, involvement in a road accident or witnessing of a fire, riot or crowd accident is sufficient to produce 'post-traumatic stress disorder' – according to the most recent version of the *Diagnostic and Statistical Manual* of the American Psychiatric Association, this is a disorder with a lifetime prevalence rate of up to 14 per cent and up to 58 per cent among combat veterans and others 'at risk' (1994, p. 426). Not only is there now a whole specialist literature on the aetiology, diagnosis, treatment and prognosis of different kinds of trauma, but we can all have our own experiences of trauma – no wonder we are 'depressed' after splitting up with a partner, having a job interview, taking an exam: for of course these are 'incredibly traumatic'.

Trauma exemplifies a more general phenomenon – that the language is not a tranquil medium of description but the site, the stake and the result of conflicts, contestations and campaigns. Trauma is part of a whole politics of the psyche. A politics in the limited sense of a set of struggles around the nature, causes, reality, consequences, responsibility, funding and compensation, legislation and so forth of various forms of trauma and stress, such as childhood abuse, presence at a disaster, the emotional damage wrought by sexual harassment. But also a politics in a wider sense. For terms such as trauma – together with stress, anxiety, personality and many others – link the political and the personal. As Roger Smith has shown in his illuminating discussion of the notion of 'inhibition' in nineteenth-century political culture and psychology, such words and phrases act as translation points between rationalities of politics and ethics of conduct (Smith, 1992). How should we be required to behave? Should we exercise 'self-control over emotions' or strive for 'self-realization of our inner feelings'? Should our 'will' be disciplined by 'habits' or should we aspire to a society that accepts 'the need for each of us to enhance our self-esteem'?

The words that become powerful enable us to live particular kinds of lives. Kenneth Gergen among others argues that human beings do not just use language to recount their life to one another, they actually live out their lives as 'narratives' (Gergen, 1991). We use the stories of the self that our culture makes available to us, with their scenarios of emotions, their repertoires of motives, their cast-list of characters, to plan out our lives, to account for events and give them significance, to accord ourselves an identity as hero or victim, survivor or casualty within the plot of our own life, to shape our own conduct and understand that of others. When our culture provides us with life narratives couched in psychological terms, our lives really do become psychological in their form. Selfhood, and beliefs about the attributes of the self, feelings, intentions and the like, are properties, not of mental mechanisms but of conversations, grammars of speaking. They are both possible and intelligible only in societies where these things can properly, grammatically be said by people about people. Rules of this 'grammar' of individuals – 'language games' – produce or induce a moral repertoire of relatively enduring features of personhood in inhabitants of particular cultures, and one that has a morally constraining quality: we are obliged to be individuals of a certain sort. Talk about the self actually makes up the types of self-awareness and self-understanding that human beings acquire and display in their own lives, *and* makes up social practices themselves, to the extent that such practices cannot be carried out without certain self-understandings (cf. Shotter, 1985; Shotter and Gergen, 1989).

Psychological language is thus one of the key components of the modern soul. Ian Hacking terms this 'the looping effects of human kinds' (1995, pp. 21 and 239). At certain historical moments, particular issues or problems are *constructed* in certain ways – as melancholia or depression, as hysteria or post-traumatic syndrome, as cowardice or shell-shock – only through the possibilities available within language: words, vocabularies, the grammars of explanation and causation, the narratives of life events that it provides. Language makes only certain ways of being human describable, and in so doing makes only certain ways of being human possible. To be human is to act, and to act is to behave under a certain description, and the possibility of description is language. This stress on language reactivates an old theme in the philosophy of the human and social sciences about the meaningful nature of human existence, which is by no means unproblematic. However, I do not want to pursue those difficulties here. I have said enough, I think, to persuade you that the availability of psy languages of description of our actions, for our passions, for our affections and our ills, makes available new ways of describing actual or possible actions, hence of thinking about them, judging them, undertaking them or refraining from them. The words for our souls enjoined upon us by psychology transform what human beings take themselves to be, and thus what they can become.

These newly invented or psychologized psy words enable human beings to classify their experiences in particular ways and to communicate them to others. But they have a more fundamental importance. They both presuppose and open out a 'psy-shaped space' within each of us, an internal zone with its own processes, laws, types of health and disease, variations, traits and so forth. Between the brain – with its nerves, its physiology, its flows, fibres, organs and tissues – and human conduct – with the dilemmas of right and wrong, and the difficult judgements of forms of life – lies an inner psy space that stands behind, originates, explains and accords meaning to any act. From now on, all our practices for the management of life, all our systems of spiritual guidance, all our cures for the anguish and the violence of the human condition and all our judgement of ourselves and others, will be obliged to make reference to this psy-shaped space that inhabits us.

MACHINATIONS OF THE SELF

But the human self is not merely a matter of the meanings of words: it is assembled through techniques, practices, 'machinated' in a hundred little machines for living within which we are all caught up. We need to focus less on what language *means* and more upon what language *does*, what components of thinking and acting it connects up, what it enables human beings to dream into existence, to do to themselves and to others. Language has to be understood in its material aspect, as integrated into a number of technologies that make human beings capable of being and doing particular things – making lists, sending messages, accumulating information from distant locations in a single spot, individualizing and ordering one another, extending new lines of force, making possible new effects. The printing press together with practices of instruction in the techniques, gestures and habits of reading and writing make it possible for human beings to be transformed into 'literate beings', identifying themselves with their signatures, committing themselves through written contracts, moving from public religious instruction based upon memorization and catechisms to the private reading of the Bible; their conduct would be civilized by being connected to treatises of civility, new spaces of interiority would be formed through establishing bodily and ocular connections with books and by means of the complex techniques of silent reading practised in libraries and other spaces set aside for contemplation and reflection (Chartier, 1989). Techniques of numeracy and systems of number enable individuals to be transformed into 'calculating beings' with a certain way of relating to themselves and their future – enabling the cultivation and generalization of foresight and prudence, say, as one calculates one's financial future in the form of a budget. Techniques of inscription, collection, tabulation and calculation together with programmes of statistics, transform human beings into members of societies, understanding their fate as shaped by social forces, their propensities as governed by social laws, their security promoted by their incorporation into social machines of welfare and insurance. The bureaucratic procedures of record-keeping, of writing, filing, referencing, cross-checking, transform human beings into cases whose dossiers embody their nature, their biography and their fate. In these ways and others, the human soul is fabricated and capacitated as it is traced through our material forms of notation, collation, circulation and utilization of inscriptions, and the senses are amplified and machinated though their connections with artefacts and bodily techniques.

Other technical accomplishments fabricate the psychological self. Take, for example, memory. The memory of oneself as a unique and continuous individual with a biography is central to our contemporary selfhood. But such biographical memory should not be thought of as a primordial capacity of the human animal. Memory is itself a set of techniques. Friedrich Nietzsche called these 'mnemotechnics': the devices whereby one 'burns' the past into oneself and makes it available in the present as a warning, a comfort, a bargaining device, a weapon or a wound (Nietzsche,

1956, p. 192). The classical art of memory, which was revived in the Middle Ages, was a particular set of techniques for remembering involving the invention of places or spaces in which items of knowledge or experience were 'placed' by the person wishing to later recall them: one could retrieve them merely by imagining oneself taking a walk past the landmarks on this territory (Yates, 1966; cf. Hirst and Wooley, 1982, p. 39). But even when not made into a conscious art, memory is a technical accomplishment. For something to be remembered it must first be given the status of an experience, then made available for reactivation though pledges, rituals, songs, pictures, libraries, contracts, debts, the design of buildings, the structuring of space and time and much more.

One's memory of oneself as a self with a unique character, an individual biography grounded in a family history and the like, is produced and assembled through family albums of photographs, birthday cards, portraits, the dossier of school reports, the curriculum vitae and a whole series of other practical accomplishments. Psy is important here, not only because it provides the languages in which these artefacts are written or by means of which they are read, but also because it has invented a series of technologies of memory which reactivate the past in the present as a set of feelings and needs, emotions experienced or repressed, blows to self-esteem or contributors to the stability of personality. These range from the case history to the psychotherapeutic confessional, from hypnosis to techniques of 'recovered memory'. Each produces memory in a particular codified form, a language, but also a grammar of causes and effects, a diagram of interior forces and flows of affect. Since their earliest uses, psy memory techniques have been particularly controversial: are the memories produced through these 'artificial' devices 'artefacts'? No doubt this is because what has been produced through the application of such techniques is often scandalous – memories of infantile desire or of childhood abuse. But for our present purposes, the salience of these psychological memory techniques is different. It lies in their wide dissemination in practices far removed from the analyst's couch or the doctor's consulting room – into magazines, newspapers, the ubiquitous interview of celebrities, radio recollection programmes, confessional television talk shows and so on. The impact of these new memory technologies is not merely as a pedagogy of reminiscence; our relation to them is also one of mimesis. We come to inhabit particular styles of remembering ourselves, and accounting for our present in terms of our past. Only through being assembled together with an array of non-natural, non-individualized techniques which extend far beyond the boundaries of the human skin is one capable of being a self with an autobiography.

These truths of the psychological self do not reside in a tranquil universe of meanings but in a set of conflicts and battles over truth – and there is only truth where there is authority. One can know the truth of oneself only through the intermediary of a mediator – whether this be a spiritual guide, a priest or a scientific expert – whose pronouncements carry the effects of truth because they are spoken from a certain position. Today these may be spoken from the chair positioned just behind the therapist's couch, from the desk upon which are laid out the scores of one's personality test, or from the ward round wherein the diagnosis of the multi-disciplinary team is pronounced. Or they may be spoken by the expert on the television documentary or confessional talk show, mediated by the agony aunt in the newspaper or magazine, 'black boxed' as indisputable facts in the common sense of television soap operas or popular novels. And not all stories are equal: only some statements can be 'in the true' and only those authorized can speak with authority when it comes to the truths of the placid or troubled self.

When I speak of my trauma, my stress, my neurosis, my low self-esteem, I thus activate more than words, meanings, narratives – I engage myself with a whole regime of truth, an array of relations of authority. As Foucault put it, what are significant are 'the various statuses, the various sites, the various positions' that must be occupied in particular regimes if something is to be sayable, hearable, operable': the physician, the scientist, the therapist, the counsellor, the lover (Foucault, 1972, p. 54). These relations emplace both the object spoken about – emotions, mental pathologies, normal development and the like – and those who are the subjects of their speech – clients, patients, users, survivors, ordinary people. Relations among words are always assembled within other relations. The language of psy, even when it is spoken and dialogic rather than the written monologue of the scientific text, is manifested only within particular practices: confessing, diagnosing, sharing, interpreting, assessing, classifying, predicting, evaluating, treating, explaining. These practices do not inhabit an amorphous and functionally homogeneous domain of meaning and negotiation among individuals. They are located in particular sites and procedures which have yet to be fully investigated: the subjectifying practices of our contemporary schools and courts, of the social work interview and the consultation with the doctor, of the ward group of the psychiatric hospital, of the interview with the personnel officer, the session in the analyst's consulting room, the therapeutic group meeting, the marriage guidance encounter, the radio phone-in. Together with the psychological reconfiguring of the spaces of domesticity or erotics, and less evident spaces such as the gym, the sports field, the supermarket, the cinema, we have here a whole series of little machines for fabricating and holding in place the psychological self.

The subjectifying effects of psy are not simply a matter of the 'symbolic violence' of a particular meaning system: language is structured into variegated relations which grant powers to some and delimit the powers of others, which enable some to judge and some to be judged, some to cure and some to be cured, some to speak truth and others to acknowledge its

241

NIKOLAS ROSE

authority and embrace it, aspire to it or submit to it. And if, in our vernacular speech, we think of ourselves in psy terms, we do so only through the relations we have established with this truth regime: for we each play our own part, as parents, teachers, partners, lovers, consumers and sufferers, in these contemporary psychological machinations of the self.

EXERCISING THE SELF

Many have decried the influence of psy on our culture by suggesting that it has undermined and replaced theology in our moral codes. Of course, they are right that our ethical language is more likely to be psychological than spiritual. Yet the journalistic argument that psy has taken the place of religion, that psychotherapy has taken the place of confession and the psy expert has assumed the role of priest is simplistic. Regimes of ethics since the Greeks have depended in different ways upon particular and varying notions of the person who is thought to be the subject of ethics. Systems of injunction, of prescription, proscription and valuation are intrinsically bound to conceptions of what it is to be the kind of human being, man, woman, master, slave, child, freeman, serf, who is the bearer of ethics.

How should we understand the psychologization of ethics? Pierre Hadot has suggested that we approach ethics not as a set of abstract moral codes, but from the perspective of what he terms 'spiritual exercises': the instruction and practice of particular techniques for the therapeutics of the passions, of the mind, of the body, of the will (Hadot, 1995). Hadot has pointed to the ascesis, the practice of spiritual exercises in the service of the arts of living, which, albeit in different ways, lay at the heart of the teaching of the Stoics, the Epicureans, Socratic and Platonic dialogues, in Neo-platonism and in the Cynics. For Hadot, such exercises were essential to the very meaning of philosophy in antiquity. One who would lead a philosophical life must practise self-examination, cultivate attention to the present moment, devote oneself to duties, cultivate indifference to indifferent things, keep certain things 'before one's eyes'. These spiritual exercises varied widely. They variously entailed such things as practical exercises to curb anger, gossip and curiosity and to cultivate moral habits, meditation first thing in the morning and last thing at night, utilization of rhetoric and imagery to mobilize the imagination, memorization of aphorisms so as to keep the fundamental dogmas at hand, the cultivation of relaxation and serenity, the practice of dialogue with others so as to be able to undertake the internal dialogue necessary to render oneself present to oneself. But they point to a recurrent phenomenon, the utilization of practical techniques, albeit for an elite, to reshape the soul in the service of an art of living.

These practices of spiritual exercise and spiritual guidance did not die with the ancient world. They were the organizing principles of early

242

Christian communities, of the Christian brothers and 'friends of God' (Brown, 1978; 1989). The spiritual exercises of Ignatius Loyola and of the early Latin Christianity that preceded him were largely Christian versions of Greco-Roman practices (Hadot, 1995; Rabbow, 1954). Their attitude to experience was one of ascesis, not in our modern sense of asceticism as austerity and self-denial, but as the practice of exercises of attention to oneself, one's thoughts and intentions: the cultivation of an attention to oneself in order to achieve a transfiguration of the soul. From the twelfth century onwards, a new practice of Christian administration of 'the cure of souls' made advances across Europe, its priestly practitioners using such treatises as Abelard's *Sic et Non* (Yes and No) and *Ethica Scito te Ipsum* (Ethics or Know Thyself) as their manuals. They spelled out the obligations of conscience in the here and now, and the forms of action permitted or forbidden in all spheres of life from contracts to war. 'After 1215, when annual confession became the obligation of all Christians, these treatises became the guides to Christian souls everywhere' (Nelson, 1965, p. 64; cf. Leites, 1988). The rise of literacy, to which I have already referred, made possible the dissemination of a whole range of other spiritual exercises, from the daily reading of the Bible, through the exercises prescribed by books of manners and civility, to the nightly confession in the writing of the diary. The eighteenth and nineteenth centuries saw the generalization of practices of spiritual direction beyond a holy elite. Weber and others famously pointed to the way in which Protestantism universalized Christian asceticism and enjoined it upon each pious individual who lived in the mundane world. In the same period in Europe and the United States, elements of religious exercises for the formation and administration of an inner and personal conscience were incorporated within a whole range of secular practices – notably those of schooling – for the inculcation and administration of habits of life and modes of self-scrutiny and vigilance (Hunter, 1988; Rose, 1993).

It is in this sense that we might understand differently the tired analogy between therapy and religion. For a genealogy of the therapeutic would indeed trace a line between psy practices of the self and ancient spiritual exercises: a line drawn in order to diagnose the variety of ways in which human beings have made themselves the subject of ethical work. Freud, for example, did not just devise a whole language of description, as Benjamin Nelson has suggested; he was also central to the invention of a novel schema for the direction of souls (Nelson, 1965). Psychoanalysis here refers not to a series of texts but to an array of practical ways in which human beings could take themselves as the objects of their own thought and practice, and act upon themselves in the name of the talking cure, the couch, the case history, the free association, the interpretation, the transference and counter-transference and so on. Freud was not the first to utilize these devices, each of which had a longer history and a wider provenance in the practice of nerve doctors at the close of the nineteenth century. But we have witnessed a proliferation of these ways of relating to ourselves over the past hundred years. The diverse techniques of psy that have been promulgated by rival schools – from rational-emotive therapy to behaviour therapy, and from humanistic counselling to family therapy – have disseminated a variety of procedures by means of which human beings either individually or in groups, using the techniques elaborated by psychological experts, can act upon their bodies, their emotions, their beliefs and their forms of conduct in order to transform themselves, in order to improve themselves and to live a better life.

These practices of self-inspection and self-problematization in terms of an inner psychological domain and its vicissitudes become the key elements in our contemporary arts of living: a style of life whose very ethos might be termed therapeutic. They make possible a number of ways for 'setting up and developing relationships with [oneself], for self-reflection, self-knowledge, self-examination, for the deciphering of the self by oneself, for the transformation one seeks to accomplish with oneself as object' (Foucault, 1988, p. 29). We can identify a number of different aspects of these psychotherapeutic techniques for the problematization of the self.

First, there are the different techniques though which one *attends to oneself*: modes of self-inspection, vocabularies for self-description, methods of self-examination. While understandably it is the confessional practices of the therapies that have attracted most attention, we should not underestimate here the role played in self-problematization and self-management by the whole panoply of psy tools for assessing, calibrating and classifying humans: tests of intelligence and personality, charts, scales and typologies. Second, they involve different modes of *engaging with the self* – an epistemological mode, for example, which searches for past determinants of present states, an interpretative mode, in which the word or act is understood in terms of its significance in relation to other parties to the interaction, a descriptive mode which seeks to fix attention on conduct dissected into micro-competencies such as grooming, bathing, eating, eye-contact, which can be recorded, normalized and made the subject of pedagogies of social skills. Third, there are the diverse *aspects of the self* accorded significance. Some have suggested that our contemporary relation to ourselves is structured by desire. But desire is only one of the aspects in which the contemporary self is grasped. Perhaps more significant, because of its dissemination through a range of professional practices from social work to nursing, has been an attention to the superficiality of 'behaviour' itself in the form of social skills and capacities to cope. Fourth, there are the variety of modes of *evaluating the self*, diagnosing its ills, calibrating its failings and its advances in terms of the norms of the intellect or the personality propagated by psychology, the repertoires of feelings and emotions disseminated by the therapies, the forms of

244

normality certified by the proponents of cognitive behavioural systems. Fifth, there are the various ways of *disclosing the self* – ways of speaking not only in the consulting room, but to children, bosses, employees, friends and lovers. I have already remarked on the proliferation of sites within which human beings are required to reflect upon themselves in psychological terms and render this into speech, from the doctor's surgery to the radio interview. And sixth, there are the different techniques for *the curing of the self* – the purgative effects of catharsis, the liberating effect of understanding, the restructuring effect of interpretation, the little practices for the retraining of thoughts and emotions, the techniques one should adopt to raise self-confidence and to maximize self-esteem. Of particular importance here has been the invention of new methods for the therapeutics of behaviour and cognition, versatile micro-procedures which can be taught by a variety of professionals and utilized by individuals in order to reshape their psychological self to 'take control of their lives' within an ethics of 'empowerment'.

It is through such little techniques of the self that psy permeates our modes of being at a molecular level, not merely forming a context of meaning, but structuring the very texture of our ways of acting. Our contemporary ethical regimes are psychological to the extent that the forms of personhood that underpin so many of our practices have themselves become psychological.

THE PSY EFFECT

Nothing I have said should be taken as asserting the dominance of psy in our lives – for could not the same be said of, for example, the languages, images, techniques and seductions of economics? Nor have I suggested that the activities of the psy professions are themselves the 'cause' of all the mutations involved in the birth of the psychological self. But I have tried to point to something like a 'psy effect' in our contemporary experience of ourselves. An effect in the sense in which Gilles Deleuze understands the notion of an effect, such as the Kelvin effect or the Compton effect, as deployed in scientific discourse:

> An effect of this kind is by no means an appearance or an illusion. It is a product which spreads or distends itself over a surface; it is strictly co-present to, and co-extensive with, its own cause, and determines this cause as an immanent cause, inseparable from its effects.
>
> (Deleuze, 1990, p. 70, quoted in Burchell 1991, p. ix)

The psy effect, that is to say, is not to be explained by seeking a cause, but rather delineated by diagnosing the ways in which human existence has become intelligible and practicable under a certain description. The psy effect is to be located not in the abstract space of culture and meaning, but

245

in a whole variety of practical 'machines' – desiring machines, labouring machines, pedagogic machines, punitive machines, curative machines, consuming machines, war machines, sporting machines, governing machines, spiritual machines, bureaucratic machines, market machines, financial machines – which engage human beings on the condition that they relate to themselves as psychological selves. Our modern self is put together out of the ways in which, in each of these assemblages, a particular psychological relation to ourselves is presupposed, administered, enjoined and assembled.

In all these diverse machinations of being, a number of themes recur: choice, fulfilment, self-discovery, self-realization. Contemporary practices of subjectification, that is to say, put into play a being that must be attached to a project of identity, and to a secular project of 'lifestyle', in which life and its contingencies become meaningful to the extent that they can be construed as the product of personal choice. We need to examine how each of our little machines of living, our assemblages of passion and of pleasure, of labour and of consumption, of war and of sport, of aesthetics and theology, have accorded a psychological form to their subjects. We need to anatomize the relations of power and subjectification brought into existence. Perhaps most fundamental to the contemporary politics of our relation to ourselves is the way in which psychological modes of explanation, claims to truth and systems of authority have participated in the elaboration of ethical regimes that stress an ideal of responsible autonomy and have become allied with programmes for regulating individuals in the name of that autonomous responsibility (cf. Rose, 1990; 1993; Rose and Miller, 1992). For these new ethical forms have become central to the government of human conduct in advanced liberal democracies, governing humans in the name of their freedom as psychological selves.

NOTE

In this chapter I have drawn directly upon arguments made in more detail in the essays collected in Rose 1996b.

BIBLIOGRAPHY

Allport, G. W. (1935) Attitudes, in C.A. Murchison, *Handbook of Social Psychology* (pp. 1–50), Worcester, MA: Clark University Press.
American Psychiatric Association (1994) *Diagnostic and Statistical Manual of Mental Disorders* (4th edn.), Washington, DC: American Psychiatric Association.
Boring, E. (1929) *A History of Experimental Psychology*, London: Century.
Brown, P. (1978) *The Making of Late Antiquity*, Cambridge, MA: Harvard.
—— (1989) *The Body and Society: Men. Women and Sexual Renunciation in Early Christianity*, London: Faber.
Burchell, G., Gordon, C. and Miller, P. (eds) (1991) *The Foucault Effect: Studies in Governmentality*, Hemel Hempstead: Harvester Wheatsheaf.

Chartier, R. (1989) The Practical Impact of Writing, in R. Chartier, ed., *A History of Private Life. Vol. 3: Passions of the Renaissance* (pp. 111–59), trans. A. Goldhammer, Cambridge, MA: Belknap Press of Harvard University Press.

Danziger, K. (1990) *Constructing the Subject: Historical Origins of Psychological Research*, Cambridge: Cambridge University Press.

Deleuze, G. (1990) *The Logic of Sense*, trans. M. Lester with C. Stivale, New York: Columbia University Press.

Fernberger, S. W. (1932) The American Psychological Association: A Historical Summary, *Psychological Bulletin*, 29, 1–89.

Foucault, M. (1970) *The Order of Things*, London: Tavistock.

—— (1972) *The Archaeology of Knowledge*, London: Tavistock.

—— (1988) Technologies of the Self, in L. H. Martin, H. Gutman and P. H. Hutton (eds), *Technologies of the Self* (pp. 16–49), London: Tavistock.

Fryer, D. H. and Henry, E. R.(eds) (1950) *Handbook of Applied Psychology*, 2 vols, New York: Rinehart.

Geertz, C. (1979) From the Native's Point of View: On the Nature of Anthropological Understanding, in P. Rabinow and W. M. Sullivan (eds), *Interpretive Social Science*, Berkeley, CA: University of California Press.

Gergen, K.(1991) *The Saturated Self: Dilemmas of Identity in Contemporary Life*, New York: Basic Books.

Gillespie, R. (1988) The Hawthorne Experiment and the Politics of Experimentation, in Jill Morawski (ed.), *The Rise of Experimentation in American Psychology*, New Haven: Yale University Press.

Hacking, I. (1995) *Rewriting the Soul: Multiple Personality and the Sciences of Memory*, Princeton: Princeton University Press.

Hadot, P. (1995) *Philosophy as a Way of Life*, Oxford: Blackwell.

Hirst, P. Q. and Wooley, P. (1982) *Social Relations and Human Attributes*, London: Tavistock.

Hornstein, G. (1988) *Quantifying Psychological Phenomena*, in Jill Morawski (ed.), *The Rise of Experimentation in American Psychology*, New Haven, Yale University Press.

Hunter, I. (1988) *Culture and Government: The Emergence of Literary Education*, London: Macmillan.

Leites, E. (ed.) (1988) *Conscience and Casuistry in Early Modern Europe*, Cambridge: Cambridge University Press.

Mauss, M. (1979) The Category of the Person, in *Psychology and Sociology: Essays* (pp. 57–94), London: Routledge & Kegan Paul.

Musil, R. (1979) *The Man Without Qualities, Vol. 1*, London: Picador (first published in 1930).

Nelson, B. (1965) Self Images and Systems of Spiritual Direction in the History of European Civilization, in S. Klausner, ed., *The Quest for Self Control* (pp. 49–103), New York: Free Press.

Nietzsche, F. W. (1956) *The Genealogy of Morals*, trans. Francis Golffing, New York: Doubleday.

O'Donnell, J. (1985) *The Origins of Behaviorism: American Psychology, 1870–1920*, New York: New York University Press.

Porter, T. M. (1995) *Trust in Numbers: The Pursuit of Objectivity in Science and Public Life*, Princeton, NY: Princeton University Press.

Rabbow, P. (1954) *Seelenführung: Methodik der Exerzitien in der Antike*, Munich: Kösel.

Rose, N. (1985) *The Psychological Complex: Psychology, Politics and Society in England 1869–1939*, London: Routledge.

—— (1990) *Governing the Soul: The Shaping of the Private Self*, London: Routledge.

—— (1993) *Towards a Critical Sociology of Freedom*, Inaugural Lecture delivered on 5 May 1992 at Goldsmiths' College, University of London: Goldsmiths' College.

—— (1994) Government, Authority and Expertise under Advanced Liberalism, *Economy and Society*, 22, 3, 273–99.

—— (1996a) Authority and the Genealogy of Subjectivity, in P. Heelas, P. Morris and S. Lash (eds), *De-Traditionalization: Authority and Self in an Age of Cultural Change*, Oxford: Blackwell.

—— (1996b) *Inventing Our Selves: Psychology, Power and Personhood*, New York: Cambridge University Press.

Rose, N. and Miller, P. (1992) Political Power Beyond the State: Problematics of Government, *British Journal of Sociology*, 43, 2, 172–205.

Roudinesco, E. (1990) *Jacques Lacan & Co. A History of Psychoanalysis in France, 1925–1985*, London: Free Association Books.

Sampson, E., (1989) The Deconstruction of the Self, in J. Shotter and K. Gergen (eds), *Texts of Identity* (pp. 1–19), London: Sage.

Shotter, J. (1985) Social Accountability and Self Specification, in K. J. Gergen and K. E. Davies (eds), *The Social Construction of the Person* (pp. 168–90), New York: Springer Verlag.

Shotter, J. and Gergen, K. (1989) *Texts of Identity*, London: Sage.

Smith, R. (1992) *Inhibition: History and Meaning in the Sciences of Mind and Brain*, Berkeley: University of California Press.

Taylor, C. (1989) *Sources of the Self: The Making of Modern Identity*, Cambridge: Cambridge University Press.

Thomas, W. I. and Znanieki, F. (1918) *The Polish Peasant in Europe and America, Vol. 1: Primary Group Organization*, Boston: Badger.

Thurstone, L. L.(1928) Attitudes can be measured, *American Journal of Sociology*, 33: 529–54.

Yates, F. (1966) *The Art of Memory*, London: Routledge & Kegan Paul.

Yerkes, R. (ed.) (1921) *Psychological Examining in the United States Army*, Washington: National Academy of Sciences.

15

DEATH AND THE SELF

Jonathan Dollimore

In Thomas Mann's 1947 novel *Dr Faustus*, there's a memorable exchange between the humanist narrator of the story, Serenus Zeitblom, and its anti-humanist hero, Adrian Leverkühn. Adrian is fascinated by 'the blackness of interstellar space whither for eternities no weakest sun-ray had penetrated, the eternally still and virgin night'. Serenus, fearing he is hearing something like Freud's death drive – that instinct towards oblivion, the desire for a state of zero tension before or beyond consciousness – responds with a vigorous defence of life from a liberal humanist perspective:

> Piety, reverence, intellectual decency, religious feeling are only possible about men and through men, and by limitation to the earthly and human. Their fruit should, can and will be a religiously tinged humanism, conditioned by feeling for the transcendental mystery of man, by the proud consciousness that he is no mere biological being, but with a decisive part of him belong[ing] to an intellectual and spiritual world; that to him the Absolute is given, the ideas of truth, of freedom, of justice; that upon him the duty is laid to approach the consummate. In this pathos, this obligation, this reverence of man for himself, is God; in a hundred milliards of Milky Ways I cannot find him.
>
> (pp. 259, 264)

Adrian is wry in his response: like all humanists, Serenus inclines to the geocentric view of the universe (the earth and man as its centre, with the implication that it was designed that way), whereas in fact this '*homo Dei*' of which he speaks is much more likely to be the product of marsh-gas fertility on a neighbouring star.[1]

Serenus cannot acknowledge that the widely publicized death of God was also the prelude to the death of Humanist Man. He wants to believe the opposite – that the death of God announced the liberation of Man: freed from the repressions and false consciousness of doctrinaire religion, 'Man', with an eye to his main chance, could at last take centre-stage and become himself – *homo Dei*. Being without God makes one even more central, more important, albeit vulnerably so.

249

The seminal text for this position was Feuerbach's *The Essence of Christianity* (1841), a very influential book, most famously perhaps for Karl Marx (see his *Theses on Feuerbach*). It was translated into English by George Eliot in 1854. For Feuerbach, man is not made in the image of God but precisely the reverse: 'All the attributes of the divine nature are, therefore, attributes of the human nature' (p. 14). Feuerbach urges Man to take back from God what is rightfully his, to recognize himself in – indeed *as* God, and, in effect, to eliminate the latter, since 'God is the highest subjectivity of man abstracted from himself. . . . God is, *per se* [Man's] relinquished self' (Feuerbach, 1841, pp. 14, 31). This was exhilarating if not hubristic, and for the duration of what might be called a radical humanism God was, in a sense, taken into man who then becomes his own absolute. As Serenus puts it: 'In . . . this reverence of man for himself, is God.' But it couldn't last; those like Adrian Leverkühn, and Friedrich Nietzsche, on whom Adrian is based, saw a fundamental error in humanism. God was in fact a prerequisite of Man, the latter's metaphysical support; get rid of God, and Man (like the state without capitalism in Marxism) must eventually wither away, unable to survive a situation which is the metaphysical equivalent of sitting on the branch he's sawn off, or pulling himself up by his own bootlaces.

Even so, some ninety years after Nietzsche, Michel Foucault was still *predicting* the demise of Man. Foucault's cruel elegy caused something of a scandal: 'Man is an invention of recent date', he declared, *soon* to be 'erased, like a face drawn in sand at the edge of the sea' (Foucault, 1966/1974, p. 387). Now, a further thirty years on, postmodernism is still celebrating the death, and still as a prediction rather than an established fact. But with a difference, in that now it is much more the demise of the humanist individual which excites. This isn't surprising, since the individual was only ever the incarnation of Man, just as the latter was the incarnation of God. But this development is also partly due to the fact that postmodernism is a reaction against the existentialism of our own century. Existentialism was an anxious humanism, emphatically situating man and the individual at the centre of things, but without the optimism of Feuerbach. The individual of existentialism was always in crisis because without the metaphysical support of God, but at least the resulting angst seemed to offer the potential for authentic being. Not according to post-modernism, where the individual, anguished or confident, is as illusory a category as 'Man'; as a consequence, the very term 'individual' is replaced with the more technical term 'subject' – a subject now endlessly 'decentred'; that is, *subjected* to the historical, social and linguistic structures which precede, exceed and create it. The claim that Man and the individual are illusions in this sense I'll refer to henceforth as anti-humanism.

Looking back over this long and continuing demise it seems that, where the death of Man and the decentring of the individual are concerned, it's no longer the empirical, historical or painful truth of these propositions which animates contemporary thinking (and it definitely once was), so much as their reassertion, or ritual re-enactment. There is an obscure postmodern pleasure in rehearsing Man's death – one might almost say in reliving it. And if this is nihilism, it reminds us that nihilism may be as often intellectually invigorating as not. It suggests too that those few brave souls who still worry about politics, and, as a result feel that perhaps we have gone too far, and wouldn't it be a good idea if we could just half-resurrect the subject in the name of, say, a 'strategic essentialism' – it suggests that, sadly, they may be missing the postmodern point. Getting rid of the individual, at least in recent postmodern theory, is paradoxically less about politics or even truth than about pleasure: though the anti-humanist sees the individual as unfree rather than free, determined rather than self-determining, an effect rather than a cause, a fabrication rather than an essence, this way of thinking inspires a sense of imploding liberation; freedom is no longer a question of praxis, as it crucially was for humanism, Marxism and existentialism, but is reduced to a celebration of non-being, fragmentation and dispersal. This was the destiny of humanist optimism via existential angst and the perceived failures of Marxism.

And never more so than with the latest rehearsal of the individual's death – perhaps the most risky yet most seductive to date; we hear, for instance, much of late of how the self is ecstatically shattered by desire, and if death here remains a metaphor, it is only half so. In short, *jouissance* is flirting with the death drive. And if that arch anti-humanist Michel Foucault is controversial again, it's not so much for his assault on Man as his own, alleged, literal fascination with death, personally and intellectually (the two things being inseparable). His recent biographer, James Miller, contends that

> the crux of what is most original and challenging about Foucault's way of thinking . . . is his unrelenting, deeply ambiguous and pro-foundly problematic preoccupation with death, which he explored not only in the exoteric form of his writing, but also, and I believe critically, in the esoteric form of sado-masochistic eroticism.
>
> (Miller, 1993, p. 7)

This suggests that postmodern thought is finding its way back to something rather old: in Western thought death was always at the heart of identity. The humanism of those like Feuerbach and Marx radically altered this, but only for a while.

In modern thought, anti-humanism often gets traced back no further than the tortuous and enigmatic pronouncements of the psychoanalyst Jacques Lacan. Earlier precedents are much more significant. I've already mentioned Nietzsche. Others include Hegel, whose dialectic locked the master into his slave, the subject into its other; Marx, who insisted that social being in all its contradictions determines consciousness rather than vice versa; and, later, Freud who showed that the ego is imprisoned, and forever being ruined, by the unconscious. Just going back this far gives a very different view of the subject's demise than that found in post-modernism. It's for this reason that I welcome the historical sweep of the seminars from which this collection of essays grows, if only as a counter to that facile kind of postmodernism which competes to occupy the forward edge of our own contemporary moment, clamouring to announce a profound new insight into the recent moment, convinced that today all is radically changed, that something is radically new, while knowing that tomorrow it will all change again and anxious to be in on the diagnosis when it does. If I have a sub-text, it's simply that much postmodern theory desperately needs intellectual history.

Another nineteenth-century figure, Arthur Schopenhauer, though rather less fashionable for contemporary theory, can help explain modern thought's renewed fascination with death. In 1919, elucidating his theory of the death drive, Freud made his shocking yet seductive claim that 'the aim of all life is death'. Some seventy years before that, Schopenhauer had said, 'Dying is certainly to be regarded as the real aim of life' (Schopenhauer, 1966, Vol II. p. 637). Schopenhauer was rework-ing a philosophical tradition that goes back a very long way – to early Christian writers, Eastern religion and, perhaps most significantly of all, to the uncanny mythologies to be found in the gnostic heresies. Emerging from these distant precedents is the realization that what tra-ditionally subverted the subject was death working through desire; most radically, death experienced *as desire*. Not simply the familiar welcoming of death as the end of desire, the cancelling of the pain which is the heart of desire, but rather death as the motor of desire.

A line from Philip Sidney written some 400 years ago suggests the complexity of this vision: 'Leave me, O Love, which reachest but to dust' ('Leave me, O Love'). Here, 'love' is both the beloved object, *and* the poet-lover's desire: the beloved will turn to dust, even or especially as she (or he) reaches for the poet, who will likewise turn to dust. That's to say, we not only decay, but desire hastens the process of decay: desire itself (re)turns us to dust; desire is a self-defeating aberration: '*reachest but to dust*' – the embrace of love, the very reaching out towards the other which love impels, is itself a dynamic of self-dissolution. As Shakespeare puts it in Sonnet 147, 'Desire is death'. John Donne is just one of many poets at that time who played with the idea that 'to die' meant to come, as in orgasm. Some believed that orgasm literally shortened or expended life; the ejaculation of semen was literally the expenditure of one's life force: 'profusely blind / We kill ourselves to propagate our kind' (*Anniversaries* in Donne, 1971). Death and sex were inseparable. Another early modern poet, George Herbert, imagines 'this heap of dust; / To which the blast of death's incessant motion, / . . . / Drives all at last' ('Church Monuments)'.

Here, energy and movement – ostensibly the essence of life – are more truly the dynamic of its dissolution, the 'blast', the 'incessant motion' of death. Donne in his own perverse way theorized this in the first of his *Paradoxes* which is entitled 'That all Things Kill Themselves' and which begins. 'To . . . effect their own deaths, all living [things] are importun'd.' As Freud was to put it later, we make our own way back to death. In the pessimistic vision of the early modern period, death does not merely end life but, in the form of a vicious, death-driven energy called mutability, disorders and decays it from within; mutability effects not just an ending but an internal undoing. The ultimate undoing is the infinite stasis of the eternal – i.e. death, the ultimate unity, the final dissolution.

I've all too briefly invoked these early modern writers, first, to try and indicate the complex sensibility which welds death to desire; second, to register the early modern period in which it occurred most significantly; third, because by doing that I can make a further observation about modern anti-humanism. Typically the current, orthodox argument goes something like this: once there was the full, or confident, individual subject: unified, self-determining, self-sufficient, unique, the source and focus of meaning, etc. Then this subject was thrown into crisis, undermined, demystified and fell apart under the pressure of, for example, historical contradictions. Often the complete subject was said to emerge in the Enlightenment, growing to full stature in the nineteenth century, and thrown into crisis in the twentieth century. But academics researching the topic also attribute the full subject to just about every other period as well, though rarely the one they are researching. This is partly because, and for reasons alluded to already, everyone wants to write *not* about the full subject, but rather the subject in crisis – it's that which endlessly fascinates us and which we 'discover' in our 'own' period, while the pedestrian old full subject gets attributed to the period immediately preceding. And increasingly the history of the subject in crisis is written from a postmodern perspective; that is, one which claims to be more or less emancipated from the ideologies of Man and the individual.

The model at work here – from unity and fullness to disunity and crisis – far from being the critical act of demystification which it so often aspires to be, can actually collude with – by repeating, often unawares – one of the founding myths of Western European culture, namely the Fall. I remarked earlier that there is something seductive about the death of Man as pronounced in anti-humanism. This is relatively recent. More usually, as with existentialism but also psychoanalysis and modernism more generally, the crisis of subjectivity was typically a source of anguish. But even this was post-lapsarian. Of course, there are resonant, historically specific and crucial differences: Lacan is not Augustine. But the fact remains that the crisis of subjectivity was there at the inception of individualism in early Christianity.

And it remained acute at the time of the supposed flowering of the unified individual, the Renaissance. Put another way, what we might now call the neurosis, anxiety and alienation associated with the subject in crisis are not so much the consequence of its recent breakdown as the very stuff of its creation, and of the culture – Western European culture – which it sustains.

Which means that the crisis of the self isn't so much the subjective counterpart of the demise, disintegration or undermining of Western European culture, as what energizes both the self and that culture, at least since Saint Augustine (and probably before), in whose *Confessions* subjectivity is founded in its own crisis – a crisis that imparts the restless energy which is the making of civilization itself. Augustine suggests how individualism was from the beginning energized by an inner dynamic of loss, conflict, doubt, absence and lack which feeds into our culture's obsession with control, its sense that the identity of everything, from self to nation, is under centrifugal and potentially disintegrative pressures which have to be rigorously controlled. This is a kind of control that is always exceeding and breaking down the very order it restlessly seeks and so is forever re-establishing its own rationale even as it undermines it. The threat of disintegration is inherited by Augustine and radically inflected into a kind of religious praxis.

If the so-called 'unified subject' is in part a retrospective projection of contemporary theory, a convenient fiction which highlights the contrasting, subsequent drama of the subject's fall from unity, that is not to say that there have not been times when the optimistic ideologies of man and the individual made a profound difference. Of course there have been such times, and Feuerbach for one shows us exactly that. But even then it was rarely as complacent as theory implies, often being wrestled from the threat of disintegration and death, or being used to defend against them, or to struggle beyond them. This is precisely the case in Thomas Mann's *Dr Faustus*, the novel with which I began. Because its time-scale spans the two world wars, the defence of humanism in this novel is anything but confident. Indeed, it is obvious that humanism seems an obsolete philosophy, but what we are also forced to take seriously is not only that it was a necessary resistance to fascism, but, even more provocatively, that anti-humanism was implicated in these movements. Unusually, yet crucially, Mann explored the ethics of humanism, and the aesthetic seductions of anti-humanism, on an epic canvas – political, historical, cultural and mythological.

I've suggested that in the Western tradition the individual is always in crisis, energized and driven forward by the same inner divisions and deprivations which threaten its disintegration, and that at the heart of that threat is the force of a death which is doubly *before* (ahead and behind). Notoriously, for Christianity, man, through sin, brought death into the world and his existence never escapes the fact that death pervades life and is the source of all suffering. But it is one of the supreme paradoxes of religion that death, even as it becomes the reason for a renunciation of life, keeps man reluctantly forward-looking and forward-driven; savaged internally by death, the individual is also driven on by it. But death was also a promise of release and an attraction in the form of the infinite stasis of the eternal, expressed in life as world-weariness, nostalgia, loss, resignation and regressive desire; to be reunited with God in a transcendent heaven is to gain *the peace that passeth all understanding*. God always held out the promise of death – he was death – and when humanists like Feuerbach took God back into man they took back death too. Modern thought internalizes death as never before. This is true of writers as diverse as Hegel, Heidegger and Bataille – and Freud.

According to Freud, whereas Eros is a binding force for unification, coherence and integration, the death drive is exactly the opposite: a force of disintegration, of unbinding. And the death drive does not come *after* Eros but is in some paradoxical, seductive sense always already before it; again, there's that terrible yet fascinating sense that death drives life. Which means that life at its most intense is always on the edge of its own ruin. As life flickered in inanimate substance it 'endeavoured to cancel itself out. In this way the first instinct came into being: the instinct to return to the inanimate state. It was still an easy matter at that time for a living substance to die' (Freud, 1920 (1984), p. 311). This is the beginnings of the death drive, which seeks to dissolve life back into its 'primaeval inorganic state' (Freud, 1929/1930 (1984), p. 310). This leads Freud to reject the idea that there is a human instinct towards perfection. On the contrary, 'What appears in a minority of human individuals as an untiring impulsion towards further perfection can easily be understood as a result of the instinctual repression upon which is based all that is most precious in human civilization' (Freud, 1920 (1984), p. 315). In other words, beneath the apparent aspiration to perfection is at heart a restless wish to die: because 'the backward path that [would lead] to complete satisfaction' is prevented by the repressions which constitute social and psychic life (and which are themselves the basis of civilization); the desired regressive backward movement is blocked, and the instinct reluctantly, against its will so to speak, proceeds forward because that is the only direction in which it can go. But this forward movement has no possibility of completion or of reaching a goal. And what drives the instinct forward is not energy as such, but lack:

> it is the difference in amount between the pleasure of satisfaction which is *demanded* and that which is actually *achieved* that provides the driving factor which will permit of no halting at any position attained, but in the poet's words, 'presses ever forward unsubdued'.
>
> (Freud, 1920 (1984), p. 315)

Once again, desire is conceptualized as a lack; more remarkably, it is energized by lack: *the lack of death itself.* What this means experientially is that the restless, dissatisfied energy which is the stuff of life is always shadowed by that desire to *become unbound*; that is, the desire for oblivion, for a dissolution of consciousness, the irresistible desire to regress back to a state of zero tension before consciousness, before life, before effort, before lack.

Freud's theory was, on his own admission, a mythology, and not even a new one; he willingly acknowledged origins as distant as Empedocles. Freud was never more provocative, crazier or seductive than when, as here, he was invoking, yet also trying to avoid, an ancient, shocking vision – at different times a metaphysic, a theology, a mythology – whereby death is not simply the end of life but its driving force: put simply, 'the aim of all life is death'. Or as John Donne put it in 1611, 300 years earlier:

> We seem ambitious, God's whole work to undo;
> Of nothing he made us, and we strive . . .
> To bring ourselves to nothing back.
>
> (*Anniversaries*, in Donne, 1971)

The point here is not that Donne somehow anticipated Freud; rather that Freud's theory of the death drive has roots in, even as it transforms, a very old mythology. But in Freud and the modern period more generally, the desire to die, to become unbound, is justified as never before. As I've already suggested, some of the complexity, and the disturbing implications of all this as it mutates into the twentieth century, are brilliantly explored in the writing of Thomas Mann. In turning again to Mann we can see something else which is different about the modern desire to die: more fundamental than the choice between humanism and anti-humanism is that between sadism and masochism.

Throughout his life, Mann was fascinated by the idea that the intimate connections between desire and death were mediated and intensified by genius and disease.[2] The three greatest influences on Mann were Arthur Schopenhauer, Richard Wagner and Friedrich Nietzsche. Arguably, Schopenhauer in *The World as Will and Representation*, and Wagner in *Tristan and Isolde* give the most significant explorations in philosophy and music, respectively, of the seductive conjunction of desire and death. Not surprisingly, Schopenhauer's work was the single most important intellectual influence on Wagner, while Schopenhauer and Wagner were also two of Nietzsche's most important early influences, although he subsequently reacted vehemently against what he regarded as the 'decadence' of their deathward vision of desire. If his greatest work is energized by that reaction it is also rarely free of the seduction of the 'decadence' he rages against, and Nietzsche himself acknowledged this. So far as Mann was concerned (and the evidence is disputable) Nietzsche owed everything to illness and disease, and literally so: Mann regarded Nietzsche's development as a case history in progressive syphilis, a disease which 'was to destroy his life but also to intensify it enormously. Indeed, that disease in Nietzsche was to exert stimulating effects in part beneficial, in part deadly, upon an entire era' (Mann, 1959, p. 146). In his essay on Freud, Mann remarks that the morbid mental state associated with disease is the instrument of profound knowledge not only for the artist and the philosopher, but also the psycho-analyst discovering the truth of human nature through abnormality and neurosis (Mann, 1976, p. 414; cf. Mann, 1959, pp. 146–7).

For Mann, genius in the grip of disease nurtures an energy at once creative and lethal, giving rise to the paradox that disease and death are only life manifested in its most vigorous form. Disease – and in this sense love, or at least infatuation, is a disease – effects an unbinding which energizes even as it destroys. Mann is endlessly fascinated by all this – but it also explains why, even in his late essay 'Nietzsche in the Light of Recent History', he cannot entirely dissociate Nietzsche from the fascism that appropriated him. In Mann's *Dr Faustus* Adrian Leverkühn, its Faustian 'hero', embodies Mann's ambivalent attitude to Nietzsche, and to the daemonic, destructive aspects of his own creativity. This is nowhere more so than in two extraordinary episodes in the novel, the one where Leverkühn deliberately has sex with a prostitute suffering from syphilis, the other where he enters into a dialogue with the devil.

After having been given a tour of Leipzig, Leverkühn asks his guide to recommend a restaurant. The guide delivers him instead to a brothel. Unawares, Leverkühn enters. A prostitute approaches him and brushes his cheek with her arm. He leaves hurriedly. The encounter affects him obscurely and deeply, not so much on the occasion itself but subsequently. Fixation grows with recollection. More than a year later he returns to the brothel to look for that same woman, whom he now names Esmerelda. She has left, gone elsewhere for 'hospital treatment'. He follows and finds her. She warns him she is syphilitic, and despite or rather because of this, he has intercourse with her. There is a terrifying kind of daemonic love in the encounter, on her part because she warns him away, on his because he refuses to go. But in Leverkühn there is also another kind of love – some-thing selfless, defiant, reckless, self-destructive, impossible – in the self-destructive act of transgression there is a '*deep, deeply mysterious longing for daemonic conception, for a deathly unchaining of chemical change in his nature*' (p. 151, my emphasis). The encounter manifests the fusion of Eros and death, binding and unbinding, disintegrating and decline, as the ground of a powerful but always agonized and temporary liberation into creativity: love and poison here once and for ever became 'a frightful unity of experience; the mythological unity embodied in the arrow' (p. 150).

This is desire as compulsion, obsession and fixation; but it is also a kind of choice, a liberation, a temporary creative freedom, a momentary 'frightful unity of experience' that can be realized only in the embrace of death. Serenus Zeitblom, the humanist narrator of Leverkühn's fate, can never recall this 'brief encounter' without a shuddering sense of religious awe: in it the one partner found salvation, the other staked it. For her there was salvation in being *found* in demise, loved by one who could not, and would never, forget her. For Leverkühn, it is salvation in the form of its parodic, daemonic inversion: he is liberated into the agon of creativity, and the prostitute's name recurs 'often in its inversion' in his work in the form of six-note series 'of peculiarly nostalgic character', and especially in his late work 'where audacity and despair mingle in so unique a way' (pp. 151–2). Leverkühn's encounter with the prostitute is closely based on what Mann believed actually happened to Nietzsche; namely that the philosopher visited a brothel unawares and then fled, realizing where he was. At the time, says Mann, Nietzsche was

> unconscious of the impression the incident had made upon him. But it had been nothing more nor less than . . . a 'trauma', a shock whose steadily accumulated aftereffects – from which his imagination never recovered – testify to the saint's receptivity to sin.
>
> (Mann, 1959, p. 145)

Mann believes that Nietzsche too returned to the brothel a year later and contracted syphilis, perhaps deliberately.

The syphilitic Leverkühn, animated by disease and impending dissolution, becomes creatively potent. The paradox of life animated by death is focused in his dialogue with the devil, who tells him that life clutches with joy at that which is brought about 'by the way of death, of sickness'; thereby life is led 'higher and further' (p. 229). What this means is that

> creative, genius-giving disease, disease that rides on high horse over all hindrances, and springs with drunken daring from peak to peak, is a thousand times dearer to life than plodding healthiness. I have never heard anything stupider than that from disease only disease can come. Life . . . takes the reckless product of disease, feeds on and digests it, and as soon as it takes it to itself it is health. Before the fact of fitness for life, my good man, all distinction of disease and health falls away. A whole host and generation of youth, receptive, sound to the core, flings itself on the work of the morbid genius, *made genius by disease*; admires it, praises it, exalts it, carries it away, assimilates it unto itself and makes it over to culture.
>
> (p. 236)

This insistence that disease, precisely because it threatens permanent disintegration and impels the individual ineluctably deathward, is life-enhancing, has its counterpart in an epistemology which is radically aesthetic and amoral: 'an untruth of a kind that enhances power holds its own against any ineffectively virtuous truth' (p. 236).

In Mann's earlier novel *Death in Venice* (1912/1993), there is a no less remarkable encounter, when Aschenbach recklessly surrenders to his infatuation with a 14-year-old boy – surrenders in the sense not of consummating, but of acknowledging it. For Aschenbach, this surrender is an unbinding, a disintegration which is also a temporary, intense awakening consequent upon a partial lifting of repression. It suggests that binding, integration, unity – Freud's Eros, itself the supposedly vital force holding civilization together – is also a lifeform rooted in repression, which is to say a living death. Aschenbach's infatuation is also an instance of a further romantic intensification of the death/desire dynamic: now death not only erupts within a desire impelled by disease and death but, more specifically and urgently, as a desire for a beauty shadowed by disease. In short, and by no means for the first time, beauty itself became the focus for death.

The moment of Aschenbach's acknowledgement occurs when the boy, Tadzio, smiles at him. It is the culmination of a development whereby Aschenbach's life vision of a civilized integration of the sensual and the spiritual finally collapses. And it is Mann's achievement to make Aschenbach most intensely alive exactly then, at that moment of collapse. Tadzio's is a speaking, winning and captivating smile, the smile of Narcissus, curious, faintly uneasy and bewitching. Aschenbach literally collapses and rushes into the dark night, all composure lost. The lifting of repression can only be whispered as a hackneyed phrase – simply, 'I love you'. (Aren't we always least original when in love?) Yet this cliché, this radical *un*originality, marks Aschenbach as momentarily more alive – more *original* – than at any other time in his life:

> And leaning back, his arms hanging down, overwhelmed, trembling, shuddering all over, he whispered the standing formulae of the heart's desire – impossible here, absurd, depraved, ludicrous and sacred nevertheless, still worthy of honour even here: 'I love you!'
>
> (Mann, 1912/1993, p. 244)

It's as if de-repressed desire meets with, and momentarily animates, the ego – and then shatters it.

Later, and now shameless, Aschenbach follows Tadzio through the cholera-infested Venetian streets, it seeming as though 'the moral law' had collapsed and only the monstrous and the perverse now seemed 'full of promise' (ibid., p.261). The city's own 'guilty secret . . . merged with his own innermost secret', and just as desire has fatally re-energized Aschenbach, so the 'pestilence had undergone a renewal of its energy, as if the tenacity and fertility of its pathogens had redoubled' (ibid., p. 246, 257).

Forbidden desire, like disease, is at first latent, then spreads, then erupts. If the death drive delivers oceanic dissolution, desublimated eros drives towards Dionysiac self-destruction in a way, and to an extent, which binds together Eros and Thanatos more closely even than Freud imagined.

NOTES

1 Even when preoccupied almost exclusively with the so-called 'discursive construction' of man and the individual, modern anti-humanism is haunted by this sense of cosmic insignificance. Compare Michel Foucault's much-cited image of man being like a face drawn in the sand at the edge of the sea (above, p. 248), and the following, from the philosopher Martin Heidegger, whose influence has been equal to if not greater than Foucault's:

> For what indeed is man? Consider the earth within the endless darkness of space in the universe. By way of comparison it is a tiny grain of sand; between it and the next grain of its own size there extends a mile or more or emptiness; on the surface of this grain of sand there lives a crawling, bewildering swarm of supposedly intelligent animals, who for a moment have discovered knowledge. And what is the temporal extension of a human life amid all the millions of years? Scarcely the move of a second hand, a breath. Within the essent as a whole there is no legitimate ground for singling out this essent which is called mankind and to which we ourselves happen to belong.
>
> (Heidegger, 1935, p. 4)

2 For this as not just a continuing but intensified preoccupaton in the 1990s, see, for example, *High Risk 2: Writings on Sex, Death and Subversion* (London: Serpent's Tail, 1994). Its editors, Amy Scholder and I. Silverberg, remark that many of their contributors 'are preoccupied with death, mortality, suicide, and the disintegration of the body. . . . But what is central here is sex's relationship to death: in some cases morbid, in some cases, elegiac' (Introduction).

BIBLIOGRAPHY

Augustine, St, *Confessions*, trans. with Introduction by R. S. Pine-Coffin, Harmondsworth: Penguin, 1961.
Donne, John, *The Complete English Poems*, ed. A. J. Smith, Harmondsworth: Penguin, 1971.
—— *Paradoxes and Problems*, ed. with Introduction and commentary by Helen Peters, Oxford: Clarendon, 1980.
Feuerbach, Ludwig, *The Essence of Christianity* (1841), trans. George Eliot (1854), Introduction by Karl Barth, Foreword by H. Richard Niebuhr, New York: Harper, 1957.
Foucault, Michel, *The Order of Things: An Archaeology of the Human Sciences* (1966), London: Tavistock, 1974.
Freud, Sigmund, *Beyond the Pleasure Principle* (1920) in *The Pelican Freud Library*, Vol. 11, *On Metapsychology: the Theory of Psychoanalysis*, trans. J. Strachey, ed. A. Richards, Harmondsworth: Penguin, 1984.
—— *Civilization and its Discontents* (1929/1930), in *The Pelican Freud Library*, Vol. 12, *Civilization, Society and Religion*, Harmondsworth: Penguin, 1985.
Heidegger, Martin, *An Introduction to Metaphysics* (1935), trans. Ralph Manheim, New Haven and London: Yale University Press, 1959.
Herbert, George, *The English Poems*, ed. C.A. Patrides, London: Dent, 1974.

Mann, Thomas, *Death in Venice* (1912), in *Selected Stories*, trans. David Luke, London: Penguin, 1993.

—— *Last Essays*, trans. Richard and Clara Winston and Tania and James Stern, London: Secker & Warburg, 1959.

—— *Essays of Three Decades*, trans. H. T. Lowe-Porter, New York: Alfred A. Knopf, 1976.

Marx, Karl, *Selected Writings*, ed. with Introduction and Notes by T. B. Bottomore and M. Rubel, Harmondsworth, Penguin, 1969.

Miller, James, *The Passion of Michel Foucault*, New York: Simon and Schuster, 1993.

Nietzsche, Friedrich, *Ecce Homo: How One Becomes What One Is* (1888), trans. with Introduction by R. J. Hollingdale, Harmondsworth: Penguin, 1979.

Schopenhauer, Arthur, *The World as Will and Idea* (1819/1844), 2 vols, trans. E. F. J. Payne, New York: Dover, 1966.

Sidney, Sir Philip, *Selected Poetry and Prose*, ed. David Kalstone, New York: Signet, 1970.

16

SELF-UNDOING SUBJECTS

Terry Eagleton

Ludwig Wittgenstein once confessed himself puzzled by the fact that people spoke of the 'external world'. External to what? was maybe what he had in mind. One familiar answer to the query is 'consciousness' or 'the subject', and there is surely much to he said for it. My experience of pain is not in the world in the sense that the wasp that caused it is. But it is not not in the world either, unless you think of the world as made up of 'physical objects', a concept of which Wittgenstein professes to be able to make no sense. Physical objects as opposed to what other sorts of objects? Mental ones, perhaps? Is a concept a mental object, or the human psyche a set of non-physical processes? Is intending some kind of an event, only – unlike, say, bleeding – a ghostly, invisible one? There is something called the psyche or subject, which is absolutely the opposite of any sort of material entity, except that to give it that kind of name is precisely to imply that it is. Some of my activities go on in my psyche, as others go in my kidneys. But whereas a doctor could know what was going on in my kidneys, only I, or perhaps some peculiarly adept psychotherapist, could know what was afoot in my psyche. And this is because my psyche or subjectivity is invisible to everyone but myself.

Wittgenstein does not believe that our souls are invisible objects, which is not to say that he thinks they are visible objects either. That would just be the flipside of the same mistake, imagining the psyche as some kind of thing, though one in principle hidden from view and so just like the lower bowel only not like it at all. If you want an image of the human soul, Wittgenstein suggests in the *Philosophical Investigations*, look at the human body. It is not that the body reveals glimpses of a spectral entity within it, just that talk of the soul or subjectivity is a way of describing the behaviour of a particular sort of material body, the one we call human. It would seem as odd to speak of the world as external to our bodies (however plausible it might sound for some immaterial soul) as it would be to speak of my foot as external to the carpet, which is just a fancy way of saying that my foot and the carpet are two different things. Perhaps we would not have needed a special sort of soul-language, one that continually risks conflating the

262

language game of our activities with the language game of objects, if we had had a sufficiently sophisticated understanding of the human body in the first place; if, for example, we did not inhabit a culture in which when we hear the word 'body', as in a phrase like 'the body in the library', we sometimes tend instantly to think of a dead one. If talk of the human body falls prey to mechanical materialism, then one will find oneself in need of some spiritualistic or psychologistic language in order to cope with everything that such a view cannot account for. It is in this sense that vulgar materialism breeds idealism. The more, in such an epoch, the body is reduced to one object among others, the more overweening will wax the subjectivity which tries to compensate for this humiliation. It is just the same with human culture: the more it suffers the miseries of commodification, ensnared in a drably instrumental reason, the more stridently it will tend to insist on its transcendent value.

For the early Wittgenstein of the *Tractatus Logico-Philosophicus*, the human subject is not *in* the world at all. Since the world is whatever is the case, while subjectivity is primarily a matter of the ethical, and since fact and value cannot be conjoined, the human subject is simply the outer limit or threshold of a field within which it cannot itself figure any more than the eye can figure within the field of its own vision. What founds all of our representations is itself radically unrepresentable, no more a material part of the picture it produces than is a perspective. Of course, for there to be a representation at all, a subject must be lurking around somewhere; but its presence can be felt rather than formulated, shown but not said, squinted at out of the corner of our eye but as elusive as a mirage which evaporates the moment we stare at it straight. There is a parallel here with the Freud of whom Wittgenstein was so suspicious (it takes one Viennese to know another), for whom the unconscious is the necessarily absent precondition of all our egoic representations. The later Wittgenstein of the *Investigations* will throw over this whole picture: there is no longer anything special about the supposed non-representability of the subject, since there is no longer anything special about representation. This whole treacherous metaphor for how our language works must now be discarded; what, for example, does 'well, maybe' or 'have a nice day' represent? But that is not to deny some continuity between the two phases of his work, since in neither phase is the self for Wittgenstein a matter of some unfathomable interiority. The subject of the *Tractatus* cannot be captured in philosophical discourse, which is why the *Tractatus* itself, which declares as much, is absurdly, ineluctably self-scuppering; but this just goes to show the paucity of philosophical discourse, not that we cannot talk about what is most precious to us in some other sort of idiom, say, that of ethics or religious experience. The limits of language may be the limits of my world, but the limits of logic or philosophy, thankfully enough, are not. There is always Brahms and Tolstoy and St Augustine, detective thrillers and bad

American films, all of which Wittgenstein consumed with relish in his hot pursuit of the meaning of life. The mystical is not some unfathomable mystery, just the extreme limit of the sayable, a frontier which can be fairly precisely patrolled from this side in order to warn off intruders and save them from wandering tracklessly in the uncharted regions beyond it. The philosopher is in business to erect No Entry signs.

The later Wittgenstein is virulently opposed to what he scornfully calls 'depth', a gesture which whole generations of Anglo-Saxon philosophers would gleefully rehearse to give some philosophical gloss to their own lack of profundity. But Wittgenstein was not an Anglo-Saxon, though he had other failings, and his nervousness of depth is no glib evasion of spiritual angst, of which he had more than his fair share. It is just that he is out to upturn the whole notion of the subject as some mysteriously unrepresentable entity, and part of that enterprise revolves on distinguishing between the grammatical and the ontological uses of the word 'I'. When I say 'I am in pain', I am not naming a human subject at all; it is just a trick of our grammar which encourages us to think so. I am not saying 'I am in pain' in response to the tacit query 'Who here is in pain?', as though I might hesitate for a moment between believing that the pain was mine and speculating that it was someone else's. 'I am in pain' does not have the same logical structure as 'Jane is in pain', though our deceptively homogenizing grammar conceals the fact from us. Moreover, I can know that you are in pain whereas, so Wittgenstein claims, I cannot know that I am in pain.

It would seem that solipsism has here been mischievously stood on its head: now it is you who are entirely transparent, and I who am desperately opaque to myself. But Wittgenstein's point concerns the grammar of the verb 'to know': I cannot know that I am in pain because there is no context in which I could possibly doubt it, whereas it makes sense to say that I sometimes know you are in pain just because I might always not. What falls to the ground, then, is the Romantic-humanist notion of some privileged cognitive access to my own internal affairs – not because I don't know them, but because it doesn't make sense here to speak of either knowing or not knowing. And so, perhaps, it does not make much sense to speak of 'internal affairs' in the first place, since the ways I get to know myself are much the same as the ways I get to know you. We insist on trying to hide something here, Wittgenstein points out, but the figleaf of our language is just concealing the fact that everything lies open to view. I might sometimes not know what you are feeling, but this is a bit like not knowing where I have put the rabbit; it says nothing about some ontological state of subjective privacy.

Wittgenstein's fellow Viennese might seem to demur. Isn't Freud all about the unfathomable subject of the unconscious, about the production of some eternally elusive psyche folded upon its own inscrutable depths?

Wittgenstein would certainly appear nervous of this whole way of speaking; but he would rightly insist that the phantastic or unconscious meanings which a thing might take on for me must be logically dependent on its sense in the public world. There can be no private meaning for the unconscious, in the sense of one being inherently inaccessible to another, as there can be no private meaning in waking life. Indeed, that this is so is one of the necessary conditions of psychoanalytic practice. Wittgenstein is not out to deny the inner life, and so to become a suitable case for his compatriot's treatment, but to render a different account of how we have access to it, one which entails casting some doubt on the adjective 'inner'. And this need not be – though actually it is – at odds with Freud, in the sense that Michel Foucault's positivist distaste for interiority as such inevitably is. What deconstructs the distinction between inner and outer here, one might say, is the human body itself, whose creativity is a constant passing-over, transgression or transcendence from the one to the other in that perpetual movement we call history. It is this which was grasped by the great phenomenologists of the body such as Maurice Merleau-Ponty, and so damagingly suppressed by most of our later body merchants. The human body, like language, is that which is continually to be caught in the process of surpassing itself, whose interiority is ceaselessly extrinsic to it, whose inside is always already on the point of becoming an outside. For the human subject to be embodied is for it to be constantly non self-identical – which is to say that the root cause of our non-self-identity lies in what we do, not in some ambiguous text or enigmatic discourse which could then be contrasted with the stolid, suspect certainties of action.

Nevertheless, Freud's work, along with Marx's, shows us something of the historical conditions in which imagining the subject or psyche as some sort of quasi-autonomous thing, as ontological rather than grammatical, becomes possible and indeed even necessary. As the division of mental and manual labour grows apace; as the body's capacities become specialized and packaged, increasingly subject to an analytical reason; as the affective, domestic and erotic are split off by modernity from production and utility and artificially cultivated in some relatively separate enclave; as these fragile realms (call them 'culture') are then forced to compensate for an alienated social reality, and so risk growing rapidly pathological, warped and overheated by pressures they cannot realistically sustain – as all this occurs with the emergence of modernity, so the idea of a subject which stands above this process, but whose proud autonomy is in fact a product of it, comes increasingly to the fore. We have been sufficiently reminded, by Foucault and others, of how this subject's apparent freedom is itself a product of power; what we also need to take measure of, in rather more dialectical spirit, is that autonomy is then no mere illusion but part of the vital preconditions of political critique. As with 'culture', the very disabling distance which now seems to separate the human subject from the social formation is at the same time one which allows it to turn round upon those social premises and submit them to critical scrutiny.

If the human subject in the period of modernity is at once dwindled and inflated, sidelined but centred, one might expect it to begin to exhibit certain manic-depressive symptoms, as it veers wildly between self-abasement and self-aggrandizement. Such indeed is the structure of the classical bourgeois subject, which is at once everything and nothing. It is everything because now, in an historic turn, subjectivity has become for the first time the foundation of the entire system of reality, that which brought it all to be in the first place and sustains it divinely in existence. It is nothing, because as we have seen with the early Wittgenstein, such an ultimate foundation cannot be represented within the system it grounds, and so it slips through the net of language leaving the merest spectral trace of itself behind. A foundation cannot itself be founded, without risk of infinite regress; so that at the very moment of its exuberant omnipotence, this strenuously mastering subject finds itself with its feet planted on nothing more solid than itself, and thus endures the diminishment of knowing that there is absolutely nothing outside itself to validate its existence. Its defiant boast ('I take value from myself alone!') is also in this sense its catastrophe ('I am so lonely in this universe!'), and its existence a perpetual irony, as its untrammelled sovereignty drives it to gobble up the whole world and so leave itself with no alterity in whose mirror it might confirm its own identity. The subject, like the autonomous work of art, must now confer value upon itself, but it cannot therefore know whether this value is valuable, since it can have no criteria beyond itself by which to assess it. Its existence is thus a pointless form of narcissism, and though this subject is all-knowing, the last thing it can know is itself. For the essence of the subject is freedom, and freedom in this negative sense of the term is that which can never be made determinate. The determinate is what can be known; and all we can say for sure about subjectivity is that whatever it is, it is certainly not that. It can figure only as some kind of empty excess or transcendence of any particular; once we have positively defined it, captured it in some usable image, it ceases in that moment to be itself. The subject is just whatever is the opposite of anything in particular, which is why it is puzzling how it comes to have a body, or has truck with the objects around it. And since it can only realize its freedom by objectifying it, it does so only to lose it, keeling over into the status of thinghood in the very act of possessing the world. It is the reverse of nature, a sheer quicksilver structuring force which we can never close our fists over, a vaunted liberty which is also a sort of vacancy. It is that which we can never get back behind, since to do so would imply the presence of some kind of subjectivity in the first place; but this utterly aboriginal event, upon which the whole of reality is founded, is at the same time a mere pregnant silence or enigmatic cypher.

Modernity has one particularly ingenious answer to these conundrums, and that is the Hegelian solution. The problem would seem to be that to found the subject in something other than itself is to limit its autonomy, whereas not to anchor it in this way is to leave its freedom idly tail-chasing and gratuitous. But if the world itself were merely a free spirit in thin disguise, then the human subject could be rooted in nature with no detriment to its liberty. Not many, however, will find this solution terribly plausible, given that it belongs to the very activity of this bourgeois-rationalist subject to reduce the nature around it to so much inert, manipulable matter, and so to rob it of its spirituality in the act of affirming its own. If the subject clings to its dominance, it loses any way of shoring it up from the outside; its freedom is thus struck vacuous, since being now without limits it merely implodes upon itself. There can be no liberty without constraint, no subject without some robust object against which to bounce off. So the only other feasible solution is to salvage the subject's freedom at the expense of its autonomy, and this, roughly speaking, is the agenda of Friedrich Nietzsche. Nietzsche is prepared to abolish the autonomous subject in order for the subject to come into its own – to reduce it, in effect, to a mere spin-off of the ubiquitous will-to-power, but a will-to-power which is itself infinitely mobile, plastic, plural, decentred, and which thus allows the subject who plugs into it to be just the same. We are determined down to our toenails, but what determines us is a multiple, decentred, ever-shifting network of conflicting forces which plays through us, so to that extent we could be said to be 'free'. Freedom, which for the great revolutionary bourgeois tradition meant the capacity for self-determination, must now be dramatically redefined as a self-fashioning which is enabled wholly by some force beyond the puny individual subject. And what this means, more or less, is that the liberal tradition is now in such deep-seated crisis that it is prepared at least in some quarters, to sacrifice the self-autonomy of the human subject to its limitless plurality.

This drastic strategy, which would have been quite unintelligible to John Stuart Mill, not to speak of John Milton, is the one which so-called postmodernism has inherited. For bourgeois Enlightenment, freedom conceived as radical self-determination was how to bring down a tyrannical authority; for a later phase of the same liberal capitalism, such self-determination is now the ideological enemy. No one is much enamoured any longer of the self-discipling autonomous monadic subject – neither Jean-François Lyotard nor Jacques Derrida, nor those who run the culture industry and shopping malls of late capitalist society. It is, in fact, a gross caricature of the great liberal heritage – though one which the post-modern theorists apparently have need of – to imagine that the subject was considered there to be entirely without material determinations. What was true was that this lineage of thought had extreme difficulty in reconciling those bits of the subject which it thought determined with those bits which it thought not, dividing it down the middle between an empty freedom on the one hand, and a dreary determinism on the other. But this was little more than the sign in thought of a contradiction in reality – for where but in capitalism do we feel at once disorientatingly free and utterly objectified, bereft of all traditional authority, only to be handed over to the iron grip of market forces? In the classical phase of capitalism, there was a place – call it culture, consciousness, religion, the family, the aesthetic – where we were still just about free, even if encircled on all sides by powers which laid siege to our liberty. What has happened in consumerist, so-called postmodern capitalism is that these erstwhile auratic enclaves have themselves been steadily integrated into general commodity production, as art, culture, sexuality, and (in the US at least) religion become themselves forces in material production. Freedom must accordingly be redefined as a sort of ceaseless mobility whose only enemy is that of limit; and the buzz-word for this in our own day has been desire. But this in fact is hardly an advance on the dilemma of the classical bourgeois subject. For desire is just another fashionable name for that protean, quicksilver force which resists all objectification, that groundless ground of our being which slips through our fingers as soon as we reach out to grasp it. What has changed is that the subject is no longer the root of the entire enterprise – that this power by which we live and breathe comes from beyond ourselves, whether we name it desire or discourse or textuality or signification. What Freud laid bare was the implacable impersonality of desire, the way it always pre-existed the individual subject in order to pass right through it and out the other side. In this sense, the subject is now anchored in something beyond itself, rather than being primordially self-generative; but this is not much consolation to it, since this process or text by which it finds itself constituted is no kind of sure foundation at all – it is, in fact, as elusive and limitless as was subjectivity itself for its classical bourgeois theorists. It is, so to speak, a subjectivity without a subject – as though that unstable, dynamic force which was previously thought to spring from the subject itself has now been projected outside it, but is every bit as incapable as it ever was of granting it any confirming recognition. Indeed, in a shattering irony, the 'ground' of our identity – desire, power, discourse – is now that which radically ruptures it.

There was, however, yet another response to the liberal dilemma, and this was the riposte of Marx and the socialist tradition. Marxism could never see any real contradiction between the subject as autonomous and the subject as decentred; in fact each dimension could be grasped in terms of the other. For once one has inserted the fact of human sociality into this scenario, it becomes clear that such sociality – what the young Marx dubbed our 'species being' – is at once what makes us extrinsic to ourselves, received back only through and in some other, and at the same time the ground of our collective self-determination. Once we cease to think of autonomy as a purely individual affair, which was never quite what the Enlightenment reduced it to in the first place, and once we begin to grasp the decentring of the subject as a transitive social action rather than some curious ontological condition, the terms of the problematic are swiftly altered. There is then absolutely no reason for the postmodernists to persist with their tedious straw target of human autonomy as individualist, undetermined, monadic, paranoically totalized and the rest. A self-determining human subject is not one who miraculously conjures up him- or her-self out of nothing, and indeed was not often thought of as this even by the bourgeois philosophical heritage itself, for which, as we have seen, such 'freedom' merely turns to ashes in its mouth. He or she is rather someone who has been able to negotiate his or her freedom within those determinations set upon it both by nature, and by the right to self-determination of others. It is for this reason that all the ponderous chicken-and-egg arguments between 'humanists' and '(post-)structuralists' about whether the subject or the structure came first, whether we fashion ourselves or have the job done for us, whether we are autonomous or determined, are finally beside the point. For the autonomy of the human subject simply means that it is determined in such a style as to be able to react back upon those determinations and make something new and unpredictable out of its encounter with them. It is part of the nature of such a subject that it must either continually make something of what makes it, or go under, and this is just another way of saying that its nature contains an enormous hole where, if it is to survive at all, culture and history must implant themselves.

The modern subject is an amnesiac one. One of Freud's most alarming insights, anticipated by Nietzsche, is that we become the speaking, thinking, desiring subjects that we are only by virtue of a massive repression of much that went into our making. This self-forgetting is structural rather than contingent: unless those determinations were absent from consciousness, we would not be able to operate as the creatures we are. It is a doctrine which crops up in transfigured guise in Louis Althusser's idiosyncratic theory of ideology. The hubris or depressive mania of the classical bourgeois subject involved it being pitched from extravagant self-affirmation to a wry recognition of its own fictional or arbitrary status. The equivalent bad news for the post-Nietzschean, post-Freudian subject is that we are chronically and necessarily subjects of repression. But the good news, quite inseparable from this, is that it is this which allows us to be creative in the first place; so that if we take both upbeat and downbeat stories together, we might cease to lurch from euphoria to melancholia and recognize, humbly yet hopefully, that our freedom and our constraint are given together.

INDEX

Barthes, Roland 220
Bassano, Jacopo: *Self-portrait* 24
Bataille, Henry 255
Baudelaire, Charles Pierre 174; 'Le Voyage' 144, 145
Bayard, Pierre du Terrail, chevalier de 20
Bayle, Pierre 73–4, 77
Beattie, James: *Essay on Poetry and Music* 125–6
Beauchamp, Christine 218–19
Beaumont, Francis: *Salmacis and Hermaphroditus* 106
beauty, female 52, 93, 108
Becket, Samuel: *The Unnamable* 223
behaviourism 9–10
Behn, Aphra: *History of the Nun* 117; *Oroonoko* 117
Beizer, Janet 218
Bell, Alexander Graham 206, 208
Bell, Alexander Melville: on 'visible speech' 216
Belsey, Catherine 43; *Critical Practice* 158; *Subject of Tragedy* 116–17
Benjamin, Walter 174
Bentham, Jeremy: utilitarian theory 6, 88, 91
Bergson, Henri-Louis 189, 212
Berlepsch, Emilie 137
Berlioz, Hector: *Harold en Italie* 142
Bernard, Claude 186
Beyle, Henry-Marie *see* Stendhal
Beza, Theodore 25; biography of Calvin 21
Bible 12, 37, 110, 111, 239, 243
biographies 3, 18, 20–4, 82; *see also* autobiographies
Bion, Wilfred 232
Blaise de Monluc: autobiography 22, 23
Blavatsky, H.P.: and Esoteric Buddhism 208
blindness 189, 190–2, 192–9; medical treatment of 196–7; in Victorian fiction 186–7, 192–3, 199
Blount, Martha 103
Boccaccio, Giovanni: biographies of Dante and Petrarch 20; biographies of women 21
Boehme, Jacob 30
Bonitzer, Pascal 213
Boring, Edwin: *History of Experimental Psychology* 227

Boswell, James 72, 73, 78, 86, 101
Bougainville, Louis-Antoine: *Voyage autour du monde* 135
Boyle, Hon. Robert 67, 69; on conscience 55; essays 53
Bradley, Katherine and Cooper, Edith *see* 'Field, Michael' [pseud.]
Bradshaigh, Lady Dorothy: on Richardson's *Clarissa* 119–20, 122, 123, 124
Braille, Louis 197
brain: and vision 197
Brentano, Franz *see* Arnim A. von and Brentano, F.
British Association for Counselling 233
British Journal of Psychology 228
British Psychoanalytical Society 233
British Psychological Society 228, 233
Brontë, Charlotte: *Jane Eyre* 199
Brooke, Henry: *The Fool of Quality* 125
Brooke, John Hedley 196
Browne, Sir Thomas 44
Browning, Elizabeth Barrett 156; *Aurora Leigh* 159; 'Runaway Slave at Pilgrim's Point' 162; *Soul's Expression* 159
Browning, Robert 164; 'Andrea del Sarto' 165; 'The Bishop Orders His Tomb' 165
Buccleuch, 3rd Duke of 86
Buddhism 28; Esoteric 204
Builder 171, 172
Burckhardt, Jacob 3, 8, 19, 24, 30, 53, 225; *Civilization of the Renaissance in Italy* 17–18
Burke, Edmund 94, 125, 127
Burke, Peter 2–3, 8, 17–28, 39
Burney, Fanny (Frances d'Arblay): *Evelina* 128
Burt, Sir Cyril 229
Burton, Robert 19; *Anatomy of Melancholy* 44, 108
Butler, Judith 158, 166
Buzard, James 148
Byron, George Gordon, 6th Baron: *Childe Harold's Pilgrimage* 142

Caesar, Gaius Julius 23; *Commentaries* 27
Cage, John 220
Calvin, John 3, 21
Calvinism 31
camera obscura 188, 189, 193, 196